SKYLIGHTS

SKYLIGHTS
Essays in the History and Contemporary Culture of Astrology

Edited by
Frances Clynes

SOPHIA CENTRE PRESS
Ceredigion, Wales
2022

Skylights: Essays in the History and Contemporary Culture of Astrology
edited by Frances Clynes

© Sophia Centre Press 2022

First published in 2022.

Sophia Centre Press
University of Wales Trinity Saint David
Ceredigion, Wales SA48 7ED, United Kingdom.
www.sophiacentrepress.com

Typeset by Daniela Puia
Cover design: Jenn Zahrt
Cover image: Joan Miró, *L'étoile matinale (Morning star)*, 1940. © Successió Miró / ADAGP,
Paris and DACS London 2021.

ISBN: 978-1-907767-14-2

Names: Clynes, Frances, editor.
Title: Skylights : essays in the history and contemporary culture of
    astrology / edited by Frances Clynes.
Description: Ceredigion, Wales : Sophia Centre Press, 2022. | Series:
    [Studies in cultural astronomy and astrology] ; [11] | Includes
    bibliographical references and index.
Identifiers: ISBN 9781907767142
Subjects: LCSH: Astrology--History. | Astrology--Social aspects. |
    Astrology and psychology. | Astrology--Philosophy. | Spirituality.
Classification: LCC BF1671 .S59 2022 | DDC 133.509--dc23

Printed by Lightning Source.

Grateful thanks are due to the Urania Trust for a generous grant which made this publication possible, and to the original members of the Sophia Trust for their funding of the Sophia Centre.

CONTENTS

INTRODUCTION

Frances Clynes and Nicholas Campion

Astrology is a substantial and accepted feature of popular culture and of the esoteric and spiritual milieus of the contemporary world. It is also a potent modern form of cultural astronomy, an application of our understanding of the stars and planets to questions of culture, and of our understanding of our place in the universe.[1]

Over the three thousand years or so of its recorded history, astrology's uses include describing individual character, diagnosing and curing disease, answering precise questions on daily matters, finding the most auspicious times for launching new enterprises, managing social affairs, providing high-level political advice, constructing sacred calendars, and taking care of the soul. It finds expression in the arts, architecture, religion and politics. It interprets the past, manages the present and predicts the future, sometimes in detail, sometimes in terms of general possibilities. It is situational in that it situates affairs on Earth within the wider environment, including the sky, and it is contextual in that it locates human life within a context provided by the stars and planets, whether they are seen as signs or influences, powers in themselves, agents of the divine, or indications of a deep, cosmic order of which we all are part. It presumes a universe in which all things are entangled, or to use a modern term, interconnected. That life on Earth is interconnected with the wider universe is why, astrology claims, it is possible to read one pattern in another, and to read the pattern of human life in the patterns formed by the planets. It is a hermeneutic, approaching the sky as a text, in the same way as scholars analyse literary forms. As Francesca Rochberg said of Babylonian astrology, the stars constitute a kind of 'heavenly writing'.[2] It carries into modern culture key characteristics of what we know as indigenous thought, including a respect for the unity of all things and a regard for cyclical time.

Astrology is found in some form in every human culture. The origins of the modern western tradition lie deep within the astral religion of ancient Mesopotamia of the third and second millennia BCE, from where it spread to adjacent regions, changing its form as it went, adapting to Hinduism and Buddhism in India, Platonic and Aristotelian philosophy in classical Greece, and Islam in the Arabic-speaking world. In Christian Europe, it assumed a pervasive influence over almost every activity and aspect of thought, from its revival in the eleventh and twelfth centuries, until the social and intellectual revolution of the seventeenth century. By the late 1600s the casting of horoscopes, astrology's most sophisticated technical form on which most of its applications were based, had all but died out in Europe. From then astrology flourished for a hundred or more years as a feature of printed almanacs, the mass media of popular culture. A fresh wave of interest and activity was underway by the late nineteenth and early twentieth centuries, encouraged largely by new forms of spiritual activity (as represented mainly by the Theosophical Society and its introduction of Indian cosmologies into the western world), and psychology (as represented chiefly by C. G. Jung). It offered a new theory of the self, or, rather, it updated an ancient theory of the self, in which the individual psyche is connected with the greater environment as represented by planetary patterns. Modern astrologers became less preoccupied with prediction and the details of the external world, and more concerned with self-understanding and with altering the future rather than forecasting it. There was also some interest in astrology as a science, whether in the traditional meaning of the word as a discipline with its own rules, or the modern meaning as demonstrably accurate and susceptible to statistical verification.

This new wave of modern western astrology initially flourished chiefly in Germany, France, Britain and the USA. It emphasised newness and innovation both in terms of the technical basis of horoscope reading, and its quest for new ways of establishing personal meaning in a universe which was now known to be incomprehensibly huge. It was at one with the quest for the new which characterised modernism in the arts. It developed its own institutional framework of schools and societies, along with journals and teaching manuals. A new popular vehicle was created in the form of the twelve-sign horoscope or, sometimes, 'star' column, which became a standard feature of popular newspapers and women's magazines by the 1920s. Those parts of the 1960s counter-culture which were concerned with the inner life brought a fresh wave of students and practitioners. From the 1980s technology began to play a more important role, with software which calculated horoscopes in a few seconds replacing the formerly laborious process. By the 2010s social media enabled any member of the public to access the kind of astrological information previously only available from a professional, and allowed any professional to establish a global clientele.

In general, histories of astrology deal with the ancient and medieval worlds and the Renaissance, and astrology's role in modern culture tends to be overlooked. This book is not the first academic publication to explore modern astrology. Two volumes of the *Journal of Religion, Nature and Culture* have already done so. Volume 1 no 2 (2007) was edited by Michael York, past director of the Sophia Centre, and Volume 7 no 4 (2013) was edited by Darrelyn Gunzburg, a Sophia Centre tutor. Other papers are scattered through *Culture and Cosmos* and previous Sophia Centre volumes. However, this is the first peer-reviewed book to focus on modern astrology. All the chapters are based on work conducted through and associated with the Sophia Centre, and delivered as lectures at the Centre's annual postgraduate conferences.

The book opens with three foundational chapters on the ancient and medieval worlds: Akindynos Kaniamos explores astrology as a means of engagement with the divine in late Roman philosophy; M. A. Rashed examines astrological themes in Islamic apocalyptic belief; and Chris Mitchell investigates the importation of astrology from the Islamic world into medieval England. We then move into the modern period with two chapters on the relationship between astrology and history. Karine Dilanian investigates the Russian cosmist Alexander Chizhevsky's theories of the influence of the sunspot cycle on history, along with his debt to Johannes Kepler. Jennifer Zahrt explores the seminal importance of Aby Warburg, founder of the Warburg Institute, in the study of the history of astrology. Three chapters then examine approaches to the soul and psyche in the twentieth century English-speaking world and the respective influences of classical thought, Indian philosophy and modern psychology: Alina Pelteacu on the classical theory of the daimon, Jayne Logan on theories of karma and reincarnation, and Laura Andrikopoulos on the development of astrology as a form of personality analysis. Turning to the mass media and popular culture, Kim Farnell sheds new light on the origin of the modern horoscope column, locating its origins earlier than the previously accepted foundation date of 1930. Lastly, two chapters deal with conceptual issues: Crystal Eves considers the implications of the common definition of astrology as a language and Garry Phillipson discusses panpsychism, exploring the implications of astrological claims for consciousness, and what theories of consciousness might mean for our understanding of astrological claims.

We have called the volume *Skylights*. The notion of skylight is obvious – the stars and planets are points of light in the sky. But why the plural? Modern scholarship has established that concepts of 'religion', 'society' or 'science' are not monolithic entities. Instead, they are complex, sometimes contradictory, and ultimately difficult to define. This is why we may, for example, now talk about 'histories' rather than 'history'. This is not a comment on whether there is such a thing as 'truth' or not, or objective as opposed to subjective knowledge, but is a recognition that, as we explore the subtleties, nuances and richness of human culture, there are no straight lines and no simple answers. Previous volumes in the Sophia Centre Press series of Studies in Cultural Astronomy and Astrology were therefore titled *Cosmologies* and *Astrologies*.³ It is in this spirit that *Skylights* continues our exploration of astrology's diverse nature and role in human culture.

A note on the cover image

Joan Miró painted *L'étoile matinale* in Varengeville-sur-Mer in Normandy on 16 March 1940, . The painting is number 6 in his series titled 'Constellations', which he painted partly as a response to the crisis at the beginning of the Second World War. Renee Riese Hubert wrote of no 16 in the series, 'Vers l'arc en ciel' ('Towards the Rainbow'),

'the network resembles a fragment of sky seen through a magnifying glass. The star-clustered bouquet grows on fertile nocturnal fields. Blossoms will never tarnish and cut flowers reach for a new bed among the stars ... astronomical or perhaps astrological maps and contours, erotic shapes and constant metamorphoses as well as the musical transcriptions of so many creatures are finally welded together'.⁴

Notes

¹ Nicholas Campion, 'Astrology as Cultural Astronomy', in Clive Ruggles, ed., *Handbook of Archaeoastronomy and Ethnoastronomy* (Berlin: Springer-Verlag, 2013), pp 103-116.
² Francesca Rochberg, *The Heavenly Writing: Divination, Horoscopy, and Astronomy in Mesopotamian Culture* (Cambridge: Cambridge University Press, 2004).
³ Nicholas Campion, *Cosmologies: Proceedings of the seventh Sophia Centre Conference,* (Lampeter: Sophia Centre Press, 2010); Nicholas Campion and Liz Greene, eds., *Astrologies: Plurality and Diversity* (Lampeter: Sophia Centre Press, 2ⁿᵈ edition 2017 [2010]).
⁴ Renee Riese Hubert, 'Miró and Breton', *Yale French Studies*, no. 31, Yale University Press, 1964, pp. 52–59 (p. 54).

SEEING AND LISTENING TO THE GODS IN IAMBLICHUS' *DE MYSTERIIS*: ASTROLOGY AS A PARADIGM OF INTERACTION WITH THE DIVINE

Akindynos Kaniamos

Theurgy (θεουργία, literally meaning 'god-working' or 'divine work') was a system of ritual practices which incorporated elements of Egyptian and Chaldean religious rites into the Platonic philosophical tradition, and flourished during the late Roman Empire. Theurgy may be intended as a gradual process of ritual purification and ascent which subordinated man to the gods, and aimed for the soul's contact, assimilation, and union with the divine. It was, as Sarah Iles Johnston put it, 'a religious movement that arose during the latter half of the second century CE and significantly affected subsequent Neoplatonic philosophy and mysticism'.[1] My concern in this chapter is with theurgists' ability to 'sense' the celestial gods by means of visions and sounds, as well as the epistemological status of astrology in *De Mysteriis*, a major work by the Syrian-born Neoplatonist philosopher Iamblichus Chalcidensis (ca. 240 – ca. 325 CE).[2] Iamblichus' treatise *De Mysteriis*, composed between 280 and 305 CE, constitutes one of the most extensive surviving works from Late Antiquity on complex polytheistic religious phenomena and practices such as divination, sacrifice, and theurgy.[3] The text's original title, *The Reply of Master Abamon to the Letter of Porphyry to Anebo and the Solutions to the Questions it Contains*, indicates that this treatise was a reply to Porphyry's *Letter to Anebo*.[4] Porphyry (ca. 234 – ca. 305 CE), also a Neoplatonist philosopher and probably Iamblichus' former teacher, aimed his *Letter* (ca. 263–268) at Anebo, an Egyptian priest or one of Iamblichus' disciples, and indirectly at Iamblichus himself, challenging the forms of divination practiced by theurgists and the overall role of theurgic ritual within the Platonic tradition, and inaugurated a philosophical dialogue seeking to elucidate the profound nature of those religious mysteries.[5] In his reply, which is a point by point answer to Porphyry's queries, Iamblichus assumes the *persona* of the Egyptian priest Abamon, which is either a sensible choice of an Egyptian-sounding name, or may derive from the Egyptian word for 'priest' (*w'b*), or for 'heart' (*ib*), meaning 'priest' or 'heart of Ammon'.[6] The modern title, *On the Mysteries of the Egyptians, Chaldeans and Assyrians*, was coined by the Renaissance scholar, priest and *magus* Marsilio Ficino (1433–1499), who translated parts of the book into Latin in 1497.[7] In the Introductory Argument preceding his translation, Ficino qualifies Porphyry's *Letter to Anebo* as 'very rich in asking different and important questions, pertaining to philosophy in many respects, and more in particular to god, angels, *daimones*, souls, providence, fate, prophecy, magic, miracles, sacrifices and prayers'.[8] The subject topic of *De Mysteriis* emerges, according to Ficino, from a metaphysical landscape containing constant interaction between humans and the divine. Henri-Dominique Saffrey remarks that Ficino's choice of the word '*mysteria*' in the title is a sensible one, since this term 'indicates the gods, spiritual entities and practices of our relationship to the divine'.[9]

From that perspective, astrology may be viewed as a representative example of a *mysterium*. As will be argued, astrology, which is discussed throughout the treatise, constitutes in *De Mysteriis* a paradigm of the practices connecting humans with fate (εἱμαρμένη) and the divine.[10] Although it would be preferable to refer to 'varieties of astrological experience' rather than to a single 'astrology', the term is intended in its etymological sense of the 'word' (*logos*) or 'language' of the stars'.[11] The Greek word *astêr* (ἀστήρ), which is often translated as star, included and often primarily meant planet.[12] Astrology, which assumes, according to Nicholas Campion, 'that there is a significant relationship between the stars or planets and affairs on earth', might be provisionally defined, then, as 'a unique system of interpretation of the correlation of planetary action in human experience'.[13] Astrology also represents in *De Mysteriis* the fusion of the Eastern cultic elements of its origins within the Platonic philosophical tradition.[14] Ficino's inclusion of Near-Eastern and Egyptian religious traditions in the modern title highlights Iamblichus' spirit of synthesising Greek religious practices with Egyptian and Mesopotamian ritual elements, and the Platonic philosophical discourse.[15] As Crystal Addey remarks, 'Iamblichus identifies the roots of theurgy jointly in the Egyptian, Chaldean and Greek religious traditions'.[16]

The relationship between humans and the divine is a crucial issue for Neoplatonist philosophers. Even though Iamblichus holds that the divine is impassive (ἀπαθὲς), since none of the superior classes possesses a nature that is susceptible to passion, he nevertheless maintains that the ascent of the human soul to the realm of the gods is accompanied by a simultaneous divine descent.[17] The process of human interaction with gods and semi-divine entities will be unfolded in this paper from the angle of the ritual practitioner who seeks to enhance his or her own level of receptivity in order to receive the divine, often manifested by means of visions and sounds. Astrology will be viewed in its theurgic dimension, primarily as a mathematical science (*mathēmatikē epistēmē*) with divine origins, which focuses on the sun's passage through the zodiac, on the divinity of the planets, and on the circular motion of their orbits in parallel with the circularity of the 'vehicle of the soul'. The enhancement of the ritual practitioner's receptivity (ἐπιτηδειότης) in order to perceive the manifestation of the divine through visions and sounds will be examined accordingly.

I. Astrology as a Mathematical Science with Divine Origins

The discussion regarding the epistemological status of astrology takes place in the context of the debate concerning the theurgic discovery and invocation of the personal *daimōn*. Incited by Porphyry's astrological queries seeking to discover the personal *daimōn* as a means of transcending fate (τὰ εἱμαρμένα) through sacrifices (ἐκθύσαιτο),[18] Iamblichus undertakes throughout *De Mysteriis* IX the task of investigating the *daimōn*'s origins and functions.[19] Porphyry sought to discover the *daimōn* through astrological calculations related to the discovery of the 'master of the house', the so-called *oikodespotēs*, and concentrated all his enquiries on that.[20] However, despite using astrological techniques, Porphyry suggested that the astrological science (μαθηματικὴ ἐπιστήμη) was impossible to grasp, due to the fact that there has been much 'disagreement' (διαφωνία) about it, or because Chaeremon or some other authority may have written against it.[21] Possibly Porphyry had in mind Plotinus' objections regarding the scientific validity of astrology, beginning with what the latter considered its internal contradictions.[22] Porphyry may have also considered astrology as merely a *technē*, without any apparent epistemological status.[23] Athanassiadi claims that in this discussion, Iamblichus distinguishes astronomy from astrology and that by using the term μαθηματικὴ he exclusively refers to the former.[24] However, astronomy and astrology were not separated in the Greek mentality and language of Late Antiquity and many ancient astronomers, such as Hipparchus and perhaps Ptolemy, were also practicing astrologers.[25] The split between these two notions is anachronistic when applied to the third and fourth centuries CE.[26] Nevertheless, Iamblichus seems to introduce, in relation to the practice of astrology, a subtle distinction between, on the one hand, the terms 'casting of nativities' (*genethlialogia*), or the *di'asterōn technē* – both standing for the popular form of inductive divination through the stars which was commonly practiced in the Graeco-Roman world by professional astrologers – and, on the other, the theurgic mode of apprehending cosmic events.[27]

Within the theurgic framework of understanding, the term μαθηματικὴ rather alludes to the *Timaeus*, in which the Soul is presented as a mixed entity, composed of numbers and ratios, and placed between the sensible and the intelligible cosmos.[28] In his account of the creation of the Soul by the demiurge, Plato suggests that the revolution of the Same partakes of Intellect and stands for the celestial Equator, while the revolution of the Different may be identified with the Ecliptic, or rather with the signs of the zodiac, according to Francis Cornford.[29] In either case, Plato subdivided the inner circle of the Different into seven unequal circles, standing for the seven known planets in Antiquity, three revolving at an equal speed, while the other four have different speeds from one another, each moving at different speeds and ratios.[30] The Platonic theory that the Soul itself was composed of Number, or of all numbers by means of which the cosmos was organised, gave credence to what Johnston qualifies as 'the Platonic equation of the Ideas or Forms with mathematical entities'.[31] Johnston argues that 'number, in Pythagorean and Platonic theory, was responsible for the organization of physical space and thereby for the construction of the physical Cosmos'.[32] Moreover, the term ἐπιστήμη, which derives from the verb ἐπίσταμαι, meaning 'to know substantially, to understand in depth', takes on in *Republic* V the additional meaning of philosophical knowledge whose objects are the pure Forms or Ideas.[33] Socrates defines *epistēmē* as the ability to know the real as it is, in a context that shows that when Socrates talks about the real, he is referring to the Forms.[34] Thus, by viewing it as *mathēmatikē epistēmē*, Iamblichus introduces astrology as a body of knowledge of philosophical significance which seeks to unveil the metaphysical dimension of the manifest cosmos by means of abstract mathematical symbols.

For Iamblichus, Porphyry's arguments do not devalue the epistemological status attributed to astrology, since 'all sciences have attracted countless sceptics, and the points of controversy that they contain are innumerable'.[35] Furthermore, Iamblichus does not only claim that astrology is a science, but also that those who contradict it do so because of ignorance. As he puts it, 'so also in the case of astrology our response is that it itself is true, but those who are wrongly informed about it fall into contradictions, since they know nothing about the truth'.[36] Iamblichus justifies this ignorance on the basis that astrology is among the sciences handed down by the gods to men.[37] In such cases, 'progressively, through the repeated admixture of much that is mortal, the divine character of the knowledge contained in them comes to be extinguished'.[38]

Despite the substantial loss of the original knowledge revealed by the gods *in illo tempore*, Iamblichus offers two sets of arguments providing 'clear proof' (τεκμήριον τῆς ἀληθείας) of the scientific validation of astrology. His first argument is empirical and concerns the mathematical aspect of this science, 'for the signs of the measuring function of the heavenly circuits are manifest to our eyes, when they announce eclipses of the sun and moon and conjunctions of the moon with the fixed stars, and the experience of our sight is seen to confirm their prognostications'.[39] Iamblichus' second set of arguments in favour of the scientific validity of astrology is historical, pertaining to the observations and the records of celestial phenomena preserved through the centuries by the Chaldeans and the Egyptians.[40] Additionally, Iamblichus alludes to many other manifest proofs testifying to the scientific status of astrology but, since the discussion topic concerns the personal *daimōn*, he leaves them aside.[41]

Nevertheless, Iamblichus discusses the scientific validity of astrology in other sections of *De Mysteriis*. Various passages confirm the essential epistemological presupposition of astrology, namely that there is a link between the physical cosmos, its metaphysical dimension, and the place of humans within, even though this correspondence is not to be intended exclusively on the physical level of events. In *De Mysteriis* III.28–30, where Iamblichus explains his objections against the makers of images (οἱ τῶν εἰδώλων ποιητὲς), he clearly draws from Plato's portrayal of the demiurge and the creation of the cosmos in the *Timaeus*, and views subsequently the whole cosmos as a divine unified creation, in which the demiurge, 'by his conceptions, his volitions, and his immaterial forms, and by means of the eternal soul, whether mundane or supramundane, fashions the universe'.[42] Iamblichus clearly contrasts the celestial motions on the physical level, on which the makers of images depend, with the 'unlimited range of powers belonging to the celestial gods, one genus of which, and the lowest, is the physical'.[43] Therefore, Iamblichus suggests that the stars' influence is not to be intended mechanistically. The cause of events on the physical realm, he argues, represents only the lowest level of expression of the heavenly powers. Celestial powers emanating from the visible gods are always in the process of being unfolded to the whole manifest cosmos, but the image-maker is incapable of understanding and aligning himself or herself with them. As Iamblichus explains, 'the image-maker does not use the astral revolutions or the powers inherent in them, or the powers found naturally around them, nor is he able to apply himself to them completely'.[44] Addey remarks that Iamblichus explicitly contrasts here the 'technical' skill of the wonder-worker operating only on the horizontal level of the realm of nature with the theurgic skill which operates on a vertical axis by connecting material objects with their divine causes.[45] It is crucial, however, to note that Iamblichus does not dismiss the astral influence upon the realm of generation. On the contrary, he claims that 'even the lowest beings in the realm of generation are moved by the celestial circuits, and are affected sympathetically by the emanations descending to them'.[46] The term ἀπόρροια (emanation) is used throughout *De Mysteriis* to denote astral influence.[47]

II. The Sun and the Zodiac

In Book VII, which examines Egyptian symbolism, Iamblichus discusses the allegorical interpretation of some Egyptian symbols. According to Iamblichus, the Egyptians, 'imitating the nature of the universe and the demiurgic power of the gods, display certain images of mystical, arcane and invisible intellections by means of symbols'.[48] In VII.2, while analysing the image of 'sailing in a ship', Iamblichus views the sun in parallel with the helmsman of the *Phaedrus*.[49] The image of sailing in a ship is similarly employed by Plotinus for the soul coming into life with its *daimōn*; Porphyry uses it as well.[50] For Iamblichus, sailing in a ship 'represents the sovereignty that governs the world. Just as the helmsman presides over the ship while taking charge of its rudder, so the sun is transcendently in charge of the helm of the whole world'.[51] Based on their reception of the myth of the cave in the *Republic*, Neoplatonist philosophers used the sun as an image and a symbol of the One and of the divine Intellect.[52] Plotinus views the sun as a physical example of the One, comparing the supreme Good to light and divine Intellect to the sun.[53] By comparing the sun to the helmsman, Iamblichus considers it a reflection of the Platonic demiurge which also resembles the Aristotelian 'Prime-mover'.[54] Iamblichus discovers through the sun 'the god from on high [who] gives out, indivisibly, from the first principles of nature, the primordial causes of movement'.[55] Shaw argues that the sun, besides being a conceptual analogue of the noetic demiurge, was also for Iamblichus a *sunthema* of the One itself.[56]

Furthermore, at *De Mysteriis* VII.3, Iamblichus asserts that the potencies emanating from the sun activate 'the entire zodiac' (πᾶν ζῴδιον), along with every portion of the heavens, all the heavenly motions, all time, according to which the cosmos is moved, and all things in the universe.[57] Like all divine entities, the powers emanating from the sun are immanent and transcendent simultaneously.[58] Therefore, the scientific validation of astrology lies in the symbolic method of signification of the sun's powers as they activate the zodiac. Hence, the astrological discourse expresses the different qualities of time, intended not only as ordered and measured *chronos*, but also as *kairos*. Dorian Greenbaum analyses thoroughly this double aspect of time in relation to providence (*pronoia*), and suggests that *kairos*, which is connected with the divine and the immortal, 'seems to be above *chronos*, or at any rate to regulate it'.[59] As Iamblichus maintains,

... the symbolic method of signification represents the forms [of the sun] shaped by the signs of the zodiac and its [the sun's] hourly changing forms by means of signifying them through words, while indicating its [the sun's] immutable, stable, unfailing, and complete gift to the whole universe at once.[60]

Iamblichus refers here to the movement of the sun through the signs of the zodiac and the perpetual change of the *hōroscopos* (Ascendant), both of which can be expressed by means of a signifying system of discourse, despite the fact that their origins derive from observation and mathematical calculations. From that perspective, astrology emerges as an epiphany of the divine, and the powers descending from the sun designate the constantly changing face of the gods emanating from the One. Nevertheless, philosophic henotheism is not to be confused with the monotheistic religions. As Niketas Siniossoglou notes, 'Neoplatonic philosophic monotheism was substantiated with reference to the exegesis of Plato's ontology'.[61] According to Iamblichus, the Egyptian teaching indicates that 'he [the god] is actually one and the same, but allots to his recipients a variety of forms and changing configurations.[62] Hence it indicates that he is changed, according to the zodiac, every hour, just as these are around the god, according to the many modes of receiving him'.[63] Iamblichus describes this procedure as a 'symbolic mystagogy' (συμβολικὴ μυσταγωγία) and concludes his chapter with the comment that the Egyptians address their visions and prayers to the sun in accordance with the above-mentioned astrological mystical doctrine, which was in line with sun worship in Late Antiquity.[64] Therefore, as Shaw remarks, 'man's prayers must be presented to Helios through the many zodiacal *schemata* that the god assumes'.[65] As a result, humans may interact with the divine through vision and prayer based on astrological knowledge.

Moreover, Iamblichus affirms that the observation of the critical time (καιρός) for action is a necessary measure before engaging with theurgic rituals.[66] This remark is a clear reference to katarchic astrology, the branch of astrology seeking to determine the appropriate moment for engaging with a specific action in accordance with the most auspicious astrological configuration for the action in question.[67] Thus, it may be argued that the scientific foundations of astrology merge its physical components (observations and mathematical calculations) with its metaphysical dimension (divine epiphany of the sun as manifested through its interaction with the degrees of the zodiac). In order to clarify the interaction between the sensible and the intelligible in Iamblichus' understanding of astrology, we will examine the divine nature of the planets.

III. The Divinity of the Planets, the Circle, and the Realm of Intellect

Neoplatonist philosophers follow Plato and view the heavenly bodies as gods.[68]
Iamblichus claims that 'the entities visible in heaven are all gods, and in a certain
way incorporeal'.[69] The divine nature of the planets is mostly discussed in Book
I. In I.17, Iamblichus examines Porphyry's query about the paradox surrounding
the divinity of the planets. Porphyry wonders how the heavenly bodies were
divine in spite of their corporeal substance, since the gods ought to be exclusively
incorporeal.[70] Iamblichus' reply stresses the dialogical interaction between the
sensible and the intelligible, inasmuch as the latter is ontologically superior
to the former and may guide it into a single unified action. Iamblichus asserts
that 'they [the heavenly gods] are not enveloped by bodies, but it is rather they
that envelop bodies in virtue of their divine forms of life and activity'.[71] In I.8,
Iamblichus advances the principle that 'the genera of superior entities are not
even present in bodies, but rule them from outside; and there is no question of
their sharing in the changes to which bodies are subject'.[72] Appearing to allude
to the procession of the gods in the heavens from the *Phaedrus*, Iamblichus views
the heavenly bodies following the gods in a unified action of ascent to the One.[73]
Shaw remarks that 'the only body that exemplifies unified action is the sphere, so
the bodies of the gods were spheres, the geometric complement of their unity'.[74]
In his *Commentary on the Timaeus*, Iamblichus views the spherical shape as the
only one in the cosmos capable of taking in all shapes, and 'which is both itself
one and capable of containing multiplicity, which indeed makes it truly divine, in
that while not departing from its oneness it dominates all the multiple'.[75] Hence,
the planets are closely akin to the incorporeal essence of the gods.[76]

The planets' spherical shape is complemented by the spherical motion of
their orbits and of the universe itself. In a passage echoing the choric dances of
the planets in the *Timaeus*, and also Plotinus' trope of the cosmic choral dance,
Iamblichus presents the whole cosmos performing its circular revolution in
imitation of the divine illumination:[77]

> It is, indeed, in imitation of it [the light emanating from the gods] that
> the whole heaven and cosmos performs its circular revolution, is united
> with itself, and leads the elements round in their cyclic dance, holds
> together all things as they rest within each other or are borne towards
> each other, defines by equal measures even the most far-flung objects,
> causes lasts to be joined to firsts, as for example earth to heaven, and
> produces a single continuity and harmony of all with all.[78]

In Iamblichean cosmology, the interaction between the sensible and the intelligible may be explained through the inextricable link which puts in parallel the planets, the circular motion, and the realm of Intellect (νοῦς). The relationship between Intellect and circle is explicitly analysed through the Egyptian symbol of 'sitting on a lotus', which signifies transcendency over the materiality represented by the symbol of the 'mud', and also indicates intellectual leadership.[79] According to Iamblichus,

> For everything to do with the lotus is seen to be circular, both the forms of the leaves and the produce of the fruit, and it is the circular motion that is uniquely connatural with the activity of intellect, and which exhibits itself consistently in one order and according to one principle.[80]

It appears that through its contact with the circular shape or motion, materiality is transformed and consequently transposed into the intelligible realm in a reinvented form. In *De Mysteriis* V.4, while explaining the reasons for which terrestrial vapours of sacrifices cannot approach the heavens, Iamblichus holds that the body of the heavens is unmixed with the material elements from the realm of generation and qualifies the heavens as 'a cyclic and immaterial body'.[81] The circle purifies matter by liberating it from its changeable form, which is liable to corruption and decay, and by transforming each heavenly body into an 'aetherial body' (αἰθέριον σῶμα). As Iamblichus claims,

> For it is agreed that the aetherial body is exempt from all contrariety, and is free from all variation, completely purified from any capacity for changing into something else, and utterly liberated from any tendency towards the centre or away from the centre, because it is free of tendency, or rather is borne around in a circle.[82]

Taking into account the Aristotelian definition of substance as 'that which, being numerically one and the same, is able to receive contraries', Clarke points out in this passage that 'at the heavenly level the contraries are present, but simultaneously, in contrast to what is true of sublunar substance'.[83] Nevertheless, within the elaboration of the interaction between the sensible and the intelligible in Iamblichus' understanding of astrology, it is sufficient to mention that Iamblichus views astrology as a discipline focused not only on the sun, but also around the planets, which, through their spherical shape and their circular revolutions, manifest the pattern of noetic deities on a lower ontological level. In the following section, emphasis will be placed on the visual interaction with the divine through the intermediary function of the soul's vehicle.

IV. Seeing the Gods by means of the Soul-Vehicle

In the context of that unified cosmic dimension which is capable of receiving contraries, the planets emerge as the *agalmata*, the visible bodies and images of the gods.[84] In *De Mysteriis* I.19, while seeking to demonstrate the essential unity which attaches the visible to the incorporeal gods, Iamblichus maintains that the visible gods are mounted on the heavenly spheres as incorporeal, intelligible, and unified entities, whose originating principles are in the realm of the intelligible.[85] According to Iamblichus, 'the visible gods are outside their bodies, and for this reason are in the intelligible realm, and the intelligible gods, by reason of their infinite unity, embrace within themselves the visible ones, and both take their stand alike according to a common unity and a single activity'.[86] Hence, the gods are a totality in unity, a communion of indissoluble connection.

Iamblichus stresses that the gods may be apprehended visually by means of the ὄχημα-πνεῦμα, the soul's vehicle. Combining the Platonic 'vehicle' (ὄχημα), in which the demiurge placed the soul in the *Timaeus*, and the 'chariots' (ὀχήματα) of the gods in the *Phaedrus*, with the Aristotelian πνεῦμα, which was analogous to the element comprising the stars, Neoplatonist philosophers viewed the pneumatic soul-vehicle as a way to join the incorporeal soul with the corporeal body.[87] In the section discussing the gifts arising from the manifestation of the gods, Iamblichus states that their presence 'shows what is not body as body to the eyes of the soul by means of those of the body'.[88] Iamblichus' reference to corporeal vision as the means by which to see the formless and invisible divine epiphany points to the 'image-making faculty' of the soul (*phantasia*).[89] Within Neoplatonism, the vehicle was considered as the seat of *phantasia* and sense perception.[90] Shaw remarks that, 'by means of images, the "eyes of the soul" clothed the gods in an interior space. Clearly, a contribution on the part of the soul was necessary to reveal what was invisible, and Proclus explains that it was the soul's "body of light" (*augoeides soma*)'.[91] Proclus asserts that 'those who see the gods witness them in the luminous garments of their souls'.[92]

In his description of different types of divine possession throughout Book III, Iamblichus merges the element of circularity accompanying the divine epiphanies with the luminous soul-vehicle which provides extrasensory perception. In dream divination, 'sometimes an intangible and incorporeal spirit encircles those lying down, so that there is no visual perception of it, but some other awareness and self-consciousness'.[93] Iamblichus claims that those who are truly possessed by the gods 'have subjected their entire life as a vehicle (ὄχημα) or instrument (ὄργανον) to the gods who inspire them'.[94] Iamblichus explicitly links the illumination of the soul-vehicle with the procedure of 'evoking the light' (φωτὸς ἀγωγή), which was a way of making higher entities visible through light shining on water or oil. This procedure, 'somehow illuminates the aether-like and luminous vehicle surrounding the soul with divine light, from which vehicle the divine appearances, set in motion by god's will, take possession of the imaginative power in us'.[95] In the Delphic oracle, 'when the fiery spirit coming up from the aperture, dense and abundant, envelops her [the prophetess] entirely in a circle, she is filled by it with a divine brightness'.[96] As Addey explains, 'during oracular and other types of divination rituals, the *phantasia* is [...] emptied of all the ritual practitioner's images and human images, and thus is receptive to and able to receive the images sent from the gods'.[97]

Therefore, the ritual practitioner constantly seeks to purify his/her soul-vehicle which serves as a medium to receive the divine illumination. Through the process of purification, which includes ritual, intellectual, and ethical means, the theurgist and the prophet enhance their level of receptivity (ἐπιτηδειότητης) regarding the appearances or messages emanating from the gods. According to Iamblichus, the most useful results of purification (κάθαρσις) are 'removal of foreign elements, restoration of one's own essence, perfection, fulfilment, self-sufficiency, ascent to the engendering cause, conjoining the parts to wholes, and the gift of power, life, and activity from wholes to individuals'.[98] Addey argues that receptivity is 'implicitly coded as a developable sacred space which is marked by a subtle blend of openness and humbleness combined with an active and simultaneous cultivation of intellectual, ritual, and ethical discipline and praxis'.[99] While describing the oracular procedure at the oracle at Colophon, Iamblichus explains that the water, from which the prophet drinks, 'only bestows the receptivity and purification of the luminous spirit in us, through which we are able to receive the god'.[100] Thus, the vehicle, purified and lifted above through theurgic rites, may house the rational soul's return to the gods.

The doctrine of the soul-vehicle provides the theoretical background for the scientific validation of astrology, at least according to Iamblichus' metaphysics. There are striking similarities in the way Iamblichus perceives the vehicle's shape and movement with his understanding of the planets. Like the planets, the vehicle is spherical and composed of aether. In his *Commentary on the Timaeus*, Iamblichus argues that the demiurge 'constructed the universe in the form of a sphere, to be an image of the Soul's self-motion. For which reason also our vehicle is made spherical, and is moved in a circle, whenever the Soul is especially assimilated to Intellect (*Nous*)'.[101] Iamblichus suggests here that Intellect is spherical and therefore the soul-vehicle, when the soul becomes perfected and enlightened, becomes spherical, imitating *Nous*. As Addey discloses, 'Iamblichus emphasises that the vehicle is made more spherical whenever the human soul is assimilated to the Divine Mind (*Nous*)'.[102] The key point is that the human soul and the World Soul both imitate the shape and motion of *Nous*, which is circular.[103] Moreover, in fragment 84 of the same *Commentary*, Iamblichus affirms that the substance of the soul-vehicle is produced from the aether as a whole, which has a generative (ἀπογεννωμένη) power.[104] Iamblichus modifies Porphyry's view of the vehicle as composed of successive subtractions from the planets' substance in such a way that it would diminish them.[105] Iamblichus holds that 'the individual pneumatic vehicle is composed and given shape in accord *with the life-principles* of the encosmic gods'.[106] Dillon argues that τὰς ζωὰς τὰς θείας refers to the planets, since, in theological terms, 'these are the aethereal source of the individual πνεύματα/ὀχήματα'.[107] The expression *life-principles* (of the planets) points to the particular principles that each heavenly god conveys to humans. It appears that Iamblichus complements the astrological connotations of Porphyry's explanation on a metaphysical level.

Furthermore, in John Finamore's view, the doctrine of the sowing of the vehicles, that is to say the dispersion of souls together with their vehicles around the visible gods, is the philosophical basis upon which is founded the Neoplatonic theory of astrological influences on human life.[108] As he argues, 'Iamblichus would have seen the sowing of souls into the gods as the cause of both similarity and differences between the souls: similar in that all souls are given a leader [planetary god], different in that each leader exerts a different influence on the soul under its power'.[109] From that viewpoint, each planet has a different influence which may be perceived in a double manner. Iamblichus suggests that there is a constant 'participation' (μετάληψις) intermingling the material elements with immaterial emanations in the cosmos.[110] Therefore the influence of each planet is different on the physical level of the realm of generation and on the pneumatic sphere of the noetic world. As Iamblichus explains,

> For example, the emanation (ἀπόρροια) deriving from Saturn tends to pull things together, while that deriving from Mars tends to provoke motion in them; however, at the level of material things the passive generative receptacle receives the former as rigidity and coldness, and the latter as a degree of inflammation exceeding moderation.[111]

Iamblichus stresses that 'since the feebleness of the material and earthly realm is not able fully to take in the unsullied power and pure life-force of aethereal elements, it transfers its own vulnerability to the primary causes'.[112] The material and earthly cannot take the pure power of aetherial elements and so humans often transfer their own vulnerability to the primary causes. Hence, humans ascribe and 'project' their own weakness onto the primary causes because they identify themselves within the realm of generation, rather than with the divine. Therefore, it may be argued that the vehicle's spherical shape and circular motion serve as a means of synchronisation with the planets' noetic emanations. From that viewpoint, the ritual practitioners who purify their vehicle and enhance their level of receptivity seek to rule their bodies from the position of their purified vehicle, and ultimately from the intellectual circuits of divine providence, imitating the visible gods' relationship with their own bodies, the planets; thus, the prophet and the theurgist can sense and 'see' the gods because of their attainment of divine assimilation and likeness.

V. Listening to the Gods

Within Book III, Iamblichus describes divinatory operations in terms of the luminous and circular descent of the divine; this account also details the sounds experienced during the divinatory episode. By repeatedly employing the Chaldean and Pythagorean term ῥοῖζος, a 'whistling' or 'rushing' sound which refers to the harmony of the spheres and the motion of the planets and stars, Iamblichus explicitly connects the audible vibrations emitted by the motion of the planets in their revolutions with the divine apparitions.[113] In dream divination, the divine spirit, 'when entering, makes a whooshing sound'.[114] Furthermore, each planet makes a distinctive sound corresponding to a separate and proper divine voice. In his unfoldment of the importance of sound and music in the phenomena of divine possession, Iamblichus claims that, 'those things such as sounds and tunes are properly consecrated to each of the gods, assigned to them in accord with their proper orders and powers, the motions in the universe itself and the harmonious sounds rushing (ῥοιζουμένας) from its motions'.[115]

In addition, each planetary voice contributes in suitable measures to the divine harmony. According to Iamblichus, 'the inspiration of the gods is not separated from the divine harmony, having been allied to it from the beginning, [and] it is shared by it in suitable measures'.[116] In a passage which strongly links cosmology and metaphysics, and echoes the Platonic theory of Recollection and the myth of Er from the *Republic*, Iamblichus justifies the innate knowledge that humans hold from the gods as the result of the soul's descent through the planetary spheres before incarnation.[117] As Iamblichus puts it,

Before it gave itself to the body, the soul heard the divine harmony. And accordingly, even when it entered the body, such tunes as it hears which especially preserve the divine trace of harmony, to these it clings fondly and is reminded by them of the divine harmony; it is also borne along with and closely allied to this harmony, and participates in it (μεταλαμβάνει) as much as can be shared (μετέχειν) of it.[118]

The verbs μεταλαμβάνειν and μετέχειν highlight the process of 'participation', intermingling material elements with immaterial emanations in the perception of the cosmic harmony. Iamblichus holds that there is a constant participation (μετοχὴ) between the immaterial emanation of the heavenly bodies and the divergent, material elements of each individual. As he puts it, '… there would never have been any such thing as participation in the first place, if the participant had not some divergent element in it as well'.[119] This process of intermingling of heterogenous elements is not a problem in itself. The responsibility lies with the earthly and material elements within humans, who cannot receive the full powers of the gods unless the human soul and body have been purified and made receptive, in order to experience the planets' potencies in a less distorted manner.

Thus, it can be argued that the mathematical aspect of astrology corresponds to the musical imitation of the celestial spheres, through the measurement and the identification of each planetary voice in the horoscope. This process may be technical, but it describes the mathematical ratios apportioned, or allotted, to each divinity.[120] Thus, as Addey asserts, 'astrology encompasses the entire circuit of the heavens which reflects the divine procession through which, according to Plato, we travelled with the gods before descending […] into the world of generation'.[121] True knowledge of the gods, and ultimately of ourselves, is, according to Iamblichus, the ultimate goal of every science.[122]

Conclusion

This paper has analysed the theurgic dimension of astrology as a mode of interaction with the divine in Iamblichus' *De Mysteriis*. Iamblichus views in *mathēmatikē epistēmē* a body of knowledge of philosophical significance which seeks to unveil the metaphysical dimension of the manifest cosmos by means of mathematical symbols. Even though the gods are transcendent, and therefore not subject to passions, they are simultaneously immanent and present throughout the cosmos, imparting signs to humans. The study of the sun's transformations through the zodiac, expressed via a signifying system of discourse, constitutes the epistemological foundation of astrology, by means of which humans may see and honour the constantly changing patterns of the deities emanating from the One. In the Neoplatonic metaphysical landscape, the planets are the visible images and bodies of the encosmic gods. Through their spherical shape and motions, the planets were seen as inextricably linked to Intellect and the immaterial gods. The ritual practitioners who enhance their own level of receptivity, through ritual, intellectual, and ethical means, may purify their aethereal soul-vehicle, rendering it spherical and akin to the noetic emanations of planets. Through the inner sight of the image-making faculty (*phantasia*), residing in the purified vehicle, humans may see and listen to the gods. Hence, astrology as *epistēmē* may free the soul from its sensible attachments, initiating a noetic procedure in which knowledge of the gods and knowledge of ourselves merge in a continuum.

Iamblichus' soteriological system proposes that humans follow the theurgic path aiming for the soul's contact, assimilation, and union with the divine. In a multi-layered but unified cosmos, in which different planetary voices resonate and form a single melody, the soul follows the sounds emitted by the gods in the course of their heavenly procession. Through a cumulative level of intimacy with them, the ritual practitioner may 'sense' the gods, approach them further in order to decrypt their messages, and act consequently according to divine providence instead of passively suffering fate. Thus, as a paradigm of the interaction with the divine, astrology may be performed throughout the spectrum of ritual and contemplative practices uniting humans to the gods, and provide substantial ontological knowledge.

Acknowledgment

This chapter constitutes an abbreviated version of the Introduction and the first chapter of my dissertation 'Human and Divine Interaction in Iamblichus' *De Mysteriis*: Astrology as a Paradigm of the Interaction with the Divine', which received 'the University of Wales Trinity Saint David Master of Arts' with distinction in 2017 and was awarded the 'MA Cultural Astronomy and Astrology Dissertation Prize' for 2018. I would like to express my sincerest gratitude to all of my MA tutors, and especially to Crystal Addey and Dorian Greenbaum, my dissertation supervisors, for their precious aid and guidance, as well as to Nicholas Campion for his valuable insights towards my understanding of the history of astrology and astral religion.

Notes

1. Sarah Iles Johnston, 'Cavalier Gods and Theurgic Salvation in the Second Century A.D.', in *Classical Philology* 87, no. 4, Chicago University Press (Oct. 1992): pp. 303–21, here p. 303. For a comprehensive discussion on theurgy, see Gregory Shaw, *Theurgy and the Soul: The Neoplatonism of Iamblichus* (University Park, PA: Pennsylvania State University Press, 1995; revised edn, Kettering, OH: Angelico Press/

Sophia Perennis, 2014) [hereafter Shaw, *Theurgy and the Soul*]; Carine Van Liefferinge, *La théurgie. Des Oracles Chaldaïques à Proclus* (Liège: Presses universitaires de Liège, 1999); Algis Uždavinys, *Philosophy and Theurgy in Late Antiquity*, with Foreword by John F. Finamore (Kettering, OH: Angelico Press/Sophia Perennis, 2010), pp. 79–142; Ilinka Tanaseanu-Döbler, *Theurgy in Late Antiquity. The Invention of Ritual Tradition* (Göttingen: Vandenhoeck & Ruprecht, 2013), pp. 95–135; Crystal Addey, *Divination and Theurgy in Neoplatonism. Oracles of the Gods*, (Farnham and Burlington, VT: Ashgate, 2014), pp. 24–40 [hereafter, Addey, *Divination and Theurgy in Neoplatonism*].

    2.   For a comprehensive discussion on Iamblichus' dates, see John M. Dillon, *Iamblichi Chalcidensis In Platonis Dialogos Commentariorum Fragmenta* (1973; Westbury: Prometheus Trust, 2009), pp. 5–10 [hereafter Dillon, *Iamblichus. The Platonic Commentaries*]. For an account of Iamblichus' life, see Dillon, *Iamblichus. The Platonic Commentaries*, pp. 3–18; John M. Dillon and Wolfgang Polleichtner, *Iamblichus of Chalcis: The Letters* (Boston, MA, and Leiden: Brill, 2010), pp. xiii–xiv [hereafter Dillon and Polleichtner, *Iamblichus of Chalcis: The Letters*]; Emma C. Clarke, John M. Dillon and Jackson P. Hershbell, eds and trans, *Iamblichus: De Mysteriis* (Atlanta, GA: Society of Biblical Literature, 2003), pp. xviii–xxvi [hereafter Clarke et al., *Iamblichus: De Mysteriis*]; Henri-Dominique Saffrey, Alain-Philippe Seconds and Adrien Lecerf, eds and French trans, *Jamblique: Réponse à Porphyre (De Mysteriis)* (Paris: Les Belles Lettres, 2013), pp. xxxiii–lix [hereafter Saffrey et al., *Jamblique: Réponse à Porphyre*]. The term 'Neoplatonism' was artificially coined by eighteenth-century German scholars seeking to distinguish the movement inspired by Plotinus (204–270 CE) from the Platonic Academy (ca. 387–383 BCE) and from the so-called 'Middle-Platonists' (80 BCE–220 CE).

    3.   For the dating of *De Mysteriis*, Dillon suggests a date around 280 CE (Dillon, *Iamblichus. The Platonic Commentaries*, p. 13), while Saffrey, Athanassiadi and Clarke assign it to ca. 300 CE See Henri-Dominique Saffrey, 'Abamon, Pseudonyme de Jamblique', in R. B. Palmer and R. G. Hamerton-Kelly, eds, *Philomathes: Studies and Essays in the Humanities in Memory of Philippe Merlan* (The Hague: Martinus Nijhoff, 1971), pp. 227–239, here pp. 231–233, reprinted in Henri-Dominique Saffrey, *Recherches sur le néoplatonisme après Plotin* (Paris: Vrin, 1990), pp. 95–107) [hereafter Saffrey, 'Abamon, Pseudonyme de Jamblique']; Polymnia Athanassiadi, 'Dreams, Theurgy and Freelance Divination: The Testimony of Iamblichus', *Journal of Roman Studies* 83 (1993): pp. 115–130, here p. 116, n. 13 [hereafter Athanassiadi, 'Dreams, Theurgy and Freelance Divination: The Testimony of Iamblichus']; Emma C. Clarke, *Iamblichus' De Mysteriis: A Manifesto of the Miraculous* (Aldershot and Burlington, VT: Ashgate, 2001), p. 6 [hereafter Clarke, *Iamblichus' De Mysteriis: A Manifesto of the Miraculous*].

    4.   Porphyry, *Epistula ad Anebo* (*Letter to Anebo*), ed. A.R. Sodano (Naples: L' Arte Tipografica, 1958); Porphyre, *Lettre à Anébon l'Égyptien*, eds and French trans, Henri-Dominique Saffrey and Alain-Philippe Seconds (Paris: Les Belles Lettres, 2012) [hereafter Porphyre, *Lettre à Anébon l'Égyptien*]. The original title of Iamblichus' treatise, Ἀβάμμωνος διδασκάλου πρὸς τὴν Πορφυρίου πρὸς Ἀνεβὼ ἐπιστολὴν ἀπόκρισις καὶ τῶν ἐν αὐτῇ ἀπορημάτων λύσεις, appears in the prefatory note from the eleventh-century Byzantine scholar Michael Psellus, see Clarke et al., *Iamblichus: De Mysteriis*, pp. 2–3, n.1.

    5.   For a comprehensive synthesis of the discussion pertaining to the relationship between Porphyry and Iamblichus in the *De Mysteriis*, see Addey, *Divination and Theurgy in Neoplatonism*, pp. 128–33. For Iamblichus as Porphyry's disciple, see Eunapius, *Lives of Philosophers*, 458.1–4, in Philostratus, *Lives of the Sophists*; Eunapius, *Lives of the Philosophers and Sophists*, trans. Wilmer C. Wright (Cambridge, MA: Harvard University Press, Loeb Classical Library 134; Clarke, *Iamblichus' De Mysteriis: A Manifesto of the Miraculous*, p. 15, n. 27. For Anebo as one of Iamblichus' (or, rather, 'Abamon's') disciples, see Iamblichus, *De Mysteriis*, I.1 (2.6), [hereafter, Iamblichus, *DM*]. All references,

quotations and translations are from Clarke et al., *Iamblichus: De Mysteriis*, unless otherwise stated. Clarke et al., *Iamblichus: De Mysteriis* reproduces the Greek text of Jamblique, *Les Mystères d'Égypte*, ed. and French trans. Éd. Des Places (1966; Paris: Budé-Les Belles Lettres, 1996) and the pagination of the Parthey edition. For practical reasons, the Scutellius division into ten books has been maintained. For the Greek text, the more recent reference edition of Saffrey et al., *Jamblique: Réponse à Porphyre*, has also been taken into consideration. English translations of other non-English texts will be quoted accordingly.

6.   Or might even mean 'father of Ammon'. For the scholarly debate regarding the exact meaning of this pseudonym, see Clarke et al., *Iamblichus: De Mysteriis*, pp. xxxiii–xxxviii; Addey, *Divination and Theurgy in Neoplatonism*, p. 138. For 'Abamon' as 'Father of Ammon', since 'aba' is Syriac, Chaldean and Hebrew for 'father', see Saffrey, 'Abamon, Pseudonyme de Jamblique', pp. 234–35.

7.   The title in Latin is *De Mysteriis Aegyptiorum, Chaldeorum, Assyriorum*.

8.   [epistolam] '…uariarum & grauium quaestionum plenam ad omnes philosophiae partes spectantium, praesertim ad deum, atque angelos, daemonesque, & animas ad prouidentiam. ad fatum. uaticinia. magicen. miracula. sacrificia. uota' (my translation). For Ficino's text in Latin, see Saffrey et al., *Jamblique : Réponse à Porphyre*, p. xvii, n. 1. I use the term *daimōn* (italicised) and its derivatives throughout this paper as semantically equivalent to the concept and the uses of the Greek δαίμων and the Latin *daemon*, and also in order to avoid confusion with the 'demon' or 'daemon' in a Christian context.

9.   (Les *mysteria*) 'désignent les dieux, les êtres spirituelles et les pratiques de notre relation à dieu', Saffrey et al., *Jamblique: Réponse à Porphyre*, p. xviii (my translation).

10.   Astrology is discussed indirectly, through the different forms it assumes, throughout the *De Mysteriis*, but especially in Books I, III, VII, VIII and IX.

11.   I have borrowed the term 'varieties of astrological experiences' from Patrick Curry and Roy Willis, *Astrology, Science and Culture. Pulling Down the Moon* (Oxford and New York: Berg, 2004), p. 65 [hereafter Curry and Willis, *Astrology, Science and Culture. Pulling Down the Moon*]. Curry and Willis have in turn borrowed and amended the phrase from William James, *Varieties of Religious Experience* (1912; New York: Mentor/New American Library, 1958). For the etymological definition, see Curry and Willis, *Astrology, Science and Culture. Pulling Down the Moon*, p. 1.

12.   Marilynn Lawrence, 'Who Thought the Stars are Causes? The Astrological Doctrine Criticized by Plotinus', in John F. Finamore and Robert M. Berchman, eds, *Metaphysical Patterns in Platonism. Ancient, Medieval and Modern Times* (University Press of the South, 2007; Westbury: Prometheus Trust, 2014), pp. 13–25, here p. 17, n. 17 [hereafter Lawrence, 'Who Thought the Stars are Causes?'].

13.   Nicholas Campion, *Astrology and Cosmology in the World's Religions* (New York and London: New York University Press, 2012), p. 11; definition of the influential British astrologer Margaret E. Hone, *The Modern text-Book of Astrology* (1951; Romford: L. N. Fowler & Co. Ltd., 1995), p. 16.

14.   For the Babylonian origins of astrology, see Francesca Rochberg, *The Heavenly Writing: Divination, Horoscopy, and Astronomy in Mesopotamian Culture* (Cambridge: Cambridge University Press, 2004), p. i, p. x, p. 13, *passim*; Nicholas Campion, *A History of Western Astrology. Vol. 1: The Ancient World* (New York and London: Continuum, 2008), pp. 35–85. For the Egyptian influence in the development of the horoscope, see Dorian Gieseler Greenbaum and Micah T. Ross, 'The Role of Egypt in the Development of the Horoscope', in Ladislav Bares, Filip Coppens and Kveta Smolarikova, eds, *Egypt in Transition. Social and Religious Development of Egypt in the First Millennium BCE* (Prague: Charles University, 2010), pp. 146–82.

15.   See Iamblichus, *DM* I.1 (4.10–5.1). For the suggestion of such synthesis, see

also Garth Fowden, *The Egyptian Hermes. A Historical Approach the Late Pagan Mind* (Princeton, NJ: Princeton University Press, 1986), p. 132.

16. Crystal Addey, 'Oracles of Fire: The Ritual Formation of the *Chaldean Oracles*', in *Fortune et Réception des textes oraculaires dans l'Antiquité tardive et le monde médiéval* (Conference), Université de Libre Bruxelles, Bruxelles (5-6 September 2016), p. 13.

17. For the impassibility of the divine, see Iamblichus, *DM* I.10 (33.12–34.5). For the ascent of the human soul through *anagogē*, it is essential to stress that, for Iamblichus, the highest purpose of the hieratic art is the ascent to the One, which constitutes the supreme master of the whole multiplicity of divinities (Iamblichus, *DM* V.22, 230.12–14). However, very few individuals may ever attain this stage of supreme union (Iamblichus, *DM* V.22, 230.14–231.2). Nevertheless, the path leading to the soul's salvation follows an unbroken line of continuity, comprising intermediate semi-divine and divine entities extending from souls, heroes, *daimones* and angels to the visible and the invisible gods (Iamblichus, *DM* I.5, 16.5–17.5 & *DM* II.3, 70.14–71.7). For the simultaneous divine descent and human ascent, Iamblichus, *DM* I.9 (28.11–29.3); *DM* III.2 (103.8–104.10); *DM* III.17 (139.8–140.4); see also Addey, *Divination and Theurgy in Neoplatonism*, pp. 221–36.

18. Porphyry, *Lettre à Anébon l'Égyptien* Fr. 84 Saffrey-Segonds (=*DM*, IX.3, 275.1–3). Reading ἐκθύσαιτο, with Parthey, for the ἐκθήσαιτο of the MSS.

19. For an overview of Iamblichus' understanding of the personal *daimōn*, see John Dillon, 'Iamblichus on the Personal Daemon', *The Ancient World* 32 (2001): pp. 3–9. (=*The Platonic Heritage*, Essay XXII); Andrei Timotin, *La Démonologie Platonicienne. Histoire de la notion de daimon de Platon aux derniers néoplatoniciens* (Leiden and Boston, MA: Brill, 2012), pp. 142–46, pp. 215–228, pp. 300–305 and especially pp. 309–22; Akindynos Kaniamos, 'The Personal *Daimōn* in Iamblichus' *De Mysteriis*: Astral Origins, Ritual and Divinization', in John F. Finamore and Mark Nyvlt, eds, *Plato in Late Antiquity, the Middle Ages and Modern Times. Selected Papers from the Seventeenth Annual Conference of the International Society for Neoplatonic Studies* (Lydney: The Prometheus Trust in association with the ISNS, 2020), pp. 27–58 [hereafter, Kaniamos, 'The Personal *Daimōn* in Iamblichus' *De Mysteriis*: Astral Origins, Ritual and Divinization'].

20. Iamblichus, *DM*, IX.2 (274.13). For the various astrological connotations of the *oikodespotēs* and the different methods for its discovery, see Auguste Bouché-Leclercq, *L'astrologie grecque* (Paris: Ernest Leroux, 1899), pp. 385–90, pp. 403–406; Dorian Gieseler Greenbaum, *The Daimon in Hellenistic Astrology. Origins and Influence* (Leiden and Boston, MA: Brill, 2016), pp. 255–66 [hereafter Greenbaum *The Daimon in Hellenistic Astrology*]. In the *Introduction to Ptolemy's Tetrabiblos* (chapter 30), in CCAG V/4, edited by Emilie Boer and Stephan Weinstock (Brussels: Henri Lamartin, 1940), pp. 185–228 [hereafter Porphyry, *Introduction to the Tetrabiblos*], Porphyry suggests a method based on two steps for the discovery of the *oikodespotēs*: first it was necessary to determine the predominator (*epikratētōr*), the planet which was most prominent in the horoscope. Then, the planet dominating the astrological sign in which the *epikratētōr* was located would become the *oikodespotēs*. For the authorship of this work, which is generally taken to be, at least in the majority, a genuine work of Porphyry, see G. Bezza in Richard Goulet, ed., *Dictionnaire des philosophes antiques*, vol. V(b): *de Plotina à Rutilius Rufus* (Paris: CNRS, 2012), pp. 1381-1384; Greenbaum, *The Daimon in Hellenistic Astrology*, pp. 266–70. For a comprehensive analysis of this astrological treatise in relation to the discovery of the *oikodespotēs*, see Greenbaum, *The Daimon in Hellenistic Astrology*, pp. 266–79. For the translation of chapter 30, see Greenbaum, *The Daimon in Hellenistic Astrology*, p. 441. Nevertheless, a large portion of the *Introduction to the Tetrabiblos* is actually a copy or paraphrase of the *Thesaurus* by late second-century astrologer Antiochus of Athens (see David Pingree, 'Antiochus and Rhetorius', in *Classical Philology* 72 (1977): pp. 203–23; Lawrence, 'Who Thought the Stars are Causes?', p. 20, n. 32.

21. Porphyry, *Lettre à Anébon l'Égyptien* Fr. 86 Saffrey-Segonds (=Iamblichus, *DM* IX.4, 277.1–5).

22. Plotinus, *Enneads*, III.1.5.33–59 and II.3. *passim.*, in Plotinus, *Enneads*, ed. and trans. A. H. Armstrong (1966-1988), 7 vols, Loeb (Cambridge, MA, and London: Harvard University Press, 1967) [hereafter Plotinus, *Enneads*]. For Plotinus' approach to astrology, see John Dillon, 'Plotinus on Whether the Stars are Causes', *Res Orientales* 12 (1999): pp. 87–92 [republished in John Dillon, *The Platonic Heritage* (Farnham and Burlington, VT: Ashgate, 2012), Essay XIX]; Lawrence, 'Who Thought the Stars are Causes?'; Peter Adamson, 'Plotinus on Astrology', in Brad Inwood, ed., *Oxford Studies in Ancient Philosophy XXXV: Winter 2008* (Oxford: Oxford University Press, 2008), pp. 265–91.

23. Whereas *technē* is associated with the craft or technical skills of knowing how to accomplish certain activities, *epistēmē* indicates the theoretical component upon which *technē* operates. See Richard Parry, 'Episteme and Techne', in Edward N. Zalta, ed., *The Stanford Encyclopaedia of Philosophy* (Fall 2014 Edition), at http://plato.stanford.edu/archives/fall2014/entries/episteme-techne/ (accessed 29 July 2021).

24. Polymnia Athanassiadi, 'Dreams, Theurgy and Freelance Divination: The Testimony of Iamblichus', p. 121.

25. G.E.R. Lloyd, *Magic, Reason and Experience. Studies in the Origin and Development of Greek Science* (London and New York: Cambridge University Press, 1979), p. 5, p. 180, n. 16 and n. 292. It cannot be verified that Ptolemy actually practised astrology, but he certainly knew a lot about it, at least on a theoretical level, as can be attested by his *Tetrabiblos*, edited and translated by F. E. Robbins (1940; Cambridge, MA and London: Harvard University Press: Loeb, 2001) [hereafter Ptolemy, *Tetrabiblos*].

26. Addey, *Divination and Theurgy in Neoplatonism*, p. 210, n. 199; Wolfgang Hübner, 'Die Begriffe "Astrologie" und "Astronomie" in der Antike: Wortgeschichte und Wissenschaftssystematik, mit einer Hypothese zum Terminus', *Quadrivium* 1989/7, Abhandlunger der Geistes-und sozialwissenschaftliche Klasse, Akademie der Wissenschaften und der Literatur Mainz (Wiesbaden: Franz Steiner Verlag, 1989).

27. Following Shaw's excellent suggestion to distinguish 'astral theurgy' from the 'astrology practiced by the Greeks', see Gregory Shaw, 'Astrology as Divination: Iamblichean Theory and its Contemporary Practice', in John Finamore and Robert Berchman, eds, *Metaphysical Patterns in Platonism: Ancient, Medieval, Renaissance and Modern Times* (New Orleans: University Press of the South, 2007; repr. Westbury: The Prometheus Trust, 2014), pp. 73–86, here p. 74. For the occurrences of *genethlialogia*, see: *DM* I.18 (53.2), IX.1 (273.5–6), IX.2 (274.5–6), IX.5 (279.10). For *di'asterōn technē*, see *DM* III.15 (135.4). For astrology as an inspired and inductive form of divination in *DM*, see Crystal Addey, 'Oracles, Dreams and Astrology in Iamblichus' *De Mysteriis*', in Angela Voss and Patrick Curry, eds, *Seeing with Different Eyes: Essays on Astrology and Divination* (Newcastle: Cambridge Scholars Publishing, 2008), pp. 35–57, here pp. 47–52 [hereafter Addey, 'Oracles, Dreams and Astrology in Iamblichus' *De Mysteriis*']; Kaniamos, 'The Personal *Daimōn* in Iamblichus' *De Mysteriis*: Astral Origins, Ritual and Divinization', pp. 29–35. For the astral dimension of theurgy in Proclus, see José Manuel Redondo's papers: 'The Celestial Imagination; Proclus the Philosopher on Theurgy', *Culture and Cosmos* 19 no. 1 and 2 (Spring/Summer and Autumn/Winter 2015): pp. 25–46; 'The Transmission of Fire: Proclus' Theurgical Prayers', in John M. Dillon and Andrei Timotin, eds, *Neoplatonic Theories of Prayer* (Leiden and Boston, MA: Brill, 2016), pp. 164–91. For the category of inspired or natural divination (*mantikē*) as opposed to the artificial, or inductive, form of divination (augury), see Plato, *Phaedrus* 244 c-d, trans. Harold North Fowler, in Plato, *Euthyphro. Apology. Crito. Phaedo. Phaedrus* (Loeb, Cambridge, MA and London: Harvard University Press, 1914) [hereafter Plato, *Phaedrus*];

Cicero, *De Divinatione*, I.vi.10–12; II.xi.26–27, trans. W.A. Falconer, in Cicero, *On Old Age. On Friendship. On Divination* (Cambridge, MA, and London: Loeb, 1923).

28. Plato, *Timaeus* 35A ff. in Plato, *Timaeus. Critias. Cleitophon. Menexenus. Epistles*, Loeb Vol. IX, trans. R.G. Bury (Cambridge, MA, and London: Harvard University Press). in *Plato: Lysis, Symposium, Gorgias*, ed. and trans. W.R.M Lamb (1925; Cambridge, MA and London: Harvard University press, 1975) [hereafter Plato, *Timaeus*].

29. Plato, *Timaeus* 36C-D. See also *ibid.*, p.72, n.1. For the idea that the circle of the Different must be identified with the Zodiac, rather than the ecliptic, see Francis M. Cornford, *Plato's Cosmology, The Timaeus of Plato*, (1937; Indianapolis, IL and Cambridge: Hackett Publishing, 1997), p. 76 [hereafter Cornford, *Plato's Cosmology*].

30. Plato, *Timaeus* 36D. At 38D it appears that the three planets that revolve at equal speed are the Sun, Venus, and Mercury (viewed from Earth as the 'inner planets'); the other four are the Moon and Mars, Jupiter, Saturn (the last three are seen from Earth as the 'outer planets'). See also Cornford, *Plato's Cosmology*, p. 80.

31. Sarah Iles Johnston, *Hekate Soteira. A Study of Hekate's Roles in the Chaldean Oracles and Related Literature* (Atlanta, GA: The American Philological Association, 1990), p. 17 [hereafter Johnston, *Hekate Soteira*]; see also Wallis, *Neoplatonism*, pp. 50–51.

32. Sarah Iles Johnston, *Hekate Soteira*, p. 17. The Pythagorean idea that the cosmos is governed by numerical laws is also recurrent in other works of Iamblichus: Iamblichus, *De Vita Pythagorica* (*On the Pythagorean Way of Life*), eds and trans J. Dillon and J. Hershbell (Atlanta, GA: Scholars Press, 1991); Iamblichus, *The Theology of Arithmetic. On the Mystical, Mathematical and Cosmological Symbolism of the first Ten Numbers* [attributed to Iamblichus], trans. R. Waterfield (Grand Rapids, MI: Phanes Press: Kairos, 1988).

33. Plato, *Republic* V 477a–478a, ed. and trans. P. Shorey, 2 vols, Loeb (1925; Cambridge, MA and London: Harvard University Press and Heinemann, 1975) [hereafter Plato, *Republic*].

34. Plato, *Republic*, 477b.

35. Iamblichus, *DM* IX.4 (277.5–6), Μυρίους γὰρ ἐσχήκασιν αἱ ὅλαι ἐπιστῆμαι τοὺς ἀμφισβητοῦντας, καὶ τὰ ἐν αὐταῖς ἀπορήματα ἀναρίθμητα γέγονεν.

36. Iamblichus, *DM* IX.4 (277.9–10), ...οὕτω καὶ περὶ τῆς μαθηματικῆς ἀντεροῦμεν, ὡς ὑπάρχει μὲν ἀληθής, οἱ δὲ πλανώμενοι περὶ αὐτῆς οὐδὲν εἰδότες τῶν ἀληθῶν ἀντιλέγουσιν.

37. Iamblichus, *DM* IX.4 (277.10–12)

38. Iamblichus, *DM* IX.4 (277.12–14), προϊόντος γὰρ ἀεὶ τοῦ χρόνου, πολλῷ τῷ θνητῷ καὶ πολλάκις ἀνακεραννύμεναι, ἐξίτηλον τὸ θεῖον ἦθος τῆς γνώσεως ἀπεργάζονται.

39. Iamblichus, *DM* IX.4 (278.2–5), Ἐπεὶ καὶ τῆς τῶν θείων περιόδων ἀναμετρήσεως ἐν ὀφθαλμοῖς ἐστι κατάδηλα τὰ σημεῖα, ὁπόταν ἐκλείψεις ἡλίου καὶ σελήνης καὶ παραβολὰς πρὸς τοὺς ἀπλανεῖς ἀστέρας τῆς σελήνης προμηνύῃ, καὶ συνομολογουμένη φαίνεται τῇ προσημασίᾳ τῆς ὄψεως ἡ πεῖρα.

40. Iamblichus, *DM* IX.4 (278.5–8). See also Iamblichus, *In Timaeum*, Book I, Fr. 11, in John Dillon, *Iamblichus. The Platonic Commentaries* [hereafter, Iamblichus, *In Timaeum*].

41. Iamblichus, *DM* IX.4 (278.8–11).

42. Plato, *Timaeus*, 29E-30D; Iamblichus, *DM* III.28 (168.14–169.2), ταῖς δὲ ἐννοίαις καὶ βουλήσεσι καὶ τοῖς ἀύλοις εἴδεσι διὰ τῆς ἀιδίου τε καὶ ὑπερκοσμίου καὶ ἐγκοσμίου ψυχῆς δημιουργεῖ τοὺς κόσμους· (translated by Clarke et al., *Iamblichus: De Mysteriis* with slight emendations).

43. Iamblichus, *DM* III.28 (169.4–6), Οὐσῶν γὰρ περὶ τοὺς οὐρανίους θεοὺς ἀπείρων δή τινων δυνάμεων, ἓν γένος τῶν ἐν αὐταῖς πάντων ἔσχατόν ἐστι, τὸ φυσικόν. (my translation)

44. Iamblichus, *DM* III.28 (170.2–6), οὕτω δεῖ καὶ ἀποφαίνεσθαι, ὅτι δὴ αὐταῖς μὲν ταῖς

περιφοραῖς ἢ ταῖς ἐνυπαρχούσαις ἐν αὐταῖς δυνάμεσιν ἢ ταῖς κατὰ φύσιν περὶ αὐτὰς ἐνιδρυμέναις οὔτε χρῆται εἰδωλοποιός, οὔθ᾽ ὅλως δυνατός ἐστιν αὐτῶν ἐφάπτεσθαι· (trans. Clarke et al., *Iamblichus: De Mysteriis* with emendations).

45. Addey, *Divination and Theurgy in Neoplatonism*, p. 254. Iamblichus' remarks echo the differences between inspired and artificial forms of divination.

46. Iamblichus, *DM* III.30 (173.10–12), Καὶ γὰρ τὰ ἔσχατα τῶν ἐν τῇ γενέσει κινεῖται τοῖς οὐρανίοις δρόμοις καὶ συμπάσχει πρὸς τὰς ἀπ᾽ αὐτῶν κατιούσας ἀπορροίας· (my translation).

47. For the use of the term ἀπόρροια, Iamblichus, *DM* I.18 (55.4), I.18 (55.6), III.16 (137.13), III.30 (173.12), IV.10 (194.10), IX.2 (274.5), IX.3 (276.12). Porphyry uses that same word in his *Introduction to the Tetrabiblos* as an astrological term, usually translated loosely as 'separation' of one planet from another; see Porphyry, *Introduction to the Tetrabiblos*, chapters 12 and 13, pp. 185–228, here p. 199. For ἀπόρροια in a similar astrological context, see also Paulus Alexandrinus, in Emilie Boer, ed., *Elementa Apotelesmatica (Introduction to Astrology)* (Leipzig: Teubner, 1958, chapter 17.

48. Iamblichus, *DM* VII.1 (249.11–250.2), ...οὗτοι γὰρ τὴν φύσιν τοῦ παντὸς καὶ τὴν δημιουργίαν τῶν θεῶν μιμούμενοι καὶ αὐτοὶ τῶν μυστικῶν καὶ ἀποκεκρυμμένων καὶ ἀφανῶν νοήσεων εἰκόνας τινὰς διὰ συμβόλων ἐκφαίνουσιν... (trans. Clarke et al., *Iamblichus: De Mysteriis* with emendations). I have considered it more appropriate for this passage to translate εἰκόνας as 'images' rather than 'signs'. The choice of the verb ἐκφαίνουσιν and the series of archetypal images which Iamblichus will analyse further point in the direction of 'images'.

49. Plato, *Phaedrus*, 247c.

50. Plotinus, *Enneads* III.4 (6.47–60). Dorian Greenbaum analyses thoroughly the use of κυβερνήτης in Porphyry's works in relation to the personal *daimōn* and the *oikodespotēs*, see Dorian Gieseler Greenbaum, 'Porphyry of Tyre on the *Daimōn*, Birth and the Stars', in Luc Brisson, Seamus O'Neill, and Andrei Timotin, eds, *Neoplatonic Angels and Demons* (Leiden and Boston, MA: Brill, 2018), pp. 102–139, here pp. 117–22; Greenbaum, *The Daimon in Hellenistic Astrology*, pp. 266–75.

51. Iamblichus, *DM* VII.2 (252.8–12), Ὁ δ᾽ ἐπὶ πλοίου ναυτιλλόμενος τὴν διακυβερνῶσαν τὸν κόσμον ἐπικράτειαν παρίστησιν. Ὥσπερ οὖν ὁ κυβερνήτης χωριστὸς ὢν τῆς νεὼς τῶν πηδαλίων αὐτῆς ἐπιβέβηκεν, οὕτω χωριστῶς ὁ ἥλιος τῶν οἰάκων τοῦ κόσμου παντὸς ἐπιβέβηκεν.

52. Plato, *Republic* VII, 514a2–517a7.

53. Plotinus, *Enneads* I.7 (*On the Primal Good*) 1.25–29; *Enneads* V.6 (*What is Beyond Being Does Not Think*) 4.15–16; *Enneads* V.6 (*On Numbers*) 7.1–7.

54. For the Platonic demiurge, Plato, *Timaeus* 29d-30c, *passim*; Cornford, *Plato's Cosmology*, pp. 34–39. For the Aristotelian prime-mover, Aristotle, *Metaphysics*, XII(Λ), VII–VIII (1072a ff.) in Aristotle, *Metaphysics, Volume II Books 10-14. Oeconomica. Magna Moralia*, trans. Hugh Tredennick and G. Cyril Armstrong (1933; London and Cambridge, MA: Harvard University Press, 1961); Joseph G. Defilippo, 'Aristotle's Identification of the Prime Mover as God', *The Classical Quarterly* 44, no. 2 (1994): pp. 393–409.

55. Iamblichus, *DM* VII.2 (252.14–15), οὕτω πολὺ πρότερον ὁ θεὸς ἄνωθεν ἀπὸ τῶν πρώτων ἀρχῶν τῆς φύσεως τὰς πρωτουργοὺς αἰτίας τῶν κινήσεων ἀμερίστως ἐνδίδωσι.

56. Gregory Shaw, *Theurgy and the Soul*, p. 195.

57. Iamblichus, *DM* VII.3 (253.2–4).

58. Iamblichus, *DM* VII.3 (253.4–5).

59. Greenbaum, *The Daimon in Hellenistic Astrology*, pp. 43–45, here p. 44.

60. Iamblichus, *DM* VII.3 (253.6–9), ...παρίστησι καὶ ταύτας ὁ συμβολικὸς τρόπος τῆς σημασίας, τὸ σχηματίζεσθαι μὲν κατὰ ζῴδιον καὶ τὰς μορφὰς ἀμείβειν καθ᾽ ὥραν τοῖς ῥήμασι

διασημαίνων, ἐκδεικνύμενος δὲ τὴν ἀμετάβλητον αὐτοῦ καὶ ἑστῶσαν καὶ ἀνέκλειπτον καὶ ὁμοῦ πᾶσαν καὶ ἀθρόαν εἰς ὅλον τὸν κόσμον δόσιν. (my translation).

61. Niketas Siniossoglou, 'From Philosophic Monotheism to Imperial Henotheism: Esoteric and Popular Religion in Late Antique Platonism', in Stephen Mitchell and Peter Van Nuffelen (eds), *Monotheism between Pagans and Christians in Late Antiquity* (Leuven: Peeters, 2010), pp. 127–48, here p. 129.

62. There are a number of spells relating to the changing appearance of the sun in the *PGM*, many of which have Egyptian origins. See, for example, *PGM* IV.633–639 in the so-called 'Mithras Liturgy' (*PGM* IV.475–829); *PGM* IV.1596–1715 ('Spell to Helios'); *PGM* 1928–2005 ('Spell of Attraction to King Pitys over any skull cup', with prayer/petition to Helios), in Karl Preisendanz, *Papyri Graecae Magicae. Die griechischen Zauberpapyri*, 2 vols, ed. and trans. Karl Preisendanz (Stuttgart: Teubner, 1973-1974); Hans Dieter Betz, ed., *The Greek Magical Papyri in Translation* (Chicago, IL, and London, University of Chicago Press, 1986).

63. Iamblichus, *DM* VII.3 (253.14–254.4), διὸ καί φησιν αὐτὸν ἕνα εἶναι καὶ τὸν αὐτόν, τὰς δὲ διαμείψεις τῆς μορφῆς καὶ τοὺς μετασχηματισμοὺς ἐν τοῖς δεχομένοις ὑποτίθεται. Διόπερ κατὰ ζῴδιον καὶ καθ' ὥραν μεταβάλλεσθαι αὐτόν φησιν, ὡς ἐκείνων διαποικιλλομένων περὶ τὸν θεὸν κατὰ τὰς πολλὰς αὐτοῦ ὑποδοχάς. The hourly change of the sun is also reminiscent of the *dodekaoros*, which is two-hour segments each assigned to an Egyptian animal.

64. Iamblichus, *DM* VII.3 (254.4–7). For the prominence of the solar cult in the Roman Empire in Late Antiquity, see Franz Cumont, 'La théologie solaire du paganisme romain', *Extrait des mémoires présentés par divers savants à l'académie des inscriptions et belles-lettres*, Tome xii, 11epartie (Paris: Imprimerie Nationale, 1913), pp. 447–79. Franz Cumont highlights the Babylonian and Egyptian elements in the solar cult and its implication with astrological doctrines, see Franz Cumont, *Astrology and Religion Among the Greeks and Romans* (1912; New York: Kessinger Publications, 1960), xxiii–xxiv, *passim*.; Franz Cumont, *The Oriental Religions in Roman Paganism* (Chicago, IL: The Open Court Publishing Company, 1911), pp. 133–34. Giuseppe Muscolino points out that the solar cult of Mithras, which was introduced in Rome by Persian slaves in the first century BCE, was reinterpreted during the third century CE 'Platonically', and gave rise to the cult of Sol Invictus, installed by Aurelian in 274 CE, in order to serve political purposes of unification under one imperial authority; see Giuseppe Muscolino, *Porfirio: La Philosophia ex Oraculis. Per una Nuova Edizione dei Frammenti* (PhD Thesis: Università Degli Studi Di Macerata, Dipartimento Di Filosofia E Scienze Umane, 2013), pp. 36–40; see also Robert Turcan, *Mitras Platonicus. Recherches sur l'helléninisation philosophique de Mithra* (Leiden: Brill, 1975). According to Richard Gordon, the public cult of the sun was accentuated in Rome when political developments led to an affinity between the sun and the concept of monarchy, see Richard L. Gordon (Ilmmünster) and Martin Wallraff (Bonn), "Sol", in: *Brill's New Pauly*, Antiquity volumes edited by: Hubert Cancik and Helmuth Schneider, English Edition by: Christine F. Salazar, Classical Tradition volumes edited by: Manfred Landfester, English Edition by: Francis G. Gentry. Consulted online on 14 October 2021 <http://dx.doi.org/10.1163/1574-9347_bnp_e1116380>. First published online: 2006. First print edition: 9789004122598, 20110510.

65. Shaw, *Theurgy and the Soul*, p. 199 (italics by the author).

66. Iamblichus, *DM* VIII.4 (267.6–10).

67. See Greenbaum, *The Daimon in Hellenistic Astrology*, pp. 40–45, pp. 247–78; Shaw, *Theurgy and the Soul*, p. 225; Addey, *Divination and Theurgy in Neoplatonism*, pp. 105–106, p. 211. For an overview of the notion of *kairos* in relation to divination, see Crystal Addey, 'Divination and the *Kairos* in Ancient Greek Philosophy and Culture', in Crystal Addey, ed., *Divination and Knowledge in Graeco-Roman Antiquity* (London and New York: Routledge, 2021), pp. 138–73. For *kairos* in relation to katarchic astrology,

see Dorian Gieseler Greenbaum, 'Divination and Decumbiture: Katarchic astrology and Greek Medicine', in Crystal Addey, ed., *Divination and Knowledge in Graeco-Roman Antiquity* (London and New York: Routledge, 2021), pp. 109–36, especially pp. 112–21.

68. Plato was willing to call the stars 'gods', as were the Babylonians; see Plato, *Republic* VI 508a4; *Laws* 821 B, 899 B, 950 D, in Plato, *Laws*. II vols, trans. R. G. Bury (Cambridge, MA, and London: Harvard University Press, 1926; *Cratylus* 397d, in Plato, *Cratylus. Parmenides. Greater Hippias. Lesser Hippias*, trans. H. N. Fowler, (Cambridge, MA, and London: Harvard University Press, 1926]; *Apology* 26 D, in Plato, *Euthyphro. Apology. Crito. Phaedo. Phaedrus,* Loeb (Cambridge, MA, and London: Harvard University Press, 1914); *Epinomis* 983d–985b, 988b, in Plato, Volume XII. *Charmides. Alcibiades* I and II. *Hipparchus. The Lovers. Theages. Minos. Epinomis*, trans. W. R. Lamb, Loeb Classical Library 201 (Cambridge, MA: Harvard University Press, 1924; The view that the planets are divine is also expressed by Plotinus and Porphyry, see Addey, *Divination and Theurgy in Neoplatonism*, pp. 205–11. For an overview of the origin of the belief in the divinity of the planets in ancient Greece, see Martin P. Nilsson, 'The Origin of Belief among the Greeks in the Divinity of the Heavenly Bodies', *The Harvard Theological Review* 33, no. 1 (January 1940), pp. 1–8.

69. Iamblichus, *DM* I.18 (52.13–14), …οἱ κατ' οὐρανὸν ἐμφανεῖς θεοί τέ εἰσι πάντες καὶ τρόπον τινὰ ἀσώματοι·

70. Porphyry, *Lettre à Anébon l'Égyptien* Fr. 22 Saffrey-Segonds (=Iamblichus, *DM* I.17, 50.13–16).

71. Iamblichus, *DM* I.17 (50.13–51.2), ὅτι δὴ οὐ περιέχονται ὑπὸ τῶν σωμάτων, φαμὲν ἡμεῖς, ἀλλὰ ταῖς θείαις ζωαῖς καὶ ἐνεργείαις περιέχουσι τὰ σώματα· (trans. Clarke et al., *Iamblichus: De Mysteriis* with emendations).

72. Iamblichus, *DM* I.8 (24.2–3), Ἔτι οὐδὲ ἔνεστιν ἐν τοῖς σώμασι τὰ γένη τῶν κρειττόνων, ἔξωθεν δ' αὐτῶν ἡγεμονεύει· οὐκ ἄρα συναλλοιοῦται τοῖς σώμασιν.

73. Plato, *Phaedrus* 246E–247B; Iamblichus, *DM* I.17 (51.5–8).

74. Shaw, *Theurgy and the Soul*, p. 153.

75. Iamblichus, *In Timaeum*, III. fr. 49 (3.26–29), τοιοῦτον δὲ τὸ σφαιρικόν, ἅμα ἓν ὂν καὶ τὸ πλῆθος περιέχειν δυνάμενον, ὃ δὴ θεῖόν ἐστιν ὄντως, τὸ μὴ ἐξιστάμενον τῆς ἑνότητος παντὸς τοῦ πεπλυθησμένου κρατεῖν. (trans. Dillon, *Iamblichus. The Platonic Commentaries*).

76. Iamblichus, *DM* I.17 (51.9–10).

77. Plato, *Timaeus* 40C–D; Plotinus, *Enneads* (*On Difficulties about the Soul II*) IV.4.33–34. For the divine illumination in Iamblichus, see John Finamore, 'Iamblichus on Light and the Transparent', in H.J. Blumenthal and E.G. Clark, eds, *The Divine Iamblichus: Philosopher and Man of Gods* (Bristol: Bristol Classical Press, 1993), pp. 55–64.

78. Iamblichus, *DM* I.9 (31.14–32.6), ὅπερ δὴ καὶ ὁ σύμπας μιμούμενος οὐρανὸς καὶ κόσμος τὴν ἐγκύκλιον περιφορὰν περιπολεῖ, συνήνωταί τε πρὸς ἑαυτόν, καὶ τὰ στοιχεῖα κατὰ κύκλον περιδινούμενα ποδηγεῖ, πάντα τε ἐν ἀλλήλοις ὄντα καὶ πρὸς ἄλληλα φερόμενα συνέχει, μέτροις τε τοῖς ἴσοις ἀφορίζει καὶ τὰ πορρωτάτω διῳκισμένα, καὶ τὰς τελευτὰς ταῖς ἀρχαῖς οἷον γῆν οὐρανῷ συγκεῖσθαι ποιεῖ, μίαν τε συνέχειαν καὶ ὁμολογίαν τῶν ὅλων πρὸς ὅλα ἀπεργάζεται.

79. Iamblichus, *DM* VII.2 (251.1–252.2).

80. Iamblichus, *DM* VII.2 (252.2–6), κυκλοτερῆ γὰρ πάντα ὁρᾶται τὰ τοῦ λωτοῦ, καὶ τὰ ἐν τοῖς φύλλοις εἴδη καὶ τὰ ἐν τοῖς καρποῖς φαινόμενα, ἥπερ δὴ μόνη κινήσει τῇ κατὰ κύκλον νοῦ ἐνεργείᾳ ἐστι συγγενές, τὸ κατὰ τὰ αὐτὰ καὶ ὡσαύτως καὶ ἐν μιᾷ τάξει καὶ καθ' ἕνα λόγον ἐμφαίνουσα.

81. Iamblichus, *DM* V.4 (202.4–9); V.4 (202.8–9), …τὸ κυκλοφορητικὸν καὶ ἄυλον σῶμα.

82. Iamblichus, *DM* V.4 (202.10–203.1), Ὁμολογεῖται γὰρ δὴ τὸ αἰθέριον σῶμα πάσης ἐκτὸς εἶναι ἐναντιώσεως, τροπῆς τε πάσης ἀπηλλάχθαι, καὶ τὸ δύνασθαι εἰς ὁτιοῦν μεταβάλλειν

πάντη καθαρεύειν, ῥοπῆς τε τῆς ἐπὶ τὸ μέσον καὶ ἀπὸ τοῦ μέσου παντελῶς ἀπολελύσθαι, διότι ἀρρεπές ἐστιν ἢ κατὰ κύκλον περιφέρεται·

83. Aristotle, *Categories*, 4a10–12, in *The Complete Works of Aristotle*, 2 vols, trans. J. L. Ackrill (Princeton, NJ: Princeton University Press, 2014); Clarke et al., *Iamblichus: De Mysteriis*, p. 231, n. 286.

84. Iamblichus, *DM* I.19 (57.12).

85. Iamblichus, *DM* I.19 (57.3–7).

86. Iamblichus, *DM* I.19 (60.8–11), Οἵ τε γὰρ ἐμφανεῖς θεοὶ σωμάτων εἰσὶν ἔξω, καὶ διὰ τοῦτό εἰσιν ἐν τῷ νοητῷ, καὶ οἱ νοητοὶ διὰ τὴν ἄπειρον αὐτῶν ἕνωσιν περιέχουσιν ἐν ἑαυτοῖς τοὺς ἐμφανεῖς, ἀμφότεροί τε κατὰ κοινὴν ἕνωσιν καὶ μίαν ἐνέργειαν ἵστανται ὡσαύτως.

87. Plato, *Timaeus* 41e1; Plato, *Phaedrus* 247b2; Aristotle, *De Gen. An.* II, 736b37–39, in Aristotle, *Generation of Animals*, trans. A.L. Peck (London and Cambridge, MA: Harvard University Press, 1943). For an overview of the vehicle's origins and functions in Neoplatonic theory, see E.R. Dodds, 'The Astral Body in Neoplatonism', in Proclus, *The Elements of Theology*, (Revised Text with Translation, Introduction and Commentary by E.R. Dodds) (1963; Oxford: Clarendon Press, 2004), pp. 313–32; Finamore, *Iamblichus and the Theory of the Vehicle of the Soul*, pp. 1–6; Robert Christian Kissling, 'The ΟΧΗΜΑ-ΠΝΕΥΜΑ of the Neo-Platonists and the De insomniis of Synesius of Cyrene', *American Journal of Philology* 43, no. 4 (1922): pp. 318–30 [hereafter Kissling, 'The ΟΧΗΜΑ-ΠΝΕΥΜΑ of the Neo-Platonists']; Crystal Addey, 'In the Light of the Sphere: The Vehicle of the Soul and Subtle Body Practices in Neoplatonism', in Geoffrey Samuel and Jay Johnston, eds, *Religion and the Subtle Body in Asia and the West: Between Mind and Body* (London: Routledge, 2013), pp. 149–67 [hereafter Addey, 'In the Light of the Sphere'].

88. Iamblichus, *DM* II.6 (81.15–82.1), τὸ μὴ ὂν σῶμα ὡς σῶμα τοῖς τῆς ψυχῆς ὀφθαλμοῖς διὰ τῶν τοῦ σώματος ἐπιδείκνυσιν·

89. Addey, 'In the Light of the Sphere', p. 150. For the subtle differences between *phantasia* in the context of Late Antiquity and 'imagination' with modern connotations, see Addey, 'In the Light of the Sphere', p. 150. See also Anne Sheppard, 'Phantasia and Inspiration in Neoplatonism', in M. Joyal, ed., *Studies on Plato and the Platonic Tradition: Essays Presented to John Whittaker* (Aldershot: Ashgate, 1997), pp. 201–10 [hereafter, Sheppard, 'Phantasia and Inspiration in Neoplatonism'].

90. Kissling, 'The ΟΧΗΜΑ-ΠΝΕΥΜΑ of the Neo-Platonists', p. 321; Addey, 'In the Light of the Sphere', p. 150; Sheppard, 'Phantasia and Inspiration in Neoplatonism', p. 206.

91. Shaw, *Theurgy and the Soul*, p. 246.

92. Proclus, *In Remp.* I.39, 8–10, ... καὶ γὰρ τοῖς ὁρῶσιν αὐτοῖς ὁρᾶται τοῖς αὐγοειδέσι τῶν ψυχῶν περιβλήμασιν· in Proclus, *In Platonis Rem publican commentaria*, ed. G. Kroll, 2 vols (Leipzig: Teubner, 1899-1901) (trans. Shaw, *Theurgy and the Soul*, p. 246).

93. Iamblichus, *DM* III.2 (103.11–104.1), Καὶ ποτὲ μὲν ἀναφὲς καὶ ἀσώματον πνεῦμα περιέχει κύκλῳ τοὺς κατακειμένους, ὡς ὅρασιν μὲν αὐτοῦ μὴ παρεῖναι, τὴν δ' ἄλλην συναίσθησιν καὶ παρακολούθησιν ὑπάρχειν.

94. Iamblichus, *DM* III.4 (109.10–11), εἰ γὰρ τὴν ἑαυτῶν ζωὴν ὑποτεθείκασιν ὅλην ὡς ὄχημα ἢ ὄργανον τοῖς ἐπιπνέουσι θεοῖς (trans. Clarke et al., *Iamblichus: De Mysteriis* with slight emendations).

95. Iamblichus, *DM* III.14 (132.9–12), Αὕτη δή που τὸ περικείμενον τῇ ψυχῇ αἰθερῶδες καὶ αὐγοειδὲς ὄχημα ἐπιλάμπει θείῳ φωτί, ἐξ οὗ δὴ φαντασίαι θεῖαι καταλαμβάνουσι τὴν ἐν ἡμῖν φανταστικὴν δύναμιν, κινούμεναι ὑπὸ τῆς βουλήσεως τῶν θεῶν. (trans. Clarke et al., *Iamblichus: De Mysteriis*).

96. Iamblichus, *DM* III.11 (126.9–11), Καὶ ὅταν μὲν ἀθρόον καὶ πολὺ τὸ ἀναφερόμενον ἀπὸ τοῦ στομίου πῦρ κύκλῳ πανταχόθεν αὐτὴν περιέχῃ, πληροῦται ἀπ' αὐτοῦ θείας αὐγῆς.

97. Addey, 'In the Light of the Sphere', p. 154; see also Sheppard, 'Phantasia and Inspiration in Neoplatonism', p. 208.

98. Iamblichus, *De Anima* Fr. 43 (1–5), Καὶ μὴν τῆς γε καθάρσεως ἀφαίρεσις τῶν ἀλλοτρίων, ἀπόδοσις τῆς οἰκείας οὐσίας, τελειότης, ἀποπλήρωσις, αὐτάρκεια, ἄνοδος ἐπὶ τὴν γεννησαμένην αἰτίαν, συναφὴ πρὸς τὰ ὅλα τῶν μερῶν, δόσις ἀπὸ τῶν ὅλων εἰς τὰ μεριστὰ δυνάμεως καὶ ζωῆς καὶ ἐνεργείας καὶ τὰ τοιαῦτα νοείσθω ὡς πάντων χρησιμώτατα. (in Iamblichus, *De Anima*, text, translation and commentary by John Finamore and John Dillon, (Atlanta, GA: Society of Biblical Literature, 2002) [hereafter, Iamblichus, *De Anima*]).

99. Addey, *Divination and Theurgy in Neoplatonism*, p. 237, see also pp. 226–29.

100. Iamblichus, *DM* III.11 (125.4–6), ἀλλ᾽ αὕτη μὲν ἐπιτηδειότητα μόνον καὶ ἀποκάθαρσιν τοῦ ἐν ἡμῖν αὐγοειδοῦς πνεύματος ἐμποιεῖ, δι᾽ ἣν δυνατοὶ γιγνόμεθα χωρεῖν τὸν θεόν.

101. Iamblichus, *In Timaeum*, III. fr. 49 (1.12–15), οὕτω καὶ τὸ πᾶν σφαιροειδὲς ἀπετέλεσε πρὸς τὴν αὐτοκινησίαν αὐτῆς ἀπεικαζόμενον. διὸ καὶ τὸ ἡμέτερον ὄχημα σφαιρικὸν ἀποτελεῖται καὶ κινεῖται κυκλικῶς, ὅταν διαφερόντως ὁμοιωθῇ πρὸς τὸν νοῦν ἡ ψυχή (trans. Dillon, *Iamblichus. The Platonic Commentaries* with slight emendations).

102. Addey, 'In the Light of the Sphere', p. 153.

103. Addey, 'In the Light of the Sphere', pp. 150, pp. 152–53; Finamore, *Iamblichus and the Theory of the Vehicle of the Soul*, pp. 49–50.

104. Iamblichus, *In Timaeum*, IV. fr. 84 (4–5).

105. Iamblichus, *In Timaeum*, IV. fr. 84 (6–7); Proclus, *In Timaeum* V: 234.18–24 (311A), in E. Diehl, ed., *Platonis Timaeum Commentaria*, 3 vols (Leipzig: Teubner, 1903-1906); Porphyry, 'Περὶ τοῦ ἐφ᾽ ἡμῖν' 305.68–71, in Porphyry, *Fragmenta*, ed. Andrew Smith (Stuttgart/Leipzig: Teubner, 1993). For a comprehensive discussion on Porphyry's views on the vehicle, see Greenbaum, 'Porphyry of Tyre on the *Daimon*, Birth and the Stars'; Greenbaum, *The Daimon in Hellenistic Astrology*, p. 240 and n. 26.

106. Iamblichus, *In Timaeum*, IV. fr. 84 (7–8, my italics), κατὰ τὰς ζωὰς τὰς θείας προϊόντων καὶ μορφουμένων τῶν μερικῶν πνευμάτων. (my translation).

107. Dillon, *Iamblichus. The Platonic Commentaries*, p. 380.

108. Finamore, *Iamblichus and the Theory of the Vehicle of the Soul*, pp. 59–114.

109. Finamore, *Iamblichus and the Theory of the Vehicle of the Soul*, p. 68.

110. Iamblichus, *DM* I.18 (55.3–5).

111. Iamblichus, *DM* I.18 (55.5–8), Οἷον ἡ τοῦ Κρόνου ἀπόρροιά ἐστι συνεκτική, ἡ δὲ τοῦ Ἄρεος κινητική· πλὴν ἔν γε τοῖς ἐνύλοις ἡ παθητὴ γενεσιουργὸς ὑποδοχὴ τὴν μὲν κατὰ πῆξιν καὶ ψυχρότητα ἐδέξατο, τὴν δὲ κατὰ φλόγωσιν ὑπερβάλλουσαν τὸ μέτριον. (trans. Clarke et al., *Iamblichus: De Mysteriis* with slight emendations).

112. Benefic and malefic planets are an extremely common trope in Hellenistic astrology, see, for example, Vettius Valens, *Vettii Valentis anthologiarum libri ix*, I. 5.2-9, ed. W. Kroll (1908; Berlin: Weidmann, 1973). For Mars and Saturn as 'malefic' planets, see, for example, Ptolemy, *Tetrabiblos*, I.5.19; Iamblichus, *DM* I.18 (55.10–56.2), ἔτι τοίνυν ἡ ἀσθένεια τῶν ἐνύλων καὶ περιγείων τόπων τὴν ἀκραιφνῆ δύναμιν καὶ τὴν καθαρωτάτην ζωὴν τῶν αἰθερίων μὴ χωροῦσα τὸ ἑαυτῆς πάθημα μεταφέρει εἰς τὰ πρῶτα αἴτια.

113. For the term ῥοῖζος, see *Oracles Chaldaïques*, ed. and trans. Édouard Des Places (1971; Paris: Budé-Les Belles Lettres, 1996), Fr. 37, Fr. 107, Fr. 146; Hans Lewy, *Chaldean Oracles and Theurgy: Mysticism, Magic and Platonism in the later Roman Empire* , ed. Michel Tardieu (1956; 1978; Paris: Etudes Augustiniennes, 2011), p. 19, n. 46 [hereafter Lewy, *Chaldean Oracles and Theurgy*]; Shaw, *Theurgy and the Soul*, p. 101, p. 198; Clarke et al., *Iamblichus: De Mysteriis*, p. 141, n. 188; Johnston, *Hekate Soteira*, p. 104, p. 108, p. 122; Addey, 'Oracles, Dreams and Astrology in Iamblichus' *De Mysteriis*', pp. 44–45; Addey, *Divination and Theurgy in Neoplatonism*, pp. 263–64.

114. Iamblichus, *DM* III.2 (104.1–2), ῥοιζομένου τε ἐν τῷ εἰσιέναι.

115. Iamblichus, *DM* III.9 (118.13–119.3), ὡς ἠχοί τε καὶ μέλη καθιέρωνται τοῖς θεοῖς οἰκείως ἑκάστοις, συγγένειά τε αὐτοῖς ἀποδέδοται προσφόρως κατὰ τὰς οἰκείας ἑκάστων τάξεις καὶ δυνάμεις καὶ τὰς ἐν αὐτῷ <τῷ> παντὶ κινήσεις καὶ τὰς ἀπὸ τῶν κινήσεων ῥοιζουμένας ἐναρμονίους φωνάς.

116. Iamblichus, *DM* III.9 (119.9–11), ἀλλ᾽ ἐπεὶ τῆς θείας ἁρμονίας ἡ τῶν θεῶν ἐπίπνοια οὐκ ἀφέστηκεν, οἰκειωθεῖσα δὲ πρὸς αὐτὴν κατ᾽ ἀρχὰς μετέχεται ὑπ᾽ αὐτῆς ἐν μέτροις τοῖς προσήκουσιν.

117. For the theory of Recollection, Plato, *Phaedrus* 250b–251a; *Timaeus* 42c; *Phaedo* 70c–72e in Plato, *Euthyphro. Apology. Crito. Phaedo. Phaedrus,* Loeb (Cambridge, MA, and London: Harvard University Press, 1914); *Meno* 81a in Plato, *Laches. Protagoras. Meno. Euthydemus,* Loeb (1924; Cambridge, MA, and London: Harvard University Press and Heinemann, 1962). For the myth of Er, see Plato, *Republic* X, 614b–621b.

118. Iamblichus, *DM* III.9 (120.5–10), ὅτι δὴ ἡ ψυχή, πρὶν καὶ τῷ σώματι δοῦναι ἑαυτήν, τῆς θείας ἁρμονίας κατήκουεν· οὐκοῦν καὶ ἐπειδὰν εἰς σῶμα ἀφίκηται, ὅσα ἂν μέλη τοιαῦτα ἀκούσῃ οἷα μάλιστα διασώζει τὸ θεῖον ἴχνος τῆς ἁρμονίας, ἀσπάζεται ταῦτα καὶ ἀναμιμνήσκεται ἀπ᾽ αὐτῶν τῆς θείας ἁρμονίας, καὶ πρὸς αὐτὴν φέρεται καὶ οἰκειοῦται, μεταλαμβάνει τε αὐτῆς ὅσον οἷόν τε αὐτῆς μετέχειν.

119. Iamblichus, *DM* I.18 (54.12–13), Τὴν ἀρχὴν γὰρ οὐδ᾽ ἂν ἦν μετοχὴ τὸ τοιοῦτον, εἰ μή τι καὶ παραλλάττον εἶχε τὸ μεταλαμβάνον.

120. For a comprehensive discussion and analysis of the myth of Er highlighting the importance of the lot or portion which the soul chooses before each incarnation, see Greenbaum, *The Daimon in Hellenistic Astrology,* pp. 282–85.

121. Addey, 'Oracles, Dreams and Astrology in Iamblichus' *De Mysteriis*', p. 51.

122. Iamblichus, *DM* X.1 (286.7–10).

2

COSMIC CHAOS IN ISLAMIC APOCALYPTIC ESCHATOLOGY

M.A.Rashed

Introduction: Competing Eschatological Narratives and Conflict in the Middle East

Many religious and political philosophies involve an 'eschaton', an event in which history, or the world, comes to an end, or enters a final phase. We refer to such beliefs as an 'eschatology'. My concern is with the redemptive eschatology of Islam, or the end – the eschaton - as a form of salvation. Such eschatology did not merely serve as a moral deterrent, controlling individual behaviour, but had a considerable impact on the socio-political history of Islam. Islamic apocalyptic eschatology describes a sequence of terrifying celestial phenomena, or cosmic portents, that ultimately lead to a turbulent cataclysmic universal apocalypse that terminates mundane history, or profane time. The impact of this vision of the end times is as powerful today as it was in the past: my research is focused on the need to understand this element of modern Islam.

Propagandistic strategies employed by modern Islamic fundamentalists reveal an undeniable influence, coupled with deliberate political manipulation, of an eschatological discourse that promises jihadists afterlife rewards in return for their active participation in a pre-ordained, highly dualistic, apocalyptic scenario that culminates with the establishment of a messianic kingdom.[1] A study by James Fromson and Steven Simon, for instance, found that the so-called Islamic State (ISIS) heavily relies on a reinterpreted apocalyptic ideology in which ISIS is depicted as the harbinger of an imminent apocalypse.[2] The employment of the apocalyptic narrative in the Middle East is without doubt a potent strategic tool towards political dominance. According to one poll, over 50% of Muslims in the region, and more than 70% in conflict areas such as Iraq and Afghanistan, believe in the imminent appearance of the Islamic saviour-messianic figure, al-Mahdī.[3]

Apocalyptic eschatology fulfils an essential cosmological role which, as stated by Freya Mathews, defines 'the place of humankind in the cosmic scheme of things'.[4] The significance of apocalyptic thought as an archaic cosmology had been recognised and discussed by modern western scholarship, particularly in Norman Cohn's *Cosmos, Chaos and the World to Come*, Mircea Eliade's *Cosmos and History: The Myth of the Eternal Return, Myth and Reality* and *The Two and the One*, and Nicholas Campion's *The Great Year*.[5] With regards to Islamic apocalypticism and its relationship to celestial phenomena *per se*, we find a rare study by David Cook titled 'Messianism and Astronomical Events during the First Four Centuries of Islam', which is an investigative study of the apparent causal relationship between the appearance of comets and the outbreak of messianic enthusiasm in Islamic history.[6] Cook concluded his paper by urging further research into how Islamic apocalypticism is shaped and provoked by celestial phenomena, since the 'study of comets and other celestial portents are some of the most important in this regard and are essential in understanding the mass communication used by many apocalyptic leaders to gain their audiences'.[7] Considering the expanding political conflict, increasing sectarian strife, worsening violence, and growing death toll in the Middle East, such an understanding has never been as crucial as it presently is, for as Jerry L. Walls asserted, 'the most passionately contested cultural, political, and social conflicts in our world today are rooted in competing eschatological claims'.[8]

In order to explore the various cosmic eschatological narratives in Islam, and the extent to which these reflected the cosmological beliefs espoused in the studied historical period, I have adopted what Georg Hegel (1770–1831) defined as the methodologies of philosophic and reflective history.[9] To Hegel, the term 'philosophic history' denotes the 'thoughtful consideration' of history, perceiving and evaluating the rational processes that drive and form the collective history of the world.[10] Since eschatological history transcends the notion of mundane history to the metaphysics of the afterlife, adopting a philosophical perspective of history becomes essential. The term 'reflective history', on the other hand, is used by Hegel to refer to 'history whose mode of representation is not really confined by the limits of the time to which it related, but whose spirit transcends the present'.[11] In other words, reflective history may be defined as an interpretive form of historiography that reflects back onto past history in an attempt to re-evaluate and understand present historical events.

Since the investigation of religious beliefs requires a 'polymethodic' approach, as Ninian Smart recommended, I employed an interdisciplinary approach was employed drawing on relevant theories in history, mythology, cosmology, sociology, politics, philosophy and theology.[12] These theories were used at times as broad explanations to the topics addressed, and at other times to raise questions. Throughout my research, I have also taken into account the linguistic challenge of translating the Qur'ān from Arabic into English, as Abobaker Ali et al. observed.[13] Ali *et al.* stated that the sublime style and rhetoric impact of the Qur'ān are the result of the application of a variety of stylistic, linguistic and verbal features that are naturally lost in translation.[14] Nevertheless, Richard Evans argued that the reconstruction of meaning is possible through a process of linguistic and conceptual contextualisation that involves the study of numerous sources.[15] Thus, to overcome the problem of translation, I have relied on several English translations of the Qur'ān.[16] Additionally, I have also employed medieval works on Arabic lexicography, philology and syntax in order to properly convey historical meaning.[17]

Background: Islamic Apocalyptic Eschatology and the Destruction of the World

Many mythical cosmogonies depict the origin of the universe in a forceful emergence of cosmos (order) from chaos (the undifferentiated void). However, Mircea Eliade noticed that eschatological myths represent a reversal of cosmogony through a return to a state of primordial chaos.[18] While the eschatologies of many ancient and primitive cultures prophesy a periodical regeneration of a cyclical cosmos, as Eliade argued, linear and irreversible 'Judaeo-Christian' history denotes an ultimate cataclysmic end of the world prior to a moral judgment in which 'men will be judged by their acts'.[19] The linear eschatology of Abrahamic religions thus acquired a teleological (assuming a future purpose for current events), ethical and retributive angle. Perceived as a continuation of previous monotheistic revelations, the Qur'ān likewise illustrates a turbulent cataclysmic cosmic destruction that precedes the Day of Judgment.[20]

The overall aim of my research is to contribute to a better understanding of Islamic eschatological cosmology through looking at how the cosmic *ashrāṭ*, or portents, that foretell the looming disintegration of mundane history were classically understood and conceptualised in the period extending from the eighth to the seventeenth centuries CE, and the extent to which this reflects Islamic cosmological beliefs. This requires an examination of the historical, socio-political and intellectual contexts that may have actively or passively shaped the literary body of Islamic eschatology, along with the medieval interpretation of the apocalyptic cosmic portents mentioned in the Qur'ān and Qur'ān exegeses, Prophetic *ḥadīth* (which record the traditions of the Prophet of Islam, Muḥammad), and the genre of *al-Fitan wal-Malāḥim* (Tribulations and Fierce Battles).

The words 'apocalypse', 'eschatology' and 'millenarianism' or 'millennialism', have been used interchangeably by scholars in a manner that reflects a conceptual confusion that most probably resulted from their intertwined and interdependent definitions. The broad use of the term 'eschatology' tends to refer to, as mentioned previously, the reversal of the cosmogonic act or a transition from cosmos to chaos.[21] The specific definition of eschatology I employed is that adopted by the monotheistic Abrahamic religions in general and Islam in particular: it is centred on a perception of mundane history as linear and irreversible, not cyclical or regenerative, and based on a belief in an ultimate Divine justice which prevails in a transformed cosmos. Alternatively, the word apocalypse in its common modern usage tends to denote an urgent sense of the temporal proximity of the Last Day.[22] Barbara F. Stowasser and Richard Landes also associated the term with cosmic-level disasters and catastrophes. I therefore use the adjective 'apocalyptic' to denote the revelatory Islamic scriptures that describe an imminent cataclysmic cosmic annihilation of the physical world.[23]

Usually associated with the terms 'eschatology' and 'apocalypse,' and indirectly, yet unavoidably, related to the phenomenon researched, is the term 'millennialism' or 'millenarianism', which is defined as an ideological and revolutionary belief in the upcoming kingdom of peace and justice that will be established on Earth by the awaited Messiah before the cataclysmic apocalypse that precedes the Last Judgment.[24] Although the two terms, 'millennialism' and 'millenarianism', are used interchangeably for the sake of simplicity in this paper, the words differ in their connotations. While both words originate from the Latin root *mille*, indicating the numerical value of one thousand, the first term 'millennialism' implies a period of a thousand years, while the second term 'millenarianism' signifies a thousand of anything and not necessarily years.[25] It should also be noted that these terms do not accurately reflect the Islamic idea of the awaited messianic age which does not specify anywhere a period of a thousand years.[26] Despite these subtleties, it has been noticed that such a belief – whether defined as millennial, millenarian, messianic, or Mahdist – could trigger political mobilization.[27]

Norman Cohn's seminal work, *The Pursuit of the Millennium,* first published in 1957, is the first extensive historical analysis of apocalyptic millennialism in the Christian West.[28] Focusing on millenarian movements and cults of medieval Western and Central Europe, Cohn perceived millennialism as a salvationist, though greatly subversive, ideology shaped by Judeo-Christian apocalyptic scriptures and driven by social injustices.[29] Cohn noted that what differentiates millenarianism from other social struggles is that it is viewed by its participants as a divinely guided movement, transcendental to mundane history, and leading to the total transformation and redemption of a world dominated by demonic forces.[30] An eruption of messianic fervour, or what Cohn termed 'revolutionary millenarianism,' is usually preceded by a disastrous disruption of the normal flow of life that aggravates the desperation of an already disoriented and marginalised population.[31]

The cosmological significance of eschatological and apocalyptic narratives, to the primitive and modern human alike, formed the central focus of a number of works by Eliade, as mentioned previously.[32] To Eliade, eschatological and messianic beliefs reflect an innate primitive human desire to abolish history, perceived as profane time of the 'fallen' state, in order to return to the original purity, integrity and plentitude of the mythical age of the 'lost Paradise' or sacred history.[33] Naturally antihistorical, this 'archaic ontology' anticipates a progressive and irreversible deterioration in the quality of profane time, with the ultimate triumph of evil shortly before the destruction of the profane cosmos, and the restoration, or re-creation, of the original mythical cosmos.[34] As the decaying cosmos approaches its inevitable end, its order starts to disintegrate, resulting in unusual celestial phenomena coupled with cataclysmic natural catastrophes.[35] Also serving as Divine 'negative theophanies', these dramatic celestial and terrestrial occurrences are ultimate warnings meant to bring people back to the path of righteousness.[36]

Such a mythical ontology, Eliade argued, serves a crucial psychological need that enables people to 'tolerate' the natural, social and political sufferings and injustices of historical or profane time.[37] There is almost a consensus among academics who have studied apocalypticism as a social and historical phenomenon that apocalyptic faith fulfils certain psychological and socio-political needs. According to Sarah Harvey and Suzanne Newcombe, apocalyptic faith helps alleviate people's anxious helplessness in situations beyond their control through providing meaning and purpose to life.[38] Walls described it as 'a daring hope, an 'insane expectation' that refuses the consolation of stoic resignation in the face of loss and devastation'.[39] In the socio-political context, Cook noticed that apocalyptic faith liberates its believers from the agreed upon societal codes, encouraging them to deal with long submerged issues.[40]

In the same vein, James C. Scott wrote in his book, *Domination and the Arts of Resistance: Hidden Transcripts*, that millennial aspirations often exhibit a strong sense of *schadenfreude,* or pleasure derived from an eager anticipation by subordinate groups for 'negative reciprocity, a settling of scores when the high shall be brought low and the last shall be first'.[41] Yet due to the social and political helplessness of the oppressed groups, this wish for negative reciprocity remains suppressed, existing only in the form of what Scott described as 'hidden transcript', or the secret defiant discourse of the lower strata of any society that refuses to conform the 'public transcript', or the hegemonic public propagandistic discourse employed by the dominant authoritative group in that society.[42] Most importantly, Scott saw millennialism as a strategic form of 'infrapolitical' resistance which is aimed at refuting the prevalent public transcript and subsequently overthrowing the political authority of the dominant group.[43]

Cosmic Chaos in Interpretations of the Qur'ān

An important source for the classical interpretation of the cosmic portents of the Last Day mentioned in the Qur'ān in the works of the noted Sunni Qur'ān commentators; Fakhr al-Dīn al-Rāzī (1149-1209 CE) and ibn Kathīr (1300-1373 CE). A polymath with a particular interest in logic and philosophy, al-Rāzī's reason-based exegesis would be interesting to examine since it was primarily written to refute the once prevalent Greco-Islamic philosophies.[44] Ibn Kathīr, on the other hand, was chosen on account of his personal history. Born in the turbulent fourteenth century, Ibn Kathīr lived in Bosrā, a town in southern Syria which was under constant threat of the much-dreaded Mongol invasions which seem to have triggered his apocalyptic imagination and led to his authoring of his well-circulated apocalyptic work *The Book of the End on Tribulations and Battles*.[45]

Many verses in the Qur'ān vividly illustrate a final cataclysmic destruction of the world. This study, however, focuses mainly on those specified in the Prophetic *ḥadīth*, 'Whoever wishes to look at the Day of Resurrection, as if he is seeing it with his eye, then let him recite: "When the sun is darkened [the Qur'ānic chapter titled '*al-Takwīr*' or 'the Darkening']" and "When the heaven is cleft asunder [the Qur'ānic chapter titled '*al-Infiṭār*' or 'the Cleaving']" and "When the heaven is split asunder [the Qur'ānic chapter titled '*al-Inshiqāq*' or 'the Sundering']."'[46] In 'the Darkening' (*al-Takwīr*), one reads an intense depiction of a turbulent cataclysmic cosmic destruction:

> When the sun (with its spacious light) is folded up [*kuwwirat*];
> When the stars fall, losing their luster;
> When the mountains vanish (like a mirage);
> When the she-camels, ten months with young, are left untended;
> When the wild beasts are herded together (in human habitations);
> When the oceans boil over with a swell;
> When the souls are sorted out, (being joined, like with like);
> When the female (infant) buried alive, is questioned—
> For what crime she was killed;
> When the Scrolls are laid open;

When the World on High is unveiled:
When the Blazing Fire is kindled to fierce heat;
And when the Garden is brought near—
(Then) shall each soul know what it has put forward.[47]

Al-Rāzī interpreted the disintegration of the world promised in the above verses of
the Qur'ān as a refutation of the concept of the eternity of the universe proposed by
Greco-influenced philosophers, stating that the intended meaning of these verses
is to declare, 'the annihilation of the *dunyā* (mundane world), and the termination
of religious obligations, for the sky is akin to a ceiling, whilst the earth is akin
to its building, and if a particular building is to be destroyed, the ceiling should
be first demolished.'[48] The stance of al-Rāzī reveal a visible resemblance to the
orthodox worldview described in the numerous writings of the noted philosopher
and theologian al-Ghazālī (1058-1111 CE), who diligently worked towards
eradicating Greek thought from Islamic philosophy.[49] The most dangerous of such
ideas in al-Ghazālī's view is the notion of the eternity of the world and denial of
bodily resurrection, concepts that could render any person embracing them infidel
(*kāfir*).[50] Clearly thus, al-Rāzī in his exegesis was engaging in a Ghazālian polemic
against prevalent pagan philosophies of his time. By asserting the eschatological
annihilation of the world in order, al-Rāzī was attempting prove the contingency
of the cosmos, for as Jürgen Moltmann proposed, the concept of *reductio ad
nihilum* (reduction into nothing) is simply a reversal of *creatio ex nihilo* (creation
out of nothing).[51]

Another philosophy that al-Ghazālī fervently disputed is the Aristotelian
concept of secondary causes: for Aristotelians the planets possessed significance
as secondary causes, transmitting the power of the first cause, the Aristotelian
creator, the 'unmoved mover'. According to al-Ghazali such ideas could lead to
the dissemination of harmful arts and practices, including judicial astrology which
leads the inquirer astray through distorting her or his worldview:

When they [people] hear that certain effects follow the motion of
planets, it occurs to them that it is the planets that influence and effect
[the course of events], and that they are the organising deities [...] As
a result, they [the planets] become venerated [by people], and their [the
people's] hearts become attached to them [the planets], believing that
good and evil are be either sought or feared from them [the planets].[52]

The Ghazālian remedy to this problems is to wholeheartedly believe that the
whole of nature is in absolute subjection to the command of God, the only

and direct Cause of all effects, in order to protect one's faith from *shirk*; the unforgivable sin of associating partners with Allah.[53] The same orthodox Islamic cosmology is also espoused by ibn Kathīr who demonstrated how the sun and the moon are merely inanimate bodies subjugated to the supreme will of Allah and serving their assigned roles, ibn Kathīr wrote:

> And among His signs [...] is the sun with its light and brilliance, and the moon with its luminosity, and the reckoning of its [the moon's] phases through its orbital motion, and its orbit, which is distinct from the sun's, [all of this] serves to make recognisable the portions of the night and the day, and the weeks, the months and the years. And from this is discerned the advent of legal times, and the times of worship and transactions. Since the sun and the moon are the most splendid among the visible celestial bodies in both the upper and lower realms, God Almighty brought to our attention that they are merely two of his created servants, overpowered by Him and subjugated to Him.[54]

To al-Rāzī, however, such natural phenomena should also be perceived as signs to be contemplated by the believers, for when these phenomena are assessed rationally they reveal the changeability and transience of *dunyā* (mundane world).[55] The 'ruddy glow of Sunset' for instance, al-Rāzī elaborated, is a significant moment of liminality between day and night that signals the transition from alertness to idleness.[56] The phases of the Moon similarly denote the impermanency of the world, he added.[57] In such an approach, al-Rāzī was rationally establishing that the diurnal motion of the sun, the phases of the moon, and the alternation between day and night are phenomena, or signs, that reveal to thoughtful and alert minds the presence of a universal regularity so meticulous that is impossible to be deemed random, but is orchestrated by a powerful and skillful Creator who could easily resurrect the dead:

> For He who is able to affect change in the superior and inferior celestial bodies, from a moment to another, and from a quality to another, must be in His own essence able to affect all that is possible and knowing of all there is, and Who possesses such attributes is undoubtedly capable of resurrecting the dead.[58]

Cosmic Chaos in Canonical Hadīths and Apocalyptic Traditions

In order to illustrate what is regarded as a credible representation of Islamic eschatology by mainstream Islam, I will first examine what are viewed by

Muslims as the most authentic or *ṣaḥīḥ* canonical compilations of Prophetic *ḥadīths* that had undergone rigorous tests of validity. The aim here is to explore the cautious apocalyptic discourse of mainstream religious authorities, as opposed to what is deemed to be, by the same authorities, as the injudicious, radical and highly fabricated narratives found in the genre of genre of *al-Fitan wal-Malāhim* (Tribulations and Fierce Battles) which will be discussed in the second part of this section.

According to one *ṣaḥīḥ ḥadīth*, the Prophet once spoke in a prolonged sermon about the portents of the Hour after the afternoon prayer (*ṣalāt al-Aṣr*) till shortly before sunset.[59] Noticing that his companions started looking towards the west in anticipation of the shortly due sunset prayer (*ṣalāt al-Maghrib*), the Prophet concluded his sermon by stressing the imminence of the Last Day, 'Behold! The world, in relation to what has passed of it, shall not remain except as what remains of this day of yours, in relation to what has passed of it.'[60] This passage examines the most mentioned cosmic portent in canonical *ḥadīth* compilations; the rising of the sun from the west:

> The hour will not strike till the sun rises from the west; and when it rises (from the west) and the people see it, they all will believe. And that is (the time) when no good will it do to a soul to believe then.[61]

When asked about the meaning of the Qur'ānic verse, [a]nd the Sun runs his course for a period determined for him,' the Prophet further elaborated on the drastic reversal of the diurnal motion of the sun:

> It travels till it prostrates itself underneath the Throne and takes the permission to rise again, and it is permitted, and then (a time will come when) it will be about to prostrate itself but its prostration will not be accepted, and it will ask permission to go on its course but it will not be permitted, but it will be ordered to return whence it has come and so it will rise in the west.[62]

The prostration (*sujūd*) of the sun, moon and other created things is similarly stressed in the Qur'ān, 'Seest thou not that to Allah bow down in worship all things that are in the heavens and on earth — the sun, the moon, the stars; the hills, the trees the animals; and a great number among mankind?'[63] Theologian ibn Qayyim al-Jawzīyyah (1292-1350 CE) wrote that *sujūd* in this context represents the metaphorical prostration to God's will, since all creation 'is submissive to His Lordship, humbled by His Glory and subdued by His Authority.'[64] The recurrent concept of *sujūd* as it pertains to all creation therefore is indicative of total subjugation to the laws and commands of Allah.

Surrendering to the commands of the Creator therefore signifies the triumph of order over chaos, while the reverse - the triumph of chaos over order - is instigated by the arrogant refusal of humanity to submit to divine laws. The triumph of chaos is heralded by unusual celestial signs, the most significant of which is the rising of the sun from the west which marks the repudiation of penitence, for as the Prophet said, in the west lies the 'Gate of Repentance' which remains unlocked till the sun rises through it.[65] Elaborating on this 'major portent' of the Last Day, Qur'ān exegete al-Tha'labī (d. 1035 CE) wrote that due to the sins of humanity, the sun and the moon are confined for a number of days after which they are permitted to rise from the west, yet eclipsed and devoid of their light.[66] When the luminaries reach midheaven, their motion is reversed back to normal allowing them to set in the 'Gate of Repentance' in the west, locking it up once and for all till the Hour.[67] In the mythic language of the apocalypse the luminaries operate as 'negative theophanies' that according to Eliade, ominously declare the looming retribution that awaits the wrongdoers, and hence intensify the human terror of history.[68]

Unlike the cautious methodology employed by the compilers of the canonical *ḥadīth* collections, the large body of a highly speculative Islamic apocalyptica, popularly known as *al-Fitan wa-l-Malāḥim* employed little, if any, tests of authenticity.[69] In medieval historiographer ibn Khaldūn's (1332-1406 CE) view, this genre reflects an innate human desire to learn about the future of matters of great importance, such as the duration of dynasties and the world.[70] The validity of the corpus of Islamic apocalyptica had always been disputed by mainstream Islamic scholars, especially since the apocalyptist - who possessed the traits of Landes' radical 'rooster' - hyperactively announced the imminent Doomsday, threatening established theological doctrines and societal public transcripts in the process.[71] Nu'aym ibn Ḥammad's (d. 843 CE) *Kitāb al-Fitan* (Book of Tribulations) is also necessary to assess the sociopolitical impact of era of *fitan*, or tribulations, on the Islamic eschatological tradition.[72] A revolutionary who vehemently opposed the 'Abbāsid state-imposed theology, Nu'aym wrote a lengthy chapter titled 'On the Celestial Portents that Foretell the Cessation of the Reign of the 'Abbāsids,' anticipating their impending fall.[73] One of these portents, according to the numerous *ḥadīths* cited by Nu'aym, is the appearance of a star in the eastern horizon, known as *al-Qarn thul-Shafā* (the Horned Star), that radiates like a full moon, and twists like a snake, before bending up like a hook.[74] Citing a narrator by the name of al-Walīd, Nu'aym wrote:

I saw a star with a tail that appeared at dawn in the eastern horizon in the month of *Muḥarram* in the year 145 *hijrī* [circa April 762 CE]. We continued to see it every morning before sunrise for the rest of *Muḥarram*, then it disappeared, then we noticed it in the twilight that follows sunset... Then it disappeared for two or three months. Then we saw a dim star with a flame a cubit long [44 cm] near Polaris and rotating around it in the two Jumādas and Rajab [from July to October], then it disappeared. Then we saw a star which was not bright... I mentioned that to an old sheikh from al-Sakāsik tribe, but he said, 'this is not the "Awaited Star"'.[75]

Nu'aym claimed that when this 'Awaited Star' appears it will soon be followed by the emergence of al-Mahdī, the prophesised redeemer of Islam mentioned in the Prophetic *ḥadīth*:

If only one day of this world remained, Allah would lengthen that day, till He raises up in it a man who belongs to me or to my family, whose name is identical to mine, and his father's name is identical to my father's, who will fill the earth with equity and justice as it has been filled with oppression and tyranny.[76]

In line with Cohn's 'revolutionary eschatology,' *Kitāb al-Fitan* reveals an aspiration for a reversal of history through the rise of the saintly figure of al-Mahdī who will save humanity from the oppression of the 'Abbāsids, and Islam from their aberrant ideology.[77] The apocalyptic narrative of Nu'aym combines elements of both active and passive apocalypticism described by Landes, for although redemption is placed in the human hand of al-Mahdī, it is still absolutely reliable on the permission of Allah.[78] Written in the turbulent years of early Islam, Nu'aym's *Kitāb al-Fitan* clearly reveals the interwoven relationship of history and apocalyptic eschatology observed by Said Amir Arjomand.[79] Its mythic language mirrors a pessimistic subversive worldview which, as Lorenzo DiTommaso noted, is antagonistic to history and political authority.[80]

Conclusion

All the works I have mentioned reveal a strong conviction in the impending disintegration of the ordered cosmos, which in their view will collapse in subjection to the command of the Irresistible Creator, Allah, thus marking the end of an illusory *dunyā*. Through asserting the preordained obliteration of the cosmos, or in other words the principle of *reductio ad nihilum*, the Islamic scholars were, above all, confirming the contingency of the universe, or *creatio ex nihilo,* and in doing so, explicitly challenged what were perceived as heretical Greco-influenced philosophies - which seem to have been quite widespread in their times - about the eternity of the world. Through embracing such a worldview, the religious, retributive and theistic essence of Islamic eschatology and, subsequently, Islamic cosmology, were retained. The contemplation of the cyclical nature of cosmic phenomena, therefore, became an activity that rationally confirmed the most fundamental eschatological principles of Islam, namely the ephemeral nature of mundane history or *dunyā* and its inevitable future annihilation, followed by a transformation and resurrection of all creation.

The evidence also suggests that the mythical language employed in canonical *ḥadīth* compilations and by the classical apocalyptist alike conveys a strong belief in the interconnectedness of the celestial and terrestrial realms, in which life-sustaining order in the heavens above is perceived as a reflection of earthly peace and harmony, the latter being the natural consequence of submitting to the commands of the Creator. The arrogant refusal of man to comply with these Divine laws, on the other hand, leads to the predominance of chaotic forces of evil on Earth, which in its turn triggers unusual celestial phenomena such as the westward-rising of the sun, the splitting of the moon, the appearance of comets and the falling of meteors. As Eliade's 'negative theophanies', these terrifying celestial events conveyed the wrath of Allah and heralded the approach of the Hour and the ensuing Divine retribution.[81] This pessimistic worldview is chiefly noticed in the works of authors who witnessed the *fitan* of civil strife, political upheavals and military threats. During such times, the apocalyptic discourse acquires Cohn's noticeably active, subversive and revolutionary messianic tone, and operates as Scott's infra-political subterranean counter-ideology, which aspires for poetic justice in which 'the high shall be brought low and the last shall be first'.[82]

As stated earlier, the exploration of the underpinning cosmological views that shape Islamic apocalypticism and millennialism, or Mahdism, thus filling a gap in the study of the Islamic mythological, teleological and philosophical perception of history. In Islamic apocalyptic eschatology, the cataclysmic annihilation of profane time inaugurates an awaited sacred time where the pious are promised with eternal rewards; a cosmological view with remarkably contrasting societal implications. It may be speculated that, to the moderate Muslim, such an outlook may fulfil the essential therapeutic role that enables man to tolerate the hardships of mundane history, as discussed by Eliade and Harvey and Newcombe.[83] Yet to the radical extremist, it is quite evident that apocalyptic faith is actively employed in innovative millennialist ideologies that seek to manifest the providential plan of Allah through accelerating the prophesied sequence of events that lead to the termination of profane time. The particular significance of the concept of *fitan*, perceived as 'holy anarchy' and which paves the way to the imminent apocalypse, clearly explains the pervasiveness of apocalypticism in areas of conflict.

Notes

1. Jerry L. Walls, 'Introduction', in Jerry L. Walls, ed., *The Oxford Handbook of Eschatology* (Oxford: Oxford University Press, 2008), p. 10; David Cook, *Contemporary Muslim Apocalyptic Literature* (Syracuse, NY: Syracuse University Press, 2005), pp. 172–83; David Cook, 'Suicide Attacks or "Martyrdom Operations" in Contemporary Jihad Literature', *Nova Religio: The Journal of Alternative and Emergent Religions* 6, no. 1 (October 2002): pp. 10–13; David Cook, *Understanding Jihad* (Oakland, CA: University of California Press, 2015), pp. 22–25; Catherine Wessinger, 'Apocalypse and Violence', in John J. Collins, ed., *The Oxford Handbook of Apocalyptic Literature* (New York: Oxford University Press, 2014), pp. 426–27, pp. 435–37.

2. James Fromson and Steven Simon, 'ISIS: The Dubious Paradise of Apocalypse Now', *Survival* 57, no.3 (June-July 2015): p. 28, p. 37.

3. James Bell, 'The World's Muslims: Unity and Diversity', Pew Research Center, Chapter 3: 'Articles of Faith', 9 August 2012, at http://www.pewforum.org/2012/08/09/the-worlds-muslims-unity-and-diversity-3-articles-of-faith/ [accessed 28 May 2016].

4. Freya Mathews, *The Ecological Self* (London: Routledge, 1991), p. 12.

5. Norman Cohn, *Cosmos, Chaos and the World to Come: The Ancient Roots of Apocalyptic Faith* (New Haven, CT: Yale University Press, 1993); Mircea Eliade, *Cosmos and History: The Myth of the Eternal Return*, trans. Willard R. Trask (New York: Harper Torchbooks, 1959); Mircea Eliade, *Myth and Reality*, trans. Willard R. Trask (New York: Harper & Row, 1963); Mircea Eliade, *The Two and the One* (London: Harvill Press, 1965); Nicholas Campion, *The Great Year: Astrology, Millenarianism and History in the Western Tradition* (London: Arkana Penguin Books, 1994).

6. David Cook, 'Messianism and Astronomical Events during the First Four Centuries of Islam', *Revue des mondes musulmans et de la Méditerranée* 91-94 (July 2000), at http://remmm.revues.org/247 [accessed 17 January 2011].

7. Cook, 'Messianism and Astronomical Events'.

8. Walls, 'Introduction', p. 10.

9. Georg Wilhelm Friedrich Hegel, *Lectures on the Philosophy of History*, trans. J. Sibree (London: G. Bell and Sons Ltd., 1914), pp. 4–9.

10. Hegel, *The Philosophy of History*, pp. 8–9.

11. Hegel, *Lectures on the Philosophy of History*, p. 4.

12. Ninian Smart, 'The Exploration of Religion and Education', *Oxford Review of Education* 1, no. 2 (1975): p. 100.

13. Abobaker Ali et al., 'Some Linguistic Difficulties in Translating the Holy Quran from Arabic into English', *International Journal of Social Science and Humanity* 2, no. 6 (2012): p. 588.

14. Ali et al., 'Some Linguistic Difficulties in Translating the Holy Quran', p. 588.

15. Richard J. Evans, *In Defense of History* (New York: W. W. Norton & Company, 1999), p. 78.

16. *The Qur'ān*, trans. Abdel Haleem, M. A. S. (Oxford: Oxford University Press,

2005); *The Meaning of the Holy Qur'ān*, trans. by Abdullah Yusuf Ali and Muhammad Marmaduke Pickthall (Beltsville: Amana Publications, 1997); Murad, Badawi and Hutchinson, *The Majestic Qur'ān*.

17. Muḥammad b. Aḥmad al-Azharī, *Tahthīb al-Loghah* or *The Refinement of the Language* (Beirut: Dār Ihyā' al-Turāth al-'Arabī, 2001); abū al-Hasan 'Alī b. 'Ismā'īl ibn Sīdah, *al-Muḥkam wal-Muḥīṭ al-'A'tham or The Precise Book on Arabic Philology* (Beirut: Dār al-Kotob al-'Ilmīya, 2000); ibn Manẓūr, Abū al-Fadl Jamāl al-Dīn Muhammad ibn Mukarram, *Lisān Al-'Arab Or the Arabic Tongue* (Beirut: Dār Sāder, 1994).

18. Eliade, *Myth and Reality*, pp. 54–64; Eliade, *The Two and the One*, pp. 135–36; Eliade, *Cosmos and History*, p. 62–73; see also David Adams Leeming and Margaret Adams Leeming, 'Creation from Chaos', in *A Dictionary of Creation Myths* (Oxford: Oxford University Press, 2009).

19. Eliade, *Myth and Reality*, pp. 54–60; pp. 64–65.

20. See for instance, Abdal Hakim Murad, M. Badawi and U. Hutchinson, eds, *The Majestic Qur'ān: An English Rendition of its Meanings* (Chicago, IL: Nawawi Foundation, 2000), 1:1–7.

21. Eliade, *Myth and Reality*, pp. 54–64; Eliade, *The Two and the One*, pp. 135–36; Eliade, *Cosmos and History*, p. 62–73; See also Leeming and Leeming, 'Creation from Chaos'.

22. Landes, *Heaven on Earth*, p. 18; Barbara F. Stowasser, 'The End is Near: Minor and Major Signs of the Hour in Islamic Texts and Contexts', in John J. Collins and Abbas Amanat, eds, *Apocalypse and Violence* (New Haven, CT: Yale Center for International and Area Studies, 2004), p. 1; Cook, *Contemporary Muslim Apocalyptic Literature*, p. 3.

23. Barbara F. Stowasser, 'The End is Near: Minor and Major Signs of the Hour in Islamic Texts and Contexts', in *Apocalypse and Violence*, ed. by John J. Collins and Abbas Amanat (New Haven: Yale Center for International and Area Studies, 2004), <http://edoc1. bibliothek.uni-halle.de/servlets/MCRFileNodeServlet/HALCoRe_derivate_00002753/ The%20End%20is%20Near.pdf> [accessed 10 December 2015], p.1; Richard Landes, *Heaven on Earth: The Varieties of the Millennial Experience* (Oxford: Oxford University Press, 2011), p.31.

24. Norman Cohn, *The Pursuit of the Millennium: Revolutionary Millenarians and Mystical Anarchists of the Middle Ages* (London: Granada Publishing, 1970), pp. 13–14; Stowasser, 'The End is Near', p. 1; Landes, *Heaven on Earth,* pp. 12–17.

25. For more on the etymological nuances of the two terms, see the footnote in Jay Gould, *Questioning the Millennium* (Cambridge, MA: Harvard University Press, 2011), p. 130. See also Jean-François Mayer, 'Millennialism: New Religious Movements and the Quest for a New Age', in James Lewis and Inga Tøllefsen, eds, *The Oxford Handbook of New Religious Movements: Volume II* (New York: Oxford University Press, 2016), p. 403; and Cohn, *The Pursuit of the Millennium*, p. 13.

26. David Cook, *Contemporary Muslim Apocalyptic Literature,* p. 148.

27. Landes, *Heaven on Earth*, pp. 12–18.

28. Cohn, *The Pursuit of the Millennium: Revolutionary Millenarians*, p. 9; Norman Cohn, *The Pursuit of the Millennium: Revolutionary Messianism in Medieval and Reformation Europe and its bearing on Modern Totalitarian Movements* (New York: Harper Torchbooks, 1961), pp. v–vii; Bernard McGinn, 'Introduction', in *Visions of the End: Apocalyptic Traditions in the Middle Ages,* edited by Bernard McGinn (New York: Columbia University Press, 1998), p. 28.

29. Cohn, *Revolutionary Millenarians*, pp. 13–14, pp. 19–29; Cohn, *Revolutionary Messianism*, p. xiii.

30. Cohn, *Revolutionary Millenarians*, p. 21; Cohn, *Revolutionary Messianism*, p. xiii, p. 308.

31. Cohn, *Revolutionary Millenarians*, p. 282; Cohn, *Revolutionary Messianism*, p. v.

32. Eliade, *Myth and Reality*; Eliade, *The Two and the One*; Eliade, *Cosmos and History*.

33. Eliade, *Cosmos and History*, pp. 35–36, p.75, p. 85, pp. 91–92, pp. 111–12; pp. 141–42.

34. Eliade, *Cosmos and History*, pp. 112–14, p. 128; Eliade, *Myth and Reality*, p. 60.

35. Eliade, *Cosmos and History*, pp. 122–28; Eliade, *The Two and the One*, pp. 133–36.

36. Eliade, *Cosmos and History*, pp. 102–04.

37. Eliade, *Cosmos and History*, p. 75, p. 85, pp. 91–92, pp. 141–42, pp. 151–52.

38. Sarah Harvey and Suzanne Newcombe, 'From the Extraordinary to the Ordinary: An Overview of Prophecy', in Sarah Harvey and Suzanne Newcombe, eds, *Prophecy in the New Millennium* (Surrey: Ashgate Publishing, Ltd., 2013), p. 8, p. 11.

39. Walls, 'Introduction', p. 6.

40. Cook, *Contemporary Muslim Apocalyptic Literature*, p. 3.

41. James C. Scott, *Domination and the Arts of Resistance: Hidden Transcripts* (New Haven, CT: Yale University Press, 1990), pp. 41–42.

42. Scott, *Domination and the Arts of Resistance*, pp. xii–xii, pp. 2–4.

43. Scott, *Domination and the Arts of Resistance*, p. 199.

44. Abū al-'Abbās Shams al-Dīn Aḥmad b. Muḥammad ibn Khallikān, *Wafīyāt al-'Ayān w Anbā' Abnā' al-Zamān Or Deaths of Eminent Men and History of the Sons of the Epoch* (Beirut: Dār Ṣāder, 1971): IV:248-252; Shams al-Dīn Muḥammad b. 'Alī al-Dāwūdī, *Ṭabaqāt al-Mufassirīn lil-Dāwūdī Or The Ranks of Commentators by al-Dāwūdī* (Beirūt: Dār al-Kotob al-'Ilmīyyah, 1983), II:215-218; Muḥammad Ḥussaīn al-Thahabī, *al-Tafsīr w'al-Mufassirūn Or Exegesis and Exegetes* (Cairo: Maktabat Wahbah, n.d.), I:206-210; G. C. Anawati, 'Fakhr al-Dīn al-Rāzī' in *The Encyclopaedia of Islam*, ed. by P. Bearman et al. (Leiden: Brill, 2004), vol.2, pp.751-755.

45. abū al-Fidā' Ismā'īl b. 'Umar ibn Kathīr, *The Book of the End on Tribulations and Battles*, ed. by Muḥammad Aḥmad 'Abd al-'Azīz (Beirut: Dār al-Jabal, 1988). See also abū al-Fidā' 'Ismā'īl b. 'Umar ibn Kathīr, 'Kitāb al-Fitan wal-Malāḥim wal-Umūr al-'Izām Yawm al-Qiyāmah Or The Book of Fierce Battles and Tribulations and the Great Things on the Day of Resurrection', in *al-Bidāya wal-Nihāya Or The Beginning and the End,* ed. by 'Abdulla b. 'Abd al-Muḥsin al-Tirkī, Vol. 19 (Cairot: Dār Hajar lil-Ṭibā'a wal-Nashr wal-Tawzī', 1997), pp.3-444. For the sociopolitical conditions in which ibn Kathīr was born check Jean-Pierre Filiu, *Apocalypse in Islam,* trans. by M. B. DeBevoise (University of California Press, 2011), pp.34-41; Jane Dammen McAuliffe, 'The Tasks and Traditions of Interpretation', in *The Cambridge Companion to the Qur'ān*, ed. by Jane Dammen McAuliffe (Cambridge: Cambridge University Press, 2006), p.196.

46. Muḥammad b. 'Issā b. al-Dhaḥāk al-Tirmidhī, *The Great Compilation of al-Tirmidhī*, book 47 on *Qur'ān Interpretation* (Beirut: Dār al-Gharb al-Islāmī, 1998), ḥadīth 3653.

47. *The Meaning of the Holy Qur'ān,* trans. by Abdullah Yusuf Ali and Muhammad Marmaduke Pickthall (Beltsville: Amana Publications, 1997), 81:1-14.

48. abū 'Abdullah Muḥammad b. 'Umar Al-Rāzī, *al-Tafsīr al-Kabīr Or The Great Commentary* (Beirut: Dār Ihiā' al-Turāth al-'Arabī, 1999), XXXI:72-73.

49. See for instance Abū Ḥāmid al-Ghazālī, *Tahāfut Al-Falāsifah Or The Incoherence of the Philosophers*, ed. by Sulayman Dunya (Cairo: Dār al-Ma'ārif, 1972); Abū Ḥāmid al-Ghazālī, *Al-Munqith Min Al-Ḍalāl Or Deliverance from Error*, ed. by Jamil Saliba and Kamil Ayyad (Beirut: Dār al-Andalus, 1967); Abū Ḥāmid al-Ghazālī, *'Ihyā' 'Ulūm al-Dīn Or Revival of the Religious Science*, ed. by Muhammad al-Dali Balta (Beirut: al-Maktaba al-'Aṣrīyya, 2015).

50. al-Ghazālī, *Deliverance from Error*, pp.83-84.

51. Jürgen Moltmann, 'Cosmos and Theosis: Eschatological Perspectives', in *The Far Future Universe: Eschatology from a Cosmic Perspective*, ed. by George Francis Rayner Ellis (Philadelphia: Templeton Foundation Press, 2002), p.256.

52. al-Ghazālī, *Revival of the Religious Sciences*, I:44; on al-Ghazālī's attack on the Aristotelian philosophy of secondary causes see al-Ghazālī, *Deliverance from Error*, pp.83-84.

53. al-Ghazālī, *Revival of the Religious Sciences*, 4:323; 328-330; al-Ghazālī, *Deliverance from Error*, p.83. For the definition of "shirk" look at ibn Manẓūr, *The Arabic Tongue*, X:449-450.

54. Abu al-Fida' Isma'īl ibn 'Omar ibn Kathīr, *Tafsir Al-Qur'an Al-Azīm or The Commentary of ibn Kathīr* (Beirut: Dār al-Kutub al-'Ilmīya, 1988), VII:166.

55. al-Rāzī, *The Great Commentary*, XXXI:103.

56. al-Rāzī, *The Great Commentary*, XXXI:103.

57. al-Rāzī, *The Great Commentary*, XXXI:103.

58. al-Rāzī, *The Great Commentary*, XXXI:103.

59. *The Great Compilation of al-Tirmidhī*, book 33 on *Fitan*, ḥadīth no. 2191.

60. *The Great Compilation of al-Tirmidhī*, book 33 on *Fitan*, ḥadīth no. 2191.

61. *The Meaning of the Holy Qur'ān*: 6:158; abū 'Abd Allāh Muḥammad b. Ismā'īl al-Bukhārī,,, *Sahih al-Bukhari*, trans. by Muhammad Muhsin Khan, book 88 *of Afflictions and the End of the World* (Virginia: al-Saadawi Publications, 1996), book 60 on *Prophetic Commentary on the Qur'an*, ḥadīth no. 160.

62. *The Meaning of the Holy Qur'ān*, 36:38; *Saḥīh Al-Bukhārī*, book 54 on *Beginning of Creation*, ḥadīth no. 421.

63. *The Meaning of the Holy Qur'ān*: 22:18.

64. Muḥammad b. abī Bakr ibn Qayyim al-Jawzīyya, *Madārij al-Sālikīn Or The Stages of the Wayfarers*, ed. by Mohammad al-Mu'tasim bi'llah al-Baghdadi (Beirut: Dār al-Kitāb al-'Arabī, 1996): I:127-128.

65. *The Great Compilation of al-Tirmidhī*, book 48 on *Supplication*, hadith no. 3535.

66. Aḥmad b. Muḥammad b. Ibrāhīm al-Tha'labī, *al-Kashf wa'l-Bayān 'an Tafsir al-Qur'ān Or The Unveiling and Clarification on Qur'ānic Exegesis*, ed. by Imām Abū Muḥammad b. 'Āshūr (Beirut: Dār Iḥyā' al-Turāth al-'Arabi, 2002), IV:207-208; *The Meaning of the Holy Qur'ān*, 81:1; 75:9.

67. al-Tha'labī, *The Unveiling on Qur'ānic Exegesis*, IV:208-209.

68. John J. Collins, 'What is Apocalyptic Literature?', in *The Oxford Handbook of Apocalyptic Literature*, ed. by John J. Collins (Oxford: Oxford University Press, 2014), p.9; Eliade, *Cosmos and History*, p.104.

69. Cook, *Contemporary Muslim Apocalyptic Literature*, p.7.

70. ibn Khaldūn, abū Zaīd Walī al-Dīn 'Abd al-Raḥmān b. Muḥammad, *Tarīkh Ibn Khaldūn Or The History of Ibn Khaldūn*, ed. by abū Ṣuhaīb al-Karmī (Riyadh: Baīt al-Afkār al-Dawlīya), p.166.

71. Landes, *Heaven on Earth*, pp.40-46.

72. Nu'aym b. Ḥammad al-Marwazī, *Kitāb al-Fitan or Book of Tribulations*, ed. by Samir Amin al-Zuhairi (Cairo: Maktabat al-Tawḥīd, 1412 hijrī).

73. Shams al-Dīn abū 'Abdulla Muḥammad b. Aḥmad al-Thahabī, *Sīyar ‹Alām al-Nubalā› Or The Lives of Noble Figures* (Damascus: Mu'asassat al-Risālah, 1985), X:610-611; Nu'aym, *Book of Tribulations*, I:224-232.

74. Nu'aym, *Book of Tribulations*, I:224, ḥadīth nos. 622-623; I:229, ḥadīth no. 640; I:230, ḥadīth no. 643.

75. Nu'aym, *Book of Tribulations*, I:229, ḥadīth no. 639.

76. Nu'aym, *Book of Tribulations*, I:229, ḥadīth no. 641; abū Dawūd Sulaīmān b. al-Ash'ath al-Sijistānī, *The Canonical Collection of Ḥadīth by Abū Dāwūd* (Beirut: al-Maktabah al-'Asrīyah, n.d.), book 38 on *al-Mahdī*, ḥadīth no. 4282.

77. Cohn, *Revolutionary Millenarians*, 1970, p.21; pp.281-282.

78. Landes, *Heaven on Earth*, pp.33-34.

79. Said Amir Arjomand, 'Islamic Apocalypticism in the Classic Period', in *The Encyclopedia of Apocalypticism: Volume 2, Apocalypticism in Western History and Culture*, ed. by Bernard McGinn (New York: The Continuum Publishing Company, 1998), p.264.

80. Lorenzo DiTommaso, 'The Apocalyptic Other', in *The 'Other' in Second Temple Judaism: Essays in Honor of John J. Collins*, ed. by Daniel C. Harlow and others (Michigan: William B. Eerdmans Publishing Company, 2011), p.236.

81. Eliade, *Cosmos and History*, p. 104.

82. Cohn, *The Pursuit of the Millennium: Revolutionary Messianism*, p. 319; Scott, *Domination and the Arts of Resistance*, pp. 41–42, p. 199.

83. Eliade, *Cosmos and History*, p. 75. p. 141; R. Scott Appleby, 'The Unholy Uses of the Apocalyptic Imagination: Twentieth Century Patterns', in *Apocalypse and Violence*, ed. by Abbas Amanat and John Joseph Collins (2002), p. 8, p. 11.

3

SIGNS FROM HEAVEN OR A DARK ART? HOW THE CHURCH EMBRACED ARABIC ASTROLOGY AND INTRODUCED IT INTO THE CHRISTIAN WEST

Chris Mitchell

Background

In the popular imagination, the European history of the last two thousand years is often limited in its scope; the narrative is frequently presented as one in which a glorious Roman Empire collapses in the fifth century, to be followed by a millennium of ignorance until the marvels of the Renaissance of the fourteenth and fifteenth centuries see a revival of civilisation. William Manchester, whose 1992 book *A World Lit Only By Fire* appeared on the *New York Times* bestseller list, claimed that 'medieval men, crippled by ten centuries of immobility, viewed the world through distorted prisms peculiar to their age. In all that time nothing of real consequence had either improved or declined'.[1] Manchester's book made no claims of academic scholarship and was a popular account of the medieval period, but it demonstrates that such attitudes are still to be found – although the book was first published in 1992, there are now 49 versions of it available, the most recent having been published in 2018.

The academic study of the development of astrology in this period is even rarer, partly because it is the 'wretched subject', as Otto Neugebauer called it, whose very study required justification.[2] With a handful of notable exceptions, beginning with Lynn Thorndike, academic discussions of the history of science prior to the 1990s had viewed astrology as a superstitious aberration.[3] For example, Carl Boyer and Uta Merzbach writing on the history of mathematics in 1989 made a clear distinction between Ptolemy's *Almagest*, a work on astronomy from the second century CE, and his *Tetrabiblos*, a work on astrology, describing the latter as 'a kind of sidereal religion to which much of the ancient world had succumbed'.[4] Although a few medieval astrological texts had been translated into English in the first half of the twentieth century, it was left to modern astrologers, rather than academics, to take this further when, in 1992, four astrologers founded a project to translate the corpus of Greek, Arabic, and Latin astrological texts.[5] Academic authors, too, started to take the history of astrology more seriously, and the focus of texts on medieval astrology underwent a noticeable change from the start of the twenty-first century, as shown in Figure 1 below.[6]

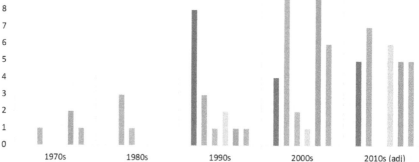

Articles published on medieval astrology

Figure 1 – Focus of texts published on medieval astrology.

Complementing the publication of astrological material, the relatively new field of cultural astronomy has recently arisen, which examines how societies interact with the sky. It is a field that combines astronomy, astrology, archaeoastronomy and anthropology, and places these disciplines into a relevant historic context. Indeed, my own PhD thesis would not have been possible without this shift of academic opinion, since it analysed a particular manuscript from my perspective as a practising astrologer. While the main focus of my thesis was an examination of the astrological techniques in one particular twelfth-century text, this chapter focuses on how astrology came to be introduced into Christian Western Europe.[7]

Christian and Muslim Attitudes Towards Astrology

Academic suspicion of astrology is also reflected in the contemporary viewpoint of the three major monotheistic religions. The *Catechism of the Catholic Church* condemns astrology as a 'form of divination... to be rejected'.[8] Contemporary Islam also tends to be hostile towards astrology, as does – with more ambivalence – Judaism.[9] The condemnation of astrology is certainly reflected in early views of Christianity. St Augustine of Hippo, writing in about 400 CE, condemned astrology on both theological and logical grounds. Theologically, he called astrologers 'cheats', and stated that 'Christian faith quite properly rejects and condemns that art', describing the 'blasphemous nonsense of astrologers'.[10] On logical grounds, he used the argument that twins often do not resemble each other, and 'yet in birth they were separated by a very brief interval of time, and in conception they were begotten at one moment, by one act of intercourse.'[11]

St Eligius of Noyon, writing in the seventh century and who converted various communities of pagans on the North Sea coast condemned astrology saying that 'nobody should attribute fate or fortune to themselves from their horoscope.'[12] The Anglo-Saxon chronicler the Venerable Bede wrote numerous texts, including ones dealing with calendars and time. In a work on the nature of time, he discussed breaking the hour down into smaller and smaller parts, ending up with the 'atom', deriving from a biblical reference where it was equivalent to 'the twinkling of an eye', and equal to 15/94 of a second.[13] Bede stated that astrologers use this time period too (without citing any sources for this claim), but that 'these [astrological] things are avoided, because such observance is futile and alien to our faith'.[14]

Despite these apparently universal condemnations, there were some cracks in the edifice of Christian objections towards astrology. St Augustine allowed celestial events for weather forecasting, and Isidore of Seville claimed that astrology was 'partly natural, and partly superstitious', distinguishing the casting of horoscopes, which he condemned, from the study of natural influences, which he permitted.[15] Nicholas Campion summed up Isidore's distinction between 'natural' astrology based on observation, and 'superstitious' astrology that assigned meanings to such observations: 'Superstitious astrology was definitely condemned, but natural astrology was not, and that simple fact was bound to lead to later confusion.'[16] The distinction between astrology as divination and astrology as the study of natural influences may have been obvious to Isidore and Augustine, but as Valerie Flint pointed out, if everyone had understood this, then it would not have been necessary for Augustine to have mentioned it.[17]

The rapid rise of Islam in the seventh century, and its conquest of the Sassanian Empire in Persia, gave Muslim scholars access to a wide range of astrological texts from Byzantium and Persia. Islam being a monotheistic religion, one might expect to find the same suspicion of astrology, with its pagan roots, that one finds in Christian objections. However, by 762, the caliph al-Mansur had set up his new capital city of Baghdad and employed a team of astrologers to determine the most auspicious date to lay the foundation, and his capital became a major centre of translation of astrological texts into Arabic, and he employed astrologers in his court.[18] This enthusiasm for astrology within early Islam is not so clear-cut, however. It appears that in early Islam during the rule of 'Abd al-Malik ibn Marwān (685-705), there was something of a political battle taking place, where, according to George Saliba, there were two competing groups: religious scholars focusing on the Qur'ān and opposed to the introduction of 'foreign sciences', and the advocates for these foreign sciences who had mastered the languages in which they were written, and who had won the day thanks to the utility of these sciences, particularly in the realm of engineering and mathematics.[19] Those advocating the use of these sciences were often Persian and Jewish scholars, with influence in the courts, and were treated with suspicion by clerics.[20]

The Persian scholar Abū Ma'šar devoted two chapters of his *Great Introduction to Astrology* to justifying astrology.[21] He did this by recourse to Aristotle, who believed in a 'Prime Mover'; Richard Lemay pointed out that Abū Ma'šar's references to 'God's will' are very similar to Aristotle's Prime Mover.[22] Since Aristotle accepted the influence of planets, and his philosophy was to an extent acceptable within some areas of Islamic scholarship, the implication is that an astrology which drew on Aristotle must have been acceptable too.[23] The argument is far more complex than this, and objections to Aristotle were to be debated by later Islamic scholars such as al-Ghazali a couple of centuries after Abū Ma'šar.[24]

Christian Attitudes Towards Islam

Bede wrote his *Reckoning of Time* in 725, and about this time the Christian West was becoming aware of Islam, and developing an interest in it. John, the Bishop of Seville in Muslim Spain, had the Bible translated into Arabic in 724. By the ninth century, the bishop of Córdoba was lamenting the fact that:

> Our young Christians... are perfected in Arabic eloquence... Scarcely one in a thousand can be found in the Christian community who is able to compose a well-written Latin letter to a friend. But there are a great many among them who can expound the Arabic pomposity of language with the greatest erudition, and adorn the final clauses of verses more elegantly than the Arabs themselves![25]

Around the year 800, Alcuin of York, an English monk who was invited to work at the court of the emperor Charlemagne in Aachen, described a disputation between a Spanish bishop and a Saracen.[26] Charlemagne himself had an interest in astronomy and was given an elaborate water clock by the caliph

Harun al-Rashid in 807, showing further links between Muslim and Christian scholars.[27] Unlike the Western Empire, where knowledge of Greek had been all but lost, Byzantium (the Eastern Roman Empire) was Greek-speaking and there were links between Constantinople and Baghdad.[28] Relations between Christians and Muslims were not always so friendly, of course – Spain was contested territory, and authors like Bede were aware of the Arab conquests following the rise of Islam; Bede referred to the appearance of two comets in 729 presaging the Umayyad attack on Aquitaine and the subsequent defeat of the Muslim army at the Battle of Tours in 732, saying that the 'Saracens, like a very sore plague, wasted France with pitiful destruction, and themselves not long after were justly punished in the same country for their unbelief.'[29]

Introduction of Arabic Science into the Christian West

One area that was not just acceptable but essential for Christianity was the ability to calculate the date of Easter in advance. The Gospels state that Christ was crucified on the eve of Passover.[30] Passover is a Jewish festival, and is always celebrated on the fifteenth day of the month of Nisan. Nisan is the first month of spring, and in the Hebrew calendar, months always start with the first visible crescent of the New Moon, so the fifteenth day is always a Full Moon (in theory).[31] Christians wished to celebrate Christ's resurrection, which happened on the first Sunday after Passover, so to calculate this date one needs to know when the spring equinox is, and when the first Full Moon after the spring equinox is. This is non-trivial – it involves understanding both lunar and solar cycles, and how they interact. While other religions that use a lunar or soli-lunar calendar (such as Islam and Judaism) can observe the sighting of the crescent Moon to announce a new month, Christians require advance notice of Easter in order to commemorate Lent.[32] This important task exercised the minds of Christians from the early days of Christianity, and because it involved computation, it was called 'computus'. However, many medieval texts call it 'compotus' – and this is not because of sloppy Latin on the part of medieval scribes, but is apparently a pun. Computus means computing, and compotus means drinking together – the idea being that computus was so complicated it was best sorted out as a group endeavour over a few jugs of ale in the local tavern![33] In the early sixth century, a Scythian monk, Dionysius Exiguus (most famously known for introducing the *Anno Domini* system of numbering years that is still used across the world today) produced a table showing the dates of Easter, based on a nineteen-year cycle.[34] Dionysius started his table from the year 532 according to his system of *Anno Domini*, replacing a system based on the accession of the Roman emperor Diocletian, which ran for a period of

95 years.[35] Debates about the correct calculation continued, but the essential method proposed by Dionysius won the day when Bede wrote his *Reckoning of Time* in 725, which according to Faith Wallis 'not only guaranteed the ultimate success of Dionysius' system, but to have made computus into a science'.[36] Bede's work differed from earlier texts because not only did he produce a full table for the 532-year cycle between 532 and 1063, but he explained the various techniques needed to calculate Easter without the need to look up the date in his table.[37] As well as its practical use, Wallis argued that Bede may have opened the door to a wider acceptance of science. Although Wallis's commentary is careful to point out Bede's wariness of anything that sounded like astrology, her commentary on chapter 24 (a chapter on the number of hours of moonlight, and not directly related to computus) claims that this demonstrates 'Bede's critical scientific mind', and whose 'importance for the history of science in the West is seriously underestimated' and that 'Bede's vision of what computus could encompass allowed monks like Gerbert and Abbo of Fleury [tenth-century scholars], well before the arrival of Greek and Arabic astronomical texts, at least to pose questions and ponder problems which were purely scientific in character, independent of their applicability to the calendar'.[38]

Thus, the Church's ambivalence towards astrology together with its need to calculate Easter, and its tentative contacts with Islam, where scholars were translating astrological texts, opened the door to examining planetary cycles in general. The study of astrology in Christian Europe took another leap forward with Gerbert d'Aurillac, who became Pope Sylvester II in 999. Legend has it that he studied in Muslim Córdoba – but according to Nothaft, this is probably not true.[39] He was, though, a keen scholar of astrological and scientific texts. Campion sums him up thus: 'We could not have a clearer instance of a scientifically inquiring mind than in Gerbert'.[40] Various astrological texts had found their way into Christian Catalonia from Islamic al-Andalus in southern Spain, which Marco Zuccato claims was through diplomatic channels facilitated by Gerbert d'Aurillac.[41] This was followed by other astrological texts, including the pseudo-astrological *Alchandreana*, Arabic texts on the astrolabe, the classical poem on astrology by the first-century Roman author Manilius, *Astronomica*, and the *Mathesis* of the fourth-century Hellenistic astrologer Firmicus Maternus.[42] Jennifer Moreton noted that there were contacts between Lotharingia (on the border of modern-day France and Germany) and the west country of England prior to the Norman Conquest, which 'reinforced interest in computus' and these links continued into the twelfth century as will be discussed shortly.[43] Wallis describes computus as 'the door through which ancient and Arabic astronomy and mathematics entered the West'.[44]

Given that Spain was contested territory and the First Crusade started around the time that these Arabic texts were coming into Christian Europe, it may seem surprising that the study of Arabic texts was tolerated. However, according to Scott Montgomery, because Arabic scholars had translated old Greek and Persian texts, these were not seen as Islamic, but rather as hidden or lost texts that Arabic scholars had safeguarded and translated. Arabic science was somehow 'exempt' from Islamic culture.[45] Another breakthrough came in 1085, when Toledo, near modern-day Madrid and a great centre of Islamic learning, fell to the Christians. This opened the doors for Christian scholars to learn Arabic and study scientific texts. The Spanish king who took over Toledo, Alfonso VI of Castile, encouraged its Arabic and Jewish scholars to stay, and Christian scholars flocked to Toledo to learn Arabic and translate Arabic texts on medicine, science, and astrology into Latin.

Many of these texts related to the astrolabe, a very useful Arabic instrument used for navigation and astronomy. An astrolabe comprises a set of rotating discs that show what stars are visible at any given time, and became an object of great interest in Christian Europe, and started to be manufactured there. Their use for navigation, astronomy, and telling the time were uncontroversial. Since an astrolabe is a map of the sky at any given time, they could also be used for drawing up the houses of an astrological chart – rather more controversial! If computus, then, was the door through which Arabic astronomy entered the west, the astrolabe was the door through which astrology entered. By the eleventh century, texts on the astrolabe were available, together with astrological texts explaining the significance of planets in houses. For example, Firmicus Maternus' *Mathesis* says that Mercury in the third house may make one an astrologer.[46] However, this information could not be used in the eleventh century; the astrological textbooks (such as *Mathesis*) were available, as was the astrolabe to be able to draw up the houses of an astrological chart, but the missing piece of the jigsaw was the ability to calculate planetary positions. Without this, horoscopic astrology was impossible, as the would-be astrologer could not calculate where Mercury was in the native's chart, and thus could not tell what house the planet was in. The classical Hellenistic astrologers did have this knowledge, as did Arabic astrologers; the second-century Hellenistic author Claudius Ptolemy had described the method of calculation in his *Almagest*, which had been translated into Arabic.[47] Arabic scholars had not only translated *Almagest*, but had used it to develop planetary tables themselves, revising some of the calculations and methods. One such set was that produced by the ninth-century Persian polymath Muhammad ibn Musa al-Khwarizmi.

Earlier mention was made of contacts between Lotharingia and the west of

England. One Lotharingian in the West Country of England in the early twelfth century was the prior of Malvern, Walcher, who collaborated with a Jewish convert to Christianity, Petrus Alfonsi. The two men worked on the production of the astronomical tables of al-Khwarizmi in 1116, which were revised by another West Country scholar, Adelard of Bath, in 1126.[48] Petrus Alfonsi was a physician who had been born as Moses Sephardi in Islamic Spain (and therefore conversant in Arabic) before converting to Christianity in 1106 and emigrating to England, where he may have served as the physician to King Henry I.[49] Adelard of Bath was a younger contemporary, who travelled to Sicily and Syria and had learned Arabic. In addition to revising al-Khwarizmi's planetary tables, he translated astrological works, wrote a treatise on the astrolabe that he dedicated to Henry II, and produced a set of horoscopes that may have related to Henry II, whom Adelard had taught when Henry was a prince in Bristol.[50] Adelard was merely one of a long line of translators in the twelfth century, which saw a huge translation movement that translated large numbers of Arabic texts on astrology, science, medicine and mathematics into Latin.[51] Roger French demonstrated that Arabic astrological texts had a particular relevance and utility for medicine, since possible religious objections about prediction did not apply to doctors in the same way, since 'their business involved prognostication'.[52]

The translation of planetary tables made horoscopic astrology possible. The missing piece of the jigsaw had been discovered, and with the use of an astrolabe, planetary tables, and astrological texts, one could now draw up an astrological chart and interpret it. Astrology had become mainstream; a Pope had introduced astrological texts into Europe at the very end of the tenth century, a prior of the Church had translated planetary tables, medics were using Arabic astrology, and a scholar from Bath was teaching astrology to the future king of England and drawing up horoscopes for him. It was clearly no longer a taboo subject.

In order to use this knowledge widely, however, it needed to be taught. The earliest teacher that we know of was a teacher called Roger in the cathedral school in Hereford, a city on the English/Welsh border: the cathedral school attached to it is still active, and is one of the oldest in England. Roger was fairly prominent, and was probably a member of the bishop's household.[53] He had been teaching computus to his students, but he also read these newly translated Arabic texts, and used them to compile a textbook for the students in his school. His prologue states that he will explain the techniques of astrology, which he is compiling into a single volume – and that this is the first time anyone has put all the rules into a single book.[54] Given the hostility of the early Church towards astrology, one might have expected Roger, like Abū Maʿšar before him, to devote some of the book to justifying why the teaching of astrology was acceptable. Far from it! 'It is the most excellent art', he boasted, 'as astrology reveals things hidden and that gives you power over other people'.[55] No Christian apologetics there! Roger did not simply repeat the Arabic sources verbatim, but developed the ideas he had found in them into a practical textbook on what we now call horary astrology, which is where one casts an astrological chart for the moment a question is asked, and determines an answer from it. Roger provided one full worked example in his text, but also gave numerous small examples, which could be quite detailed. For example, in one section on determining the intention of a questioner, he provides an example where 'if a planet were in the fifth house and the fifth house's lord is Saturn, and Saturn is in the sixth house in Taurus, in which sign Saturn signifies the stomach, one would consider sickness of the stomach of the sons', based on the definitions in Arabic texts that the sixth house relates to illness, that the fifth house relates to sons, and that Saturn in Taurus relates to the stomach.[56] This example is not in the Arabic sources from which Roger derived his book, but is a practical example based on delineations from a variety of those texts.[57]

Little is known of Roger the teacher other than his texts. Alfred of Shareshill, an early thirteenth-century translator of Aristotle and a younger contemporary of Roger, dedicated a version of *De vegetabilibus* to 'my most beloved Roger', and this, together with the fact that Roger's manuscripts were copied for many centuries, implies that he was not simply an isolated provincial schoolteacher.[58] It is not known whether his particular textbook was used by later teachers of astrology, although it was copied widely, but we do know that cathedral schools such as the one in Hereford were the forerunners of the universities that sprang up a few decades later, and that astrology became part of the university curriculum.[59] French claimed that Roger belonged to 'a circle of Anglo-Normans' interested in natural science, which included Robert Grosseteste, who was probably 'in Hereford in Roger's lifetime'.[60] Grosseteste was, according to Richard Southern, part of the household of the Bishop of Hereford in 1197 and wrote works on computus and astrology.[61] Grosseteste went on to become a very major figure in natural science, taught at Oxford University and then went to Paris to study theology before returning and eventually becoming Bishop of Lincoln.[62]

The introduction of Arabic astrology thus became embedded in the curriculum. Its practical use in medicine ensured it became an essential skill, and continued to be taught for many centuries. Guido Bonatti, whom Campion cites as 'one of the most famous astrologers in European history' wrote his astrological textbook *Book of Astronomy* in the thirteenth century, citing his Arabic sources.[63] Charles Burnett has demonstrated that al-Qabisi's

Introduction was being taught at universities in the early fifteenth century, and in the early seventeenth century Galileo Galilei was not only teaching astrology at the university in Padua, but drawing up horoscopes for clients.[64]

Conclusion

The rediscovery of astrology in twelfth-century Catholic Europe requires some explanation, especially as the astrology of the pagan Roman Empire was treated with suspicion by early Christian authorities, and had been generally condemned. However, the condemnation was ambivalent; the use of what Isidore had identified as 'natural astrology' such as weather forecasting was permitted, and the study of lunar and solar cycles was essential to determine the date of Easter, an essential requirement for Christian worship. Computus, the study of these cycles to determine Easter, thus played a very important role in monasteries, and led to the study of planetary cycles in general. Tentative contact with Islam from the eighth century onwards, sometimes hostile and sometimes friendly, led to some Arabic science finding its way into Christian Europe – in particular, the study of the astrolabe. The astrolabe led to a more general acceptance of Arabic science, which, as it had been translated from older texts, was not seen as having a specifically Islamic slant. Some of these scientific texts were astrological in nature, but not initially usable for practical astrology since the knowledge of calculating planetary positions had been lost.

That changed dramatically in the twelfth century. The capture of Toledo in 1085 by Alfonso VI of Castile, who permitted Jewish and Muslim scholars to remain and work with Christian scholars, led to a huge translation movement with scholars from across Europe going to centres of learning such as Toledo to learn Arabic and translate these texts into Latin. These texts included numerous astrological works, and, critically, the understanding of the calculations needed to determine planetary positions. Once this was understood, horoscopic astrology became possible again in the Christian West – and since Arabic astrologers had been practising astrology for centuries, and these Arabic astrological texts were now also available in Latin, this opened the door for the study and teaching of astrology.

One such teacher, Roger of Hereford, was a computist and part of the bishop's household, and taught computus to his students in the cathedral school at Hereford. When he encountered newly translated Arabic texts on astrology, he incorporated these into the curriculum there, teaching his students the principles and practice of astrology. He wrote a number of texts, including one on judicial astrology, which is a practical textbook on interrogations, the use of horoscopes to answer precise questions, now known as horary astrology. The twelfth-century rediscovery of astrology appeared to be embraced by the Church. It was taught in cathedral schools and universities, welcomed by clerics, and embraced by English kings, and the authors of astrological works felt no need to justify their art – a far cry from the condemnation of astrology by the early Church.

Note

1.   William Manchester, *A World Lit Only by Fire: The Medieval Mind and the Renaissance* (New York: Little, Brown and Co, 1992), p.26.

2.   Otto Neugebauer, 'The Study of Wretched Subjects', *Isis*, 42.2 (1951), p.111.

3.   Notable exceptions include Lynn Thorndike, *A History of Magic and Experimental Science* (New York: Columbia University Press, 1923); F.J. Carmody, *Arabic Astronomical and Astrological Sciences in Latin Translation: A Critical Bibliography* (Berkeley: University of California Press, 1956); Edward Grant, *A Source Book in Medieval Science* (Cambridge, MA: Harvard University Press, 1974).

4.   Carl Boyer and Uta Merzbach, *A History of Mathematics* (New York: Wiley, 1989), p.171.

5.   For early translations, see Al-Biruni, *The Book of Instruction in the Elements of the Art of Astrology*, R. Ramsay Wright (ed.) (London: Luzac & Co, 1934); Abraham ibn Ezra, *The Beginning of Wisdom: An Astrological Treatise*, R. Levy and F. Cantera (trans.) (Baltimore: The Johns Hopkins Press, 1939); Firmicus Maternus, *Ancient Astrology Theory and Practice: Matheseos Libri VIII*, J.R. Bram (trans.) (Park Ridge, NJ: Noyes Press, 1975); for the 1992 translation project, see 'The Early History of Project Hindsight', http://www.projecthindsight.com/archives/history.html [accessed 3 May 2021].

6.   The figures for the 2010s decade were obtained in 2018, and so have been multiplied by 1.25.

7.   This is the topic of Chapter Two of Mitchell, 'England's First Astrology Book'.

8.   Catholic Church, *Catechism of the Catholic Church*, 2nd. ed. (Vatican: Libreria Editrice Vaticana, 2012), 2116.

9.   The Islamic website Sunnah Online cites various sources in its objection to astrology in 'The Islamic Ruling on Horoscopes', *SunnahOnline.com*, https://sunnahonline.com/library/beliefs-and-methodology/70-the-islamic-ruling-on-horoscopes [accessed 3 May 2021]; the ninth-century Persian scholar Abu Dawud al-Sijistani (often cited in contemporary Islamic websites, including SunnahOnline.com) stated 'مَنِ اقْتَبَسَ عِلْمًا مِنَ النُّجُومِ اقْتَبَسَ شُعْبَةً مِنَ السِّحْرِ زَادَ مَازَاد' ('If anyone acquires any knowledge of astrology, he acquires a branch of magic'), Abu Dawud al-Sijistani, *Sunan Abu Dawood*, 3905; for a modern Jewish Orthodox perspective, the website aish.com states 'Although Judaism believes in astrological influences, we are commanded not to inquire of them' in 'Astrology, Horoscopes', www.aish.com/atr/Astrology-Horoscopes.html [accessed 3 May 2021]; for a contrary Orthodox perspective, the Hassidic site chabad.org offers a qualified "yes" to the question "Is astrology kosher?", Levi Brackman, 'Is Astrology Kosher?', www.chabad.org/library/article_cdo/aid/269721/jewish/Is-Astrology-Kosher.htm [accessed 3 May 2021].

10.   Augustine, *Confessions, Volume I: Books 1-8*, C. Hammond (trans.), Loeb Classical Library 26 (Cambridge, MA: Harvard University Press, 2014), 4.3.4, p.137; Augustine, *Confessions*, 7.6.8 p.309.

11.   Augustine, *City of God, Volume II: Books 4-7*, W.M. Green, (trans.), Loeb Classical Library 412 (Cambridge, MA: Harvard University Press, 1963), 5.1, p.139.

12.   'Nullus sibi proponat fatum vel fortunam aut genesim, quod vulgo nascentia

dicitur' from B. Krusch (ed.), *Vita Eligii Episcopi Noviomagensis* (Hannover: Hahn, 1902), II 16a, p.707.

13. The phrase 'twinkling of an eye' is in 1 Corinthians 15:52, and given in the Vulgate as 'in ictu oculi', but Bede's text gives no reference for why this is 15/94 of a second.

14. Bede, *Bede: The Reckoning of Time*, Faith Wallis (trans.) (Liverpool: Liverpool University Press, 1999), pp.15-16.

15. Augustine, *The Letters of St. Augustine*, J.G. Cunningham (trans.) (Altenmünster: Jazzybee Verlag, 2015), Letter LV Chapter VIII.15, p.100; Isidore of Seville, *Etymologies*, S. Barney, W.J. Lewis, J.A. Beach, O. Berghof (eds) (Cambridge: Cambridge University Press, 2006), 3.xxvii, p.99.

16. Nicholas Campion, *A History of Western Astrology Volume II - The Medieval and Modern Worlds* (London: Continuum, 2009), p.14.

17. Valerie Flint, *The Rise of Magic in Early Medieval Europe* (Princeton, NJ: Princeton University Press, 1994), p.96.

18. John Freely, *Aladdin's Lamp: How Greek Science Came to Europe Through the Islamic World* (New York: Alfred A. Knopf, 2009), p.71.

19. George Saliba, 'Islamic Astronomy in Context: Attacks on Astrology and the Rise of the Hay'a Tradition', *Bulletin of the Royal Institute for Inter-Faith Studies*, 4.1 (2002), pp.25-46.

20. George Saliba, *Islamic Science and the Making of the European Renaissance* (Cambridge, MA: MIT Press, 2007), p.76.

21. Keiji Yamamoto and Charles Burnett (eds), *The Great Introduction to Astrology by Abū Maʿšar* (Leiden: Brill, 2019), Chapter 2, 'The second chapter: on the existence of the science of astrology', pp.53-79, and Chapter 5, 'The fifth chapter: on giving arguments concerning the confirmation of astrology and the refutation of everyone who claims that the planets' movement has no power and no indication for the things coming to be in this world', pp.107-149.

22. Richard Lemay, *Abu Ma'shar and Latin Aristotelianism in the Twelfth Century* (Beirut: American University of Beirut, 1962), pp.68-69.

23. See for example Aristotle's discussion on the planetary influences in gestation in Aristotle, *Generation of Animals*, A.L. Peck (trans.), Loeb Classical Library 366 (Cambridge, MA: Harvard University Press, 1942), p.482.

24. See for example al-Ghazali's dismissal of planetary spheres in al-Ghazali, *Tahafut al-Falasifah (Incoherence of the Philosophers)* Sabih Kamali (trans) (Lahore: Pakistan Philosophical Congres, 1963), pp.75-78.

25. Dorothee Metlitzki, *The Matter of Araby in Medieval England* (New Haven: Yale University Press, 1977), p.5. The Muslim rulers of Spain allowed Christians and Jews to remain and worship, which is why there were bishops in these Muslim cities.

26. Metlitzki, *The Matter of Araby*, p.15.

27. Kocku von Stuckrad, 'Interreligious Transfers in the Middle Ages: The Case of Astrology', *Journal of Religion in Europe*, 1.1 (2008), pp.49-50.

28. Nicholas Campion describes how 'Stephanus the Philosopher, a student of the caliph's astrologer, Theophilus of Edessa, moved from Baghdad to Constantinople in 775.', Campion, *History of Western Astrology*, p.20; John Freely describes how Leo the Mathematician became head of a school of philosophy and science in Constantinople, while one of his students ended up at the court of a caliph translating Greek science texts into Arabic, Freely, *Aladdin's Lamp*, p.71.

29. Bede, *Ecclesiastical History, Volume II*, J.E. King (trans.), Loeb Classical Library 248 (Cambridge, MA: Harvard University Press, 1930), 5.23, p.369.

30. The day before Passover was the date of Christ's crucifixion according to John 19:14.

31. For an explanation of the Hebrew calendar and its relationship to astronomy and Passover, see Solomon Gartenhaus and Arnold Tubis, 'The Jewish Calendar – A Mix of Astronomy and Theology', *Shofar* 25.2 (Winter 2007), pp.104-124.

32. See for example Bede, *Reckoning of Time*, p.xx.

33. The etymology of "compotus" was provided by the thirteenth-century astrologer Michael Scot, according to Philipp Nothaft: 'from the drink allegedly shared by the founders of the calendar or from the drinking parties (compotationes) necessary to entertain those who were being educated in the art.', Philipp Nothaft, *Scandalous Error: Calendar Reform and Calendrical Astronomy in Medieval Europe* (Oxford: Oxford University Press, 2018), p.121.

34. A.A. Mosshammer, *The Easter Computus and the Origins of the Christian Era* (Oxford: Oxford University Press, 2008), p.72.

35. Bede, *Reckoning of Time*, p.liv.

36. Bede, *Reckoning of Time*, p.xvii.

37. For the full listing of Bede's 532-year table, see Appendix Two of Bede, *Reckoning of Time*, pp.392-404.

38. Bede, *Reckoning of Time*, p.300.

39. Philipp Nothaft, *Walcher of Malvern* (Turnhout: Brepols, 2017), p.15.

40. Campion, *History of Western Astrology*, p.32.

41. Marco Zuccato, 'Gerbert of Aurillac and a Tenth-Century Jewish Channel for the Transmission of Arabic Science to the West', *Speculum*, 80 (2005), p.743.

42. The *Alchandreana* is a curious mix of astrology and numerology with many Hebrew elements and dates from the early eleventh century – eleventh century copies of the manuscript are Barcelona, Arxiu de la Corona d'Aragó, Ripoll 225 and Paris, Bibliothèque nationale de France, Lat. 17868, ff.2r-13r, and the text is discussed in full in David Juste, *Les Alchandreana Primitifs* (Leiden: Brill, 2007); an eleventh-century edition of Firmicus Maternus' *Mathesis* is in Paris, Bibliothèque nationale de France, Lat. 7311, ff.4-49; and texts on the astrolabe are discussed in Arianna Borelli, *Aspects of the Astrolabe* (Stuttgart: Franz Steiner, 2008); David Juste, 'Hermann der Lahme und das Astrolab im Spiegel der neuesten Forschung' in F. Heinzer and T. Zotz (eds.), *Hermann der Lahme: Reichenauer Mönch und Universalgelehrter des 11. Jahrhunderts* (Stuttgart: Kohlhammer, 2016), pp.273-284; J. Drecker, 'Hermannus Contractus Über das Astrolab', *Isis*, 16.2 (1931), pp.200-219; Josep Casulleras, 'The Instruments and the Exercise of Astrology in the Medieval Arabic Tradition', *Archives Internationales d'Histoire des Sciences* 63.170-171 (2013), pp.517-540.

43. Jennifer Moreton, 'Before Grosseteste: Roger of Hereford and Calendar Reform in Eleventh and Twelfth-Century England', *Isis*, 86.4 (1995), pp.562-586.

44. Faith Wallis, 'Medicine in Medieval Calendar Manuscripts' in M.R. Schleissner (ed.), *Manuscript Sources of Medieval Medicine: A Book of Essays*, (Abingdon: Routledge, 2014), p.109.

45. Scott Montgomery, *Science in Translation* (Chicago: University of Chicago Press, 2000), p.165.

46. 'In iii loco merc[urius] ab horosc[opo] c[on]stitutus faci[et] sacerdotes magos archiatros mathematicos & p[er] se i[n]venientes atq[ue] discentes, q[uic]q[uid] ill[is] n[on] [est] alienos magisterio', Firmicus Maternus, *Mathesis*, BNF Lat. 7311, f.31r. lines 6-7, translated as 'Mercury in the third house will make priests, magicians, healers, astrologers, men who through their own efforts discover things not handed down [by tradition].' in Firmicus Maternus, *Ancient Astrology: Matheseos*, III.VII.6, p.100.

47. One of the first European translations of *Almagest* is by the prolific translator Gerard of Cremona, Bibliothèque nationale de France Lat. 14738; an English translation is Ptolemy, *Ptolemy's Almagest*, G.J. Toomer (trans.) (London: Duckworth, 1984), Books IX-XI, pp.419-554.

48. Metlitzki, *The Matter of Araby*, p.25. For a discussion of how al-Khwarizmi's tables were developed, see Julio Samsó, *Astronomy and Astrology in al-Andalus and the Maghrib* (Abingdon: Routledge, 2007).

49. John Tolan, *Petrus Alfonsi and his Medieval Readers* (Gainesville: University Press of Florida, 1993).

50. John North, *Horoscopes and History* (London: Warburg Institute, 1986), pp.96-107.

51. For a full discussion, see Mitchell, 'England's First Astrology Book', pp.40-54.

52. Roger French, 'Foretelling the Future: Arabic Astrology and English Medicine in the Late Twelfth Century', *Isis* 87.3 (1996), p.454.

53. From a personal e-mail communication with Christopher Pullin, the Chancellor of Hereford Cathedral, on 2 August 2016.

54. 'Quoniam regulas artis astronomice iudicandi no[n] n[isi] p[er] div[er]sa op[er] a disp[er]sa invenimus, u[ti]li astrologo[rum] desiderio satisfacere cupie[n]tes eis q[ui]b[us] ubi nec[ess]e fu[er]it explananatione[m] sit suppleme[n]tionem apponentes i[n] unu[m] brevit[er] colligem[us]', Roger of Hereford, *Judicial Astrology*, Cambridge University Library II1.1, f.40ra lines 3-12: 'Since we discover the rules of the art of judicial astronomy only from diverse scattered works, we will shortly gather together in one combined supplement the practices of the astrologers to satisfy that longed-for request, for those to whom an explanation would be necessary' (my translation).

55. 'Est aut[em] + hic finitissi[m]a certissi[m]a excellentissi[m]a post creatoris cog[itat] ione[m] a q[ua] + ip[s]a i[n]cipit', Cambridge II1.1, f.40rb lines 2-5; 'de h[u]i[us] utili[ta] te au[tem] sup[er]fluu[m] e[ss]et agere cu[m] ista hom[in]em sup[er] ho[min]em efferens fut[ur]a[ram] ac o[mn]iu[m] a nat[ur]a abscondito[rum] p[re]ciu[m] efficiat', Cambridge II1.1, f.40ra line 28 - f.40rb line 2.

56. Oxford, Bodleian Library Selden Supra 86, f.15v. Translation is my own.

57. In this example, a combination of *On Hidden Things* by Masha'Allah, the pains of the planets in al-Qabisi's *Introduction to Astrology*, and house definitions from various Arabic texts including Abū Ma'šar's *Great Introduction*.

58. Charles Haskins, *The Renaissance of the Twelfth Century* (Cambridge, MA: Harvard University Press, 1933), p.317; for details of the distribution of Roger's manuscript, see Mitchell, 'England's First Astrology Book', Chapter 3.

59. Unfortunately, the curriculum at Oxford, for example, cannot be reconstructed in detail prior to the fourteenth century – see Laurence Brockliss, *The University of Oxford: A History* (Oxford: Oxford University Press, 2016), p.86 – and no mention is made of Roger of Hereford's textbook; Charles Burnett cites an example from 1405 that the only astrological text studied at Bologna was al-Qabisi's *Introduction to Astrology*: Charles Burnett, 'Al-Qabisi's *Introduction to Astrology*: From Courtly Entertainment to University Textbook', *Studies in the History of Culture and Science: A Tribute to Gad Freudenthal* (Leiden: Brill, 2010), p.49.

60. French, *Foretelling the Future*, p.462.

61. Richard Southern, *Robert Grosseteste* (Oxford: Clarendon Press, 1992), p.126.

62. Southern, *Robert Grosseteste*, gives a full biography.

63. Campion, *History of Western Astrology*, p.56; Guido Bonatti, *Book of Astronomy*, B.N. Dykes (trans.) (Golden Valley, Minnesota, 2007).

64. Burnett, 'From Courtly Entertainment to University Textbook', p.49; H. Darrel Rutkin, 'Galileo as Practising Astrologer', *Journal for the History of Astronomy* 49.3 (August 2018), pp.388-391.s

4

IN SEARCH OF THE CONSCIOUS HISTORICAL PROCESS: ALEXANDER CHIZHEVSKY AND JOHANNES KEPLER

Karine Dilanian

Introduction

Alexander Chizhevsky (1897-1964) was one of the first members of a group known as the *Russian cosmists*, along with such key figures as Nikolai Fedorov (1829–1903) and Konstantin Tsiolkovsky (1857–1935), the theorist of space exploration and cosmonautics.[1] He was a graduate of the Moscow Archeological Institute and Moscow Commercial College and, in 1918, he successfully defended his PhD thesis 'On the Periodicity of the World-Historical Process' at the Scientific Council of the History and Philology Faculty of Moscow University. Six years later, he extended his thesis in his book *Physical Factors of the Historical Process*, subtitled *The influence of cosmic factors upon the behaviour of organized human masses as well as upon the universal historical process beginning with V century BC and ending at the present day. Researches and theory*, which was published in a limited edition in Kaluga in 1924.[2] In the introduction Chizhevsky questioned the aim and purpose of history as a science and added that it has no practical social significance. He pictured history as 'the knowledge of the dead', as 'an archive, where people rarely make inquiries and whose comprehension and all these "history lessons"', have, as he wrote, 'never taught anyone anything'.[3] He claimed that, 'despite the huge records collected by historians, the sophisticated methods of its development and, despite the tremendous problems that scientists have overcome, history, as it is, means no more than zero for the social practice of mankind'.[4]

Faced with what he saw as the inadequacy of historical studies, Chizhevsky suggested turning to modern science, on the grounds that it reduces psychological phenomena to physiological processes, in which it finds a physicochemical basis which is itself founded in the mechanics of elementary particles. This perspective, Chizhevsky argued, allows for deeper penetration into the essence of mental life which, in turn, is closely related to the life of the whole organism and to the external world surrounding it. Although there were other attempts to connect human activity to historical evolution and natural laws as well as to demonstrate the influence of the physical agents of nature, in Chizhevsky's opinion they all lacked a consistent theory. Chizhevsky argued that physical phenomena occur according to strict laws and that historical phenomena do not represent the result of human action and free will, but are subordinate to a certain order, which, he said, 'must be revealed eventually'.[5] Consequently, he proposed the application of physical-mathematical methods and principles to the study of the historical process and social evolution. He considered that the universe can only be understood through the study of physics and that therefore 'physics must have its say when considering any question in the world and that 'in the light of the modern scientific worldview, the fate of Humanity is undoubtedly dependent on the fate of the universe'.[6]

As far as a likely mechanism for humanity's connection to the universe was concerned, Chizhevsky speculated that any celestial body moving in space relative to the Earth produces an effect on the Earth's magnetic field. This effect then generates various changes and perturbations in meteorology and affects a number of other terrestrial phenomena. In addition, the Sun, as the primary source of all movement on Earth, is dependent on the electromagnetic life of the universe as well as on the position of other celestial bodies.[7] From this viewpoint, Chizhevsky continued:

> it is necessary to consider *a priori* that the greatest events in human societies, enveloping whole countries and nations through the participation of great masses of population must occur simultaneously with some fluctuations or variations in the forces of the environment. Indeed, any mass-public event is a very challenging complex. Dismembering, dividing this complex into many parts that are plain and clear, and then simplifying the understanding of phenomena, is the most important task of natural-historical knowledge.[8]

Taking the Sun as the main participant and the driving force of this process, Chizhevsky undertook a study of the course of historical events in connection within the Sun's periodic activities. The results of this research were presented in *Physical Factors of the Historical Process*, in which he demonstrated his concept of the correlation of the 11-year cycles of solar activity to their influence on the different terrestrial phenomena.[9] The book was dedicated to Rudolf Wolf (1816–1893), who had correlated the Sunspot cycle to observations of the Earth's magnetism.[10] Chizhevsky conducted a detailed historiometric analysis of riots, wars, battles, revolutions and epidemics in the Russian Empire and early USSR, along with dozens of other countries, and compared them to Sunspot activity records for the period 500 BCE to 1922 CE. He concluded that a significant proportion of the most important historical events involving large numbers of people occurred around the Sunspot maximum.[11] He wrote that his synthesise of historical material had enabled him to determine the following 'morphological law' of historical process:

> The course of the universal historical process is composed of an uninterrupted row of cycles, occupying a period equaling the arithmetical mean of 11 years and synchronizing with the degree of its military-political activity with Sunspot activity. Each cycle possesses the following historic-psychological peculiarities:

> In the middle points of the cycle's course, the mass activity of humanity all over the surface of the Earth, given the presence in human societies of economic, political or military factors, reaches the maximum tension, manifesting itself in psychomotoric pandemics: revolutions, insurrections, expeditions, migrations etc., creating new formations manifesting in separate states, and new historic epochs in the life of humanity. It is accompanied by an integration of the masses, full expression of their activity and a form of government dominated by the majority.

> In the extreme points of the cycle's course, military-political tension falls to the minimum, giving way to creative activity. A general decrease of military or political enthusiasm is replaced by peace and peaceful creative work in the sphere of state organizations, international relations, science and art, with a pronounced tendency towards absolutism in the governing powers and a disintegration of the masses.[12]

> In correlation with the Sunspot maximum stand:

> a. The dissemination of different doctrines – political, religious, etc.; spreading of heresies, religious riots, pilgrimages etc.

> b. The emergence of social, military and religious leaders, reformists, etc.

> c. The formation of political, military, religious and commercial corporations, associations, unions, leagues, sects, companies, etc.

It is also impossible to overlook the fact that pathological epidemics also coincide very frequently with the Sunspot maximum periods.[13] There are nine Sunspot cycles in a century and therefore nine cycles of political and military activity.[14] Each of these is then divided into four periods: three years for minimum excitability; two years for the growth of excitability; three years for maximum excitability; and three years for the decline of excitability.[15] In summary, he concluded that the correlation between Sunspot activity and human behaviour should be considered established.[16]

Russian Cosmism as a Source for Chizhevsky's Concepts

In their paper 'Fate of the term *Russian cosmism*', V. P. Rimsky and L.P. Filonenko attribute the term to Svetlana Semenova, writing in the late 1970s.[17] Semenova described what she called a special, 'space-utopian' offshoot of Russian philosophy.[18] She defined cosmism as:

> the idea of active evolution, the need for a new conscious stage in the development of the world, when Humanity guides it in the direction that the mind and moral sense dictates to it, and takes, so to speak, the helm of evolution into its own hands. Therefore, it may be more accurate to define this trend not as cosmic, but as active evolutionary.[19]

However, the earliest mention of the term 'Russian cosmism' may be found in the *Philosophical Encyclopedia*, published in 1970 in an article by Renata Galtseva dedicated to Vladimir Vernadsky (1863–1945). Here Galtseva introduces the term as

> the ideas of the so-called Russian cosmism (Tsiolkovsky, Chizhevsky, partly Fedorov and Florensky), which considers the Universe and Man as a holistic system with its regulation (homeostasis) and involves a reasonable transformation of space.[20]

Chizhevsky himself always underlined the influence of Tsiolkovsky's ideas and his personality upon him, writing,

> Indeed, our scientific interests had one common ground, one, but which one? He studied the Cosmos and theoretically constructed space rocket ships, as for me – I studied the influence of the Cosmos upon us, and air that we breathe.[21]

Chizhevsky met Tsiolkovsky in 1914 and their scientific conversation continued for more than twenty years.[22] Tsiolkovsky was the first with whom Chizhevsky shared his hypothesis concerning cycles of solar activity and their influence upon life on Earth, and it was Tsiolkovsky who suggested that Chizhevsky use statistics to prove his ideas.[23] Moreover, Tsiolkovsky supported and resolutely stood up for Chizhevsky's concept of solar influence on the dynamics of the historical process. He wrote in a local Kaluga newspaper *Communa*:

> the young scientist [Chizhevsky] tries to discover the functional relationship between human behaviour and fluctuations in the Sun's activity and to determine by calculations the rhythm, cycles and periods of these changes, thus creating a new sphere of human knowledge. Chizhevsky expresses all these broad generalizations and bold thoughts for the first time in his scientific work, which gives them great value and arouses interest. Chizhevsky's book will be read with curiosity both by historians, to whom everything in it will be new and partly alien (for astronomy breaks into history), and by psychologists and sociologists. This work is an example of the merger of various sciences together on the monistic soil of physical and mathematical analysis.[24]

Tsiolkovsky and Chizhevsky did not agree on everything. In his article on 'Chizhevsky's Cosmism', V.V. Kazutinsky points out that Tsiolkovsky believed that the 'will of Universe', which is the mental energy of the 'higher intelligent forces' is transferred to humanity and determines many aspects of its life, while Chizhevsky emphasized the impact of space energy on terrestrial processes.[25] Kazutinsky stresses the originality of Chizhevsky's contribution to cosmism but also notes out that it remains as heretical now as it was in the 1920s and 30s. Chizhevsky also discussed astrology, but as an outmoded ancestor of modern scientific astronomy. In his book *The Cosmic Pulse of Life*, in a chapter entitled 'From Astrology to Cosmic Biology', he wrote:

> Maybe the first human, who looked carefully at the starry sky, spread over him in the silence of dark blue night, realized that the choir of luminaries moving in height has something in common with its bottom - the Earth - and therefore has a direct, albeit invisible connection with it. From such an elementary observation, supported by the arguments of the most unpretentious logic, the imaginary science, called astrology, was born. All nations passed through this preliminary stage of star

science, standing between astrolatry, or star worship, and astronomy, or sky science.[26]

However, as Kazutinsky pointed out, Chizhevsky considered that ancient astrology needs a fundamental rethink from the point of view of modern science.[27] Chizhevsky claimed that the latest science has discovered a growing number of threads that connect human behaviour – the manifestation of the higher nervous activity – with the cosmic and geophysical phenomena of the world around.[28] He asserted that it is not possible to recognize the basic postulate of ancient astrology – universal sympathy – while denying the influence of celestial bodies on human fate and the state of spirit.[29] He argued that

> the more the sphere of human experience increases, the more facts science accumulates that testify the influence of the environment on the person, on his development and behaviour, the more this principle of astrology becomes still more important in our eyes – the naive and at the same time the greatest guess of the ancients about the basic properties of our world, based on the principles of cosmic monism![30]

Johannes Kepler as a Source of Chizhevsky's Concepts

Chizhevsky followed in a line of thinkers who rejected the detailed interpretative structures of horoscopic astrology but approved of the principle of a universal order which serves as a rationale for astrology, notably Johannes Kepler (1571-1630). He included a brief survey of the history of astrology in *The Cosmic Pulse of Life* in which he referred to Kepler's 1619 work *Harmonice Mundi* as 'the ingenious book', and astrology as 'the corner stone of his philosophy'.[31] Chizhevsky pointed out that Kepler acknowledged the existence of the general cosmic initial essence (*obsshee nachalo*), which operated the whole world and its separate parts, which were all strongly connected to each other. He stressed that Kepler tried to explain the structure of cosmos through Pythagorean concepts, relying on harmonic ratios. Kepler had proved his theory, Chizhevsky added, through 'the discovery of his great and at the same time simple laws of the planetary motions'.[32] A reference to Kepler's concept of Harmony occurs in Chizhevsky's early, unpublished monograph *The primary beginning of the universe. Cosmic system. Problems.* Ekaterina Zvonova considers this monograph a compendium of the main philosophical and metaphysical concepts of Chizhevky, she states that *The Primary Beginning of the Universe* 'with no less reason than the famous Kepler's work could be called *Harmonice Mundi*'.[33]

Chizhevky himself argued that

> the principle of unity brings Harmony to the world, and Harmony
> is the most important touchstone of the probability of any doctrine.
> This principle – *principium universale circulationis* – is the so-called
> universal principle of circulation.[34]

In his *Physical Factors of the Historical Process*, Chizhevsky mentioned Kepler
both in the main text and in the footnotes, demonstrating his acquaintance with
Kepler's *On the More Certain Fundamentals of Astrology*.[35] Thus in the *Physical
Factors,* Chizhevsky discussed sunspots and the phenomenon of 'the dark light
of the Sun', caused by eclipses or 'other reasons', such as meteorological effects.
He wrote:

> The evangelists Matthew, Mark, Luke point to the darkening of the
> Sun, which supposedly occurred after the death of Jesus Christ. Ovid
> (Metamorphoses, XV) and Virgil (Georgica) speak of the darkening
> of the Sun at the death of Caesar in 44 before CE. Such phenomena
> have been repeatedly described and can be explained by other reasons,
> and not by the presence of colossal spots, for example, the so-called
> 'dry haze' sometimes obscuring the light of the Sun and indicated by
> Kepler...[36]

Here Chizhevsky turns to Kepler's explanation of the effect of reflection and
refraction, which he described in Thesis 27 of his *Fundamentals*. Starting with
description of the rainbow color, he turns to the explanation of the colour of the
Sun in different conditions:

> From one side it is diminished, and from the other it is refracted; finally
> on both sides it ends in black or darkness. In the first step of diminution,
> it becomes yellow, in the second, red, then dusky, and finally, black.
> The same thing appears in the clouds either when the sun has set or is
> about to rise; the same thing appears in the stars around the horizon;
> the same thing in solar eclipses, when our eyes, in which this delusion
> occurs, are suddenly deprived of the light of the sun.[37]

Although this note does not mention the title of Kepler's work and does
not give a direct reference, it demonstrates Chizhevsky's sufficiently detailed
knowledge of the Kepler text. There are both textual and semantic coincidences
in Chizhevsky's *Physical Factors of the Historical Process* to Kepler's writings.

As Kepler wrote, 'The most general, most powerful and most certain cause, which is known to everyone, is that of the approach and withdrawal of the Sun'.[38] Chizhevsky opened his *Physical Factors* with the statement: 'Taking into account enormous amount of our light as well as its relatively short distance from Earth, we can say that the Earth is under the direct and quite powerful influence of the central body of the system'.[39]

Kepler viewed the Sun as a transcendent power: Edwin Burtt depicted him as a 'Sun-worshipper', who spoke of the Sun with some kind of exaltation, naming the Sun 'a fountain of light', 'the king of the planets for his motion', 'the heart of the world for his power' and 'the eye for his beauty'.[40] Burtt cited Kepler, who said that 'by the highest right we return to the Sun, who alone appears, by virtue of his dignity and power, suited for this motive duty and worthy to become the home of God himself, not to say the first mover'.[41] In the 'Conjectural Epilogue to the Sun' in the *Harmonice Mundi* Kepler described the Sun in a form of a solemn anthem, uniting astronomical reality, celestial mechanics with mythological images, he proclaimed:

> From the heavenly music to the hearer; from the Muses to Apollo the choirmaster; from the six planets, which go around and make the harmonies, to the Sun at the center of all orbits, motionless in his place, but revolving on his own axis. For whereas there is the most complete harmony between the extreme motions of the planets... joined to the center of the Sun.[42]

For Chizhevsky, heliocentrism was not only a theory reflecting a structure of the solar system, but a world-view, which extends its limits from astronomical factors to a human being. It connected a person's psychological, mental and physical existence by invisible links to the Sun and hence, as Zvonova mentions, makes him 'a real brainchild of the Sun and of the whole Universe'.[43] In his *Earthly echo of solar storms* Chizhevsky argued that

> we, *the children of the Sun*, represent only a weak echo of those vibrations of the natural forces of cosmos, which, passing around the Earth, slightly touch it, tuning in unison it's slumbering possibilities. We are used to taking a rude and narrow anti-philosophical view of life as the result of a random game of earthly forces alone. This, of course, is wrong. Life, as we see, is much more cosmic, than terrestrial. It was created by the impact of the cosmic creative dynamics on the Earth's inert matter. It lives by the dynamics of these forces, and each beat of

the organic pulse is coordinated with the beat of the cosmic heart - this grandiose collection of nebulae, stars, the Sun and planets.[44]

Zvonova considers this to be a world-view (*Weltanschauung* in German, *mirovozzrenie* in Russian) and called it 'heliocentricism'.[45] However, the most important shared feature of Kepler's and Chizhevsky's work is their attitude towards connections between the cosmic order and the current state of events on Earth. There is a deeply practical application, namely the prediction of mass activity and the management of social life and political affairs. Nicholas Campion describes the use of astronomy in order to support the conservation of social order through the management of the wider cosmological environment as a 'political cosmology'.[46] In pursuit of this practical purpose both Kepler and Chizhevsky suggested that astrology should be reformed. Of course, Kepler lived when astrology was still taught at universities, while in Chizhevsky's time it was considered heretical.[47] Campion points to Kepler's belief that 'astrology, modernised and purged of its medieval dogma, would offer a valuable tool for managing the state and preserving political order'.[48] Kepler declared in his famous statement that 'I am a Lutheran astrologer; I throw away the nonsense and keep the hard kernel'.[49] And he specified in the conclusion to his *Fundamentals* that he 'discussed and defended the fundamentals of astrology and the coming year 1602 on the basis of physics'.[50] Chizhevsky, expressed his view in his essay *From Astrology to Cosmic Biology* asking a question:

> Have we prematurely buried astrology in its fundamental dogmatic part? And do not the results of the mathematical analysis applied to the electromagnetic field return us millennia back to the origins of ancient Chaldean wisdom?... Maybe astrology forces human thought to find similar principles in the field of exact sciences?'[51]

Kepler's Political Cosmology and Chizhevsky's Historiometric Cycles

Campion suggests an analytical model for Kepler's methodology of political cosmology, based on Kepler's considerations expressed in his *On the More Certain Fundamentals of Astrology*.[52] He divides Kepler's methodology into four stages of study and research:

1. The first stage is historical; it provides studies of historical cycles and examines correlations between political events and planetary cycles.

2. The second stage is predictive; there are investigations of future planetary cycles in order to identify critical periods of political tension.

3. The third stage is political, that is to warn politicians of coming turbulent periods potentially leading to political crises, civil disorder, war and the like.

4. In the fourth stage, governments design and implement policy, taking the appropriate action to minimize negative course of events.[53]

Campion points out that Kepler's cosmic state 'would manage dissent by social and political reform where possible, but propaganda and repression, if necessary, to forestall violent revolution'.[54] He identifies the first, *historical*, stage of Kepler's methodology in *On the More Certain Fundamentals of Astrology*. In Thesis 71, Kepler noted the correlation of previous planetary configurations with major political events: the conjunction of Mars and Saturn at the time of the St. Bartholomew's Day massacre in Paris in 1572, and a Jupiter–Mars opposition during the battle at Eger in 1596, an important moment during the Ottoman wars in Europe. Kepler argued that these events provided evidence that, under these kinds of planetary configurations, people 'are generally stunned and frightened, or aroused in the expectation of revolts, and this fact is very significant for a multitude of people congregated in one place either for some undertaking or for destruction'.[55]

The second *predictive* stage is concerned with the projection of the *historical* stage into the future, identifying similar planetary patterns and making predictions based on past events. Theses 72–75 illustrate this approach with reference to the planetary configurations of the coming year, 1602. Thus, he proposed:

> when the conjunction of Saturn and Mars falls in Poland at sunrise, and the eclipse of the Sun is strongest in Moscow and Poland, and if there is already war there, I think that defeat is predicted by that aspect. If someone should accommodate this agitation of the horoscope to his own strengths, he himself may inflict defeat; but if a strong peace grows firm in the meantime, clearly there is no danger from the heavens alone.[56]

Kepler's model may be applied to Chizhevsky's concept of the periodicity of the historical process and its correlation with activity of the solar cycle. In 1922 Chizevsky made forecasts for the next maximum of solar activity in 1927-29, arguing that 'if we assume the existence of a period of 60 years (Young) or 35 years (Lockyer), which co-join the main oscillation of 11 years, then the nearest future maximum should be especially tense (maximum maximorum), because the maximum of 1870 was distinguished by great strength'.[57] He concluded that it is very likely that during these years,

> major historical events will occur that will change again the geographical map due to the presence of socio-political factors. It would be highly desirable to get prepared by this time, the possibility of a scientific experiment in the field of studying the behaviour of human individuals and the masses.[58]

Thus, Chizhevsky's model in this phase correlates to Kepler's second, *predictive*, stage. As it happens, the year 1929 in the USSR was called 'the Year of Great Change' (God Velikogo Pereloma).[59] The term was introduced by Stalin, who wrote in his article in *Pravda*, entitled 'A Year of a Great Change. On the Occasion of the Twelfth Anniversary of the October Revolution':

> The past year was a year of great *change (veliky perelom)* on all the fronts of socialist construction. The keynote of this change has been, and continues to be, a determined *offensive* of socialism against the capitalist elements in town and country. The characteristic feature of this offensive is that it has already brought us a number of decisive successes in the principal spheres of the socialist reconstruction of our national economy.
>
> We may, therefore, conclude that our Party succeeded in making good use of our retreat during the first stages of the New Economic Policy in order, in the subsequent stages, to organise the change and to launch a *successful offensive* against the capitalist elements.

In USA, the Stock Market Crash and the beginning of the Great Depression took place in 1929.[60] We do not, though, have a record of Chizhevsky commenting on either Stalin's propaganda or the Crash in relation to the solar cycle.

The third stage, according to Campion, is *political,* and it aims at warning politicians of coming turbulent periods potentially leading to political crises, civil disorders, wars and the like. In Thesis 71 Kepler wrote,

> I would think that it is not entirely useless for leaders and rulers of people to be taken up with such considerations; for, in order to rule the

multitude one must have great skill and an awareness of those forces that affect human dispositions in a group.[61]

In respect of the third, *political*, stage of Kepler's analytical model, Chizhevsky suggested that governing authorities should be aware of the condition of the Sun at any given moment and this be forewarned of potential disruption:

> before making a decision, the government needs to cope with the state of the light: is it bright, is its face clear or is it overshadowed by spots? The Sun is the great military and political indicator: his testimony is unmistakable and universal.[62]

Finally, looking at the fourth stage, *taking appropriate action*, in 1602 for the sake of peace and quiet Kepler proposed postponing or breaking up political meetings, or removing the reasons for people's disaffection:

> by the introduction of some new deterrent, let their minds be changed. If some bold venture must be undertaken and accomplished by exciting terror, let August be chosen. If the mind must be hardened for some labor, let it be in September.[63]

Chizhevsky, too, thought that the mental state of the masses was influenced by fluctuations in the Sun's electric energy. He argued that,

> the greatest mistakes and failures of rulers, commanders, leaders of the people could often be caused on the grounds that they did not conform to the state of mental predisposition of the masses, or required them to fulfill the impossible, not corresponding to the state of their psyche, or mistakenly counted on their support at that time, when the masses were deprived of their binding unity, external factors did not begin to exert influence on them or the latter was already ending.[64]

Moreover, Chizhevsky considered that, consequently, the nearest branches of historiometry should become one of the most important experimental sciences of state studies, and astronomy – as applied science.[65] Summing up, it is evident through the comparative study of Kepler's *On the More Certain Fundamentals of Astrology* and Chizhevsky's *Physical Factors of the Historical Process* that Chizhevsky assimilated Kepler's ideas and follows his methodology in applying cosmological theory to his historical research techniques in historiometry.

'...and nothing is absolutely predestined'

Kepler believed that his political astrology was, as Campion writes, 'a valuable tool for managing the state and preserving political order' was probabilistic by nature.[66] Kepler demonstrates his perspective in Thesis 71, writing that

> if in these months the enemy should dare some boldness, take up suitable remedies to guard against consternation in the minds of the people. For these remedies are always in our power, however things may happen, and nothing is absolutely predestined.[67]

In his speculation on the problem of the interaction between cosmic and terrestrial factors, Chizhevsky wondered:

> Are we in the bondage to the Sun, are we in slavery to its electrical forces? If you want, yes, but our bondage is relative, and we ourselves can control the chains shackling our wrists and works intended for us to perform.[68]

He considered that 'the Sun does not coerce people to do this and that, but forces people do something'.[69] However, he continued, humanity follows the line of the least resistance and immerses itself in the oceans of its own blood.[70] He asked:

> Why do not we try to fill the impulse emanating from cosmic depths with necessary, well-thought-out content? What tempting prospects would it open up to us! Then we could dream *of creating a conscious history*.[71]

Thus, Chizhevsky extended Kepler's idea that 'the remedies that are always in our power' to the idea that these 'remedies' represent possible changes to the course of events through intentional actions, and unites it with the idea expressed by Russian cosmists on what Semenova called 'active evolution, the need for a new conscious stage in the development of the world'.[72]

However, as Campion argues, Kepler's political cosmology, which served as a preparation 'for the groundwork for social democracy in the 20th century, which aimed to introduce socialism through gradual reform and so resist revolution' did not survive in the philosophical and scientific debate of the late 17th century.[73] Campion points to the tragedy of Kepler's reformed political astrology, that, 'while it provided a significant motive for his remarkable work in mathematical astronomy, it died out when astrology's intellectual credibility collapsed'.[74]

The fate of Chizhevky's concept of cosmic factors influencing the historical process in some way echoes the fate of Kepler's political cosmology. Kazutinsky stresses the paradoxical-situation of silence that developed around Chizhevsky's works and explains that Chizhevsky's book *Physical Factors of the Historical Process* later fell into the context of ideological prohibitions of Marxist theory, which considered Chizhevsky's concept to be a form of rigid determinism.[75] Chizhevsky wrote that in the 1930s,

> genuine battles were fought because of the Sun; I was required to abandon officially many years of my own research, demanded repentance and desecration his own works and renouncements of them... I suffered like Galileo, but did not abuse science.[76]

Kazutinsky stresses that Chizhevsky's ideas became a part of 'repressed science' and for many decades were cloaked with a veil of distrust, fear and oblivion and forced out of culture.[77] On January 21 1942 he was arrested on the basis of a false denunciation made by his flatmate, who wished to occupy his room in their apartment, and was placed in an internal prison of the People's Commissariat of Internal Affairs, and then spent eight years in the camps and eight years in exile.[78] Evidently, these circumstances were crucial to the fate of his scientific works. However, Kazutinsky is optimistic in respect of the future development of Chizhevsky's ideas, and he considers Chizhevsky's theories can be included into modern post-nonclassical science. He argues that:

> Chizhevsky's concept is a necessary fragment of the script a self-organizing universe and is of paramount importance for the development of the problems of *Big History*, directly including socio-historical events in the framework of the processes of space self-organization and cosmic evolution.[79]

Conclusion

Alexander Chizhevsky's cosmism and theories on the relationship between history and the Sunspot cycle were clearly influenced by Kepler's ideas. The most significant parallel that comes to light is between Kepler's methodology for the study of political cosmology and Chizhevsky's research into historiometric cycles. It is evident through the comparative study of their works that Chizhevsky assimilated Kepler's ideas and followed a similar methodology in applying cosmological theory to history. Both advocated the practical application of their astrological and astronomical concepts to society, arguing that their methods could regulate mass behaviour and maintain civil order. Though their concepts were not in demand by their contemporaries, still they can find their place in the modern cross-disciplinary theories of *Big History*, which integrate a range of methodologies in the pursuit of a global understanding of historical processes.

Notes

1.   George M. Young, *The Russian Cosmists: The Esoteric Futurism of Nikolai Fedorov and His Followers*, Oxford University Press, 2012. See also: Michael Hagemeister, 'Russian Cosmism in the 1920s and Today'in *The Occult in Russian and Soviet Culture*, ed. Bernice Glatzer Rosenthal, Cornell University Press, 1997, pp. 185–202, p. 186; 'Chizhevsky', at https://cyclesresearchinstitute.org/cycles-research/general/chizhevsky/ [accessed 25 December 2021].

2.   A.L. Chizhevsky, *Phizicheskie factory istoricheskogo processa*, (*Physical factors of the historical process*) Kaluga: 1 Gospolittipografiya, 1924.

3.   Chizhevsky, *Phizicheskie factory*, p. 7.

4.   Chizhevsky, *Phizicheskie factory*, p. 7.

5.   Chizhevsky, *Phizicheskie factory*, p. 8.

6.   Chizhevsky, *Phizicheskie factory*, p. 9.

7.   Chizhevsky, *Phizicheskie factory*, p. 9.

8.   Chizhevsky, *Phizicheskie factory*, p. 9.

9.   Chizhevsky, *Phizicheskie factory*, p. 27.

10. Britannica T. Editors of Encyclopaedia. 'Rudolf Wolf.' Encyclopedia Britannica, <https://www.britannica.com/biography/Rudolf-Wolf>. Accessed 09/07/2021.

11. Chizhevsky, *Phizicheskie factory*, p. 27.

12. Chizhevsky, *Phizicheskie factory*, p. 52.

13. Chizhevsky, *Phizicheskie factory*, p. 28.

14. Chizhevsky, *Phizicheskie factory*, p. 27.

15. Chizhevsky, *Phizicheskie factory*, p. 28.

16. Chizhevsky, *Phizicheskie factory*, p. 60.

17. V.P. Rimsky and L.P. Filonenko, 'Sud'ba termina *Russky kosmizm*' (*Fate of the term 'Russian cosmism'*), conference theses *Scientific Readings of the memory of K.E. Tsiolkovsky*, 2012, Kaluga, online publication, <https://readings.gmik.ru/lecture/2012-SUDBA-TERMINA-RUSSKIY-KOSMIZM>. [accessed 10/07/2021].

18. Rimsky and Filinenko, 'Fate of the term'.

19. S.G. Semenova, 'Introduction', *Russkii Cosmism* [*Russian Cosmism*], eds. S.G. Semenova, A.G. Gacheva, Moskva: Pedadodika-Press, 1992, pp. 3–33, p. 4.

20. R. Galtseva, 'Vernadsky V.I.', *Philophskaya Enciklopediya* [*Philosophical Encyclopedia*], ed. F.V. Konstantinov, in 5 vol., vol. 5, Sovetskaya enciklopediya, 1970, p. 624, <http://philosophy.niv.ru/doc/encyclopedia/philosophy/fc/slovar-194-3.htm#zag-541> Accessed 10/07/2021.

21. A.L. Chizhevsky, *Na beregu Vselennoy. Gody drujby s Tsiolkovskim.*

Vospominaniya [*On the shore of the Universe. Years of friendship with Tsiolkovsky. Memoirs*], Moskva: Misl', 1995, p. 30. See also p. 32.

22. Chizhevsky, *Na beregy*, p. 45.

23. Chizhevsky, *Na beregy*, p. 47.

24. *Communa* No. 77, Kaluga, 1924, 4 April cit. Chizhevsky 1995a, p. 22.

25. V.V. Kazutinsky, 'Cosmizm Chizhevskogo', *Kosmicheskoe mirovozzrenie – novoe myshlenie XXI veka* ['Chizhevsky Cosmism,' *Cosmic Worldview - New Thinking of the XXI Century*], Vol. 3, Issue 3, 2004, pp. 175–193, p. 180.

26. A.L. Chizhevsky, *Kosmichesky puls jizny. Zemlya v od'yatyah Solnca. Geliotaraksiya* [Cosmic pulse of life. Earth in the arms of the Sun], Moskwa: Mysl, 1995, p. 496.

27. Kazutinsky, 'Cosmizm Chizhevskogo', p.178.

28. Chizhevsky , *Kosmichesky puls*, p. 503.

29. Chizhevsky, *Kosmichesky puls*, p. 503.

30. Chizhevsky, *Kosmichesky puls*, pp. 503–504.

31. Chizhevsky, *Kosmichesky puls*, p. 501.

32. Chizhevsky, *Kosmichesky puls*, p. 501.

33. E.E. Zvonova, 'Philosophsko-antropologicheskie aspect metaphizicheskih rabot A.L. Chizhevskogo' ['Philosophical and anthropological aspects of the metaphysical works of A.L. Chizhevsky'], *Philosophskaya antropologiya*, no. 6, 2014, pp. 872–884, p. 875.

34. A.L. Chizhevsky, *Osnovnoe nachalo mirozdaniya. Sistema Cosmosa. Problemy* [*The fundamental genesis of the Universe. System of Cosmos. Problems*], Archive of the Russian Academy of Sciences, 1921, Fund 1703, inventory no. 1, pp. 1–106, p. 7.

35. For the main text see Chizhevsky, *Na beregu*, p. 53; for footnotes see Chizhevsky, *Phizicheskie factory*, pp. 25–26, 28.

36. Chizhevsky, *Phizicheskie factory*, pp. 25–26.

37. Johannes Kepler, "On the More Certain Fundamentals of Astrology Prague 1601", trans. J. Bruce Brackenridge and Mary Ann Rossi, *Proceedings of the American Philosophical Society*, vol. 123, no. 2 (Apr. 27, 1979), pp. 85–116, p. 95.

38. Kepler, 'On the More Certain', Thesis 5, p. 91.

39. Chizhevsky *Phizicheskie factory*, p. 11.

40. Edwin Arthur Burtt, *The Metaphysical Foundations of Modern Science*, New York: Harcourt, Brace & Company, Inc., 1925, pp. 47-48.

41. Burtt, *The Metaphysical Foundations*, p 49.

42. Johannes Kepler. *The Harmony of the World*, trans. E.J. Aiton, A.M. Duncan, J.V. Field, American Philosophical Society, Philadelphia, 1997, p. 492.

43. E.E. Zvonova, *Philosophsko-antropologicheskie vozzreniya A.L. Chizhevskogo*, [*Philosophical and anthropological aspects of the metaphysical works of A.L. Chizhevsky*], PhD thesis, 2015 p. 21.

44. Chizhevsky A.L., *Zemnoe echo solnechnyh bur'* [*Earthly Echo of Solar Storms*], Moskva: Nauka, 1976, p. 37.

45. Zvonova, *Phiosophsko-antropologicheskye vozzreniya* p. 21.

46. Nicholas Campion, 'Johannes' Kepler's Political Cosmology, Psychological Astrology and the Archaeology of Knowledge in the Seventeenth Century', *Harmony and Symmetry. Celestial regularities shaping human culture, Proceedings of the SEAC 2018 Conference in Graz*, eds. Sonja Draxler, Max E. Lippitsch & Gudrun Wolfschmidt, SEAC Publications, vol. 01, Hamburg: tradition, 2020, no pagination, 7.1.1–7.1.4.

47. Claudia Brosseder, 'The Writing in the Wittenberg Sky: Astrology in Sixteenth-Century Germany', *Journal of the History of Ideas*, Vol. 66, No. 4, 2005, pp. 557–576, esp. pp. 559–560; Kazutinsky, 'Cosmizm Chizhevskogo', p. 180.

48. Campion, 'Johannes' Kepler's Political Cosmology', 7.1.2.

49. Judith Field 'A Lutheran Astrologer: Johannes Kepler', *Archive for History of Exact Sciences*, vol. 31, 1984, pp. 190–268, p. 220.

50. Kepler, 'On the More Certain', p. 105.

51. Chizhevsky, *Kosmichesky puls*, pp. 502, 504.

52. Campion, 'Johannes' Kepler's Political Cosmology', 7.1.3; Kepler, 'On the More Certain', Thesis 67–75.

53. Campion, 'Johannes' Kepler's Political Cosmology', 7.1.3.

54. Campion, 'Johannes' Kepler's Political Cosmology', 7.1.5.

55. Kepler, 'On the More Certain', Thesis 71, p. 104.

56. Kepler, 'On the More Certain', Thesis 72, p. 104

57. Chizhevsky, *Phizicheskie factory*, p. 69.

58. Chizhevsky, *Phizicheskie factory*, p. 69.

59. J. V. Stalin, 'A Year of Great Change: On the Occasion of the Twelfth Anniversary of the October Revolution', *Pravda*, No. 259, November 7, 1929, https://www.marxists.org/reference/archive/stalin/works/1929/11/03.htm [accessed 6 November 2021].

60. See John Kenneth Galbraith, *The Great Crash*, Boston: Houghton Mifflin Co., 1929, pp. 83–84.

61. Kepler, *'On the More Certain'*, Thesis 71, p. 104.

62. Chizhevsky, *Phizicheskie factory*, p. 64.

63. Kepler, 'On the More Certain', Thesis 71, p. 104.

64. Chizhevsky, *Phizicheskie factory*, p. 64.

65. Chizhevsky, *Phizicheskie factory*, p. 65.

66. Campion, 'Johannes' Kepler's Political Cosmology', 7.1.2

67. Kepler, 'On the More Certain', Thesis 71, p. 104.

68. Chizhevsky, *Phizicheskie factory*, p. 63.

69. Chizhevsky, *Phizicheskie factory*, p. 63.

70. Chizhevsky, *Phizicheskie factory*, p. 63.

71. Chizhevsky, *Kosmichesky puls*, p. 682. Chizhevsky's enphasis

72. S.G. Semenova, 'Introduction', p. 4.

73. Campion, 'Johannes' Kepler's Political Cosmology', 7.1.3.

74. Campion, 'Johannes' Kepler's Political Cosmology', 7.1.3

75. Kazutinsky, 'Cosmizm Chizhevskogo', p. 191.

76. Chizhevsky, *Kosmichesky puls*, p.13.

77. Kazutinsky, 'Cosmizm Chizhevskogo', p. 191.

78. I. I. Nesmeyanova, 'A.L. Chizhevskij i ego dokumental'noe nasledie' ['A.L. Chizhevsky and his Documentary Heritage'], *Magistra Vitae*, 2018, no 1. pp. 99–111, p. 103, online journal < http://magistravitaejournal.ru/images/1_2018/nesmejanova.pdf>. Accessed 10/07/ 2021.

79. Kazutinsky, 'Cosmizm Chizhevskogo', p. 192. On the concept of 'Big History' see: David Christian, Cynthia Brown and Craig Benjamin, *Big History: Between Nothing and Everything*, McGraw-Hill Higher Education, 2013. On Russian cosmists and 'Big History' see Akop Nazaretyan, 'Western and Russian Traditions of Big History: A Philosophical Insight', Journal for General Philosophy of Science, vol. 36 (1), 2005, pp. 63–80. See also 'Big History' at https://www.bighistoryproject.com/home

5

AN OBSERVATION TOWER: ABY M. WARBURG AND THE TRANSMISSION OF ASTROLOGY

Jennifer Zahrt

Take a better look at the image. Martin Luther[1]

The German art historian Aby M. Warburg (1866–1929) had a lifelong preoccupation with star lore and its associated imagery, evidenced by a posthumous exhibit showcasing his decades of research into the history of astrology and astronomy mounted at the Hamburg Planetarium in 1929.[2]

Warburg's influence on the study of the history of astrology is immense. He was one of a handful of European scholars, who created the discipline, but he also had strong ideas of what astrology was. We need to unpack these ideas in order to explore his legacy and how he shaped our understanding of medieval and Renaissance astrology.

His tireless pursuit of the history of astrological symbolism in art led him to create the Warburg Institute, which has galvanized generations of scholars to research astrological imagery anew. In creating the conditions of possibility for people to encounter and study astrological texts and images, the Warburg Institute itself became a vector for the transmission of astrology in academia via the visual imagination.

It was in 1907, midway through his academic career, that Warburg first learned of astrology through the tarot. Ron Chernow reports that he 'excitedly deciphered the Tarot cards, showing they weren't simply playing cards, but had been used to make astrological predictions'.[3] These discoveries were made possible, Aby claimed to his brother Felix in December of 1909, because he had bought 'fifteen hundred books on astrology the previous year'.[4] Warburg also read, and was influenced by, *Sphaera Barbarica*, a ground-breaking academic work on Greek astrological history by Franz Boll, which was published in 1903.[5] In 1917, he actually visited an astrologer.[6] No extant evidence suggests that Warburg became a practicing astrologer himself, rather he was interested in collecting and studying the images produced by the astrological imaginary.

Warburg's attitude to astrology was not straightforward and he was deeply critical of the revival of astrological practice during the First World War.[7] Even so, he recognized that the history of astrology and its various forms of expression in different cultural contexts were potent sources for investigating the production and transmission of human knowledge. The inherently interdisciplinary qualities of astrology form the core of Warburg's approach to cultural history, enabling him toward the end of his life to develop a new model of interpretation of symbolic form, one that oscillated between expression and orientation.[8] As the Viennese art historian, and future close collaborator, Fritz Saxl put it, Warburg saw 'astrological sources of images as among the most important transmitters of the heritage of antiquity'.[9] Warburg's engagement with astrology is thus critical to his hermeneutic method, his collection of scholarly material, and his creation of an institution that continues to be pivotal for cultural studies to this day.

A Capital Promise: The Genesis of the Warburg Institute

At the age of 13, young Aby made a wager with his twelve-year-old brother Max. As the eldest child, Aby offered to abdicate his right to head the family bank – M. M. Warburg & Co. – in exchange for a lifetime supply of books. Max shared his memory of the moment: 'It was not a pottage of lentils, however, which he demanded, but a promise that I would always buy him all the books he wanted. After a very brief pause for reflection, I consented. [...] unsuspecting, I gave him what I must now admit was a very large blank cheque'.[10] Aby began collecting books in 1886 and established his library in 1909. By 1911, when Saxl first saw the library, he remarked:

> ... it had at that time about 15,000 volumes and any young student like myself must have felt rather bewildered when entering it. On the one hand he found an excellent collection of bibliographies, most of them unknown to him and apt to shorten his labours; on the other hand very detailed collections, partly on subjects like astrology with which he was hardly familiar. The arrangement of the books was equally baffling and he may have found it most peculiar, perhaps, that Warburg never tired of shifting and re-shifting them.[11]

Warburg eschewed classification systems, and preferred to arrange the books by subject in an ever evolving scheme. As Saxl put it, Warburg wanted to 'give the student a library uniting the various branches of the history of human civilization where he could wander from shelf to shelf'.[12]

The library occupied an unusual place in German culture at the time, neither qualifying for government nor university support – it had to rely on private enterprise.[13] Saxl noted that Hamburg 'was the right soil for such a private foundation'.[14] Warburg succeeded in getting his family on board with his vision. From its formation until it became exiled from Hamburg in 1933 and attached to the University of London in 1944, Warburg's library and Institute were the product of a single family investing their private capital into a cultural institution. Fortuitously, his family's international ties allowed them to escape the ravages of the 1923–24 hyperinflation in the German economy and to continue to build up their book collection.[15] Acutely aware of the value of his library, Aby stated in a letter around 1900, that 'we should demonstrate by our example that capitalism is also capable of intellectual achievements of a scope which would not be possible otherwise'.[16] In 1926, at the inauguration of the library's new building, Max Warburg designated the library 'a Warburg bank branch that would deal with cosmic instead of earthly pursuits'.[17] The comparison to stellar phenomena didn't stop there.

Inside the library, Aby designed the main lecture room in an elliptical shape as a deliberate model of planetary orbits around the Sun, with 'curving walls and tall rows of books illuminated by a circular sky light'.[18] Warburg intended for scholars to orbit the space like planets or comets and come into contact with its books and materials. As Dorothea McEwan reports:

> Warburg even saw in his library an observation tower from which 'the entire trade route of culture and symbols between Asia and America could be viewed'. A pertinent Hamburg tradition with its Colonial Academy and shipping tradition was invoked when he declared the Kulturwissenschaftliche Bibliothek Warburg to be 'a tower observing the trade routes of cultural exchange', scanning 'our field of vision'.[19]

Thus, Warburg's library itself became a post in this trade route of ideas, and more importantly, a focal point for the transmission of astrological knowledge.

Warburg's View of Astrology

Warburg's investigation of astrology intensified during the Great War. 'The First World War', historian Mark Russell writes, 'proved to Warburg that barbarism and irrationality did not belong to the past; he suffered horribly under the weight of its events. Early in the struggle, he decided to use the weapon he had at hand, his library, in a desperate effort to understand humanity's descent into unreason'.[20] Warburg began collecting ephemeral literature on predictions, which led him to an investigation into the ephemeral literature of the Reformation as a whole. Warburg became concerned with Martin Luther's relationship to astrology: 'How did this man regard the astrological pamphlets, the prognostics, and portents which at that time were pouring from the printing presses?'[21] In comparing his contemporary moment with a similar moment in German history, Warburg hoped to see if he could draw any constructive parallels for making sense of the apparent sudden surge of superstitious belief.

The results of this investigation into astrology during the Reformation were given as lectures in 1917 and finally published in 1920, as *Heidnisch-antike Weissagung in Wort und Bild zu Luthers Zeiten*, roughly translated into English as 'Pagan-ancient Prophecy in Word and Image during Luther's Era'. The main body of Warburg's study concerns the controversy over the rectified natal charts of Martin Luther. In astrology, chart rectification attempts to reckon a correct date or time from uncertain information, for example when a person's exact time of birth is not known.[22] Usually calculations tend to adjust by a matter of a few minutes or hours. That Luther's birthday was rectified by an entire year is not necessarily plausible, which makes it seem more likely that the rectified charts constituted a heated political propaganda – a type of 'fake news', as it would be called today. This propaganda seems to have worked in Luther's favour. With so many various potential natal charts circulating, muddying any confidence in the information, Luther became somewhat protected from prognostications that could serve to harm him (whether or not a prognostication was actually true, an individual could take it upon themselves to *make it true*, as in an attempted assassination, for example). Warburg refers to these astrological charts as '*kalendrische "Wahrheiten"*' ('calendrical "truths"') – a historical and a mythical truth for the biographers of Luther's time.[23]

Warburg understood astrology to be the constant, around which *its images* changed over time. Missing here is an acknowledgment that astrology has its own developmental history.[24] As Dorothea McEwan put it, Warburg felt that 'the ongoing belief in astrology had to be interpreted as one that provided continuity in discontinuity, old beliefs in changing times'.[25] Warburg resisted seeing any shift in images as perhaps symptomatic of changes in the fundamentals of astrological practice. This factor is decisive for understanding Warburg's grasp of the subject as well as the interpretations he draws from his materials. Warburg articulated his conception of the astrological images he traced through history, calling them 'Gestirngötter', or 'stellar gods', which

> ... were demoniac beings in whom uncannily contradictory powers were wedded together. As symbols of stars they helped to expand space by

guiding the soul in its flight through the universe. As images of stars they were, at the same time, idols with which man in his wretchedness and childish fear tried to achieve a mystic union through acts of worship.[26]

The distinction he drew between the signs of the zodiac (*Sternzeichen*) and constellations (*Sternbilder*) links to the tension pervading his work between reason and magic. A zodiac sign denotes a discrete, measurable region of the heavens based on the ecliptic (the path drawn by the Sun in the sky during the Earth's yearly orbit). It represented a classical, mathematical way of making sense of the celestial sphere. The images of the constellations mapped onto the heavens are 'idols' (*Götzen*). For Warburg, the 'stellar gods' represent a unification of these two principles, oscillating between two poles or contradictory powers (*entgegengesetzter Doppelmacht*). The powers that seem to be in tension with one another are two layers of interpretation superimposed: mathematical interpretation (for physical navigation) and mythological interpretation (for spiritual navigation).

The astronomer/astrologer was charged with making sense out of these portents: 'The star-gazer of the Reformation period embraces these twin poles which the modern scientist would consider incompatible. Mathematical abstraction and concrete cult of the stars as efficacious causes mark the range within which his primitive mentality is able to oscillate'.[27] Thus Warburg's definition of *Denkraum* (roughly, 'reflective space') seems to originate from his interpretation of astrological practice:

Logik, which creates the space between man and the external world by means of discursive and conceptual signs, and *Magic*, which destroys that very space through superstitious practices that confuse man and the external world and create imagined or practical links between them – these two powers still form for the fortune-telling astrologer one primitive tool with which he can carry out measurements and work magic at the same time.[28]

Warburg celebrates the overcoming of measurement (*messen*) from magic (*zaubern*). Logic allows for a separation from a unified 'primitive' state of affairs and establishes a contemplative distance between people and objects. Warburg conflates astrology with demonic magic:[29]

In astrology, two entirely heterogeneous intellectual forces, which logically should simply clash with one another, have irrefutably come together in a single method: Mathematics, the finest tool for abstract thinking, with the fear of demons, the most primitive form of religious causation. While the astrologer on the one hand measures the universe clearly and harmoniously in a sober system of lines, and knows how to precisely calculate the positions of the fixed stars and planets to the Earth and to each other in advance, in front of his mathematic tables he is animated by an atavistic and superstitious aversion to these starnames, which he handles as numerals, and which are actually demons that he has to fear.[30]

Warburg's conflation of constellations with demons rests on his understanding of astral magic, presented in texts such as the *Picatrix*, as well as a productive misreading of texts that describe alternative modalities of astrological interpretation. Warburg's focus on the transmission of images depicting astrological symbolism eclipses his appreciation for interpretational nuances at work in astrological practice, namely the many astrologies arising in Europe that sought to divorce magic from astrology both in the sixteenth century and in the early twentieth–century. The majority of contemporary practicing astrologers viewed astrology as an experiential, empirical science, engaging questions of scientific validity.[31]

The view of medieval, Renaissance and Reformation astrology inherited from Warburg has recently been updated by Claudia Brosseder, who has recently addressed the theory and practice of astrology in the social and intellectual history of sixteenth-century Germany, She showed that Martin Luther's close ally, Philip Melanchthon, 'referred to a strictly naturalist interpretation of astrology, making Aristotle's *Physica*, *De generatione et corruptione*, and *De caelo* as well as Ptolemy's *Tetrabiblos* the point of depart of his thinking'.[32] Demons are nowhere to be found. Thus she provides a corrective to Warburg's interpretation of astrologers as seeing astral demons. Brosseder adds that the astrologers who gathered at Wittenberg, where Melanchthon was Professor of Greek, 'strove to praise astrology as a hermeneutic art that yielded knowledge of universal range, for the study of nature as well as for the history and fate of mankind and of human individuals in the past and future': astrology, above all, was concerned with interpretation.[33] In analysing the practice of the Wittenberg astrologer, Petrus Hosmann, Brosseder finds that,

... he refers to Ptolemy's *Tetrabiblos*, but most importantly, to the treasure trove of his personal experiences. This treasure of experiences was the astrologer's *arcanum* and the secret of his success or failure.

This held true for an insignificant astrologer like Hosmann as well as an intellectually outstanding thinker like Girolamo Cardano.[34]

Personal experience with astrological interpretation is an important and necessary prerequisite to successful decoding of its images and figures.

Ultimately, the Wittenberg astrologers 'wanted to achieve a "marriage" between Divine Providence and the most advanced science within astrology'.[35] Warburg discussed astrology in deterministic terms; however, Melanchthon and his colleagues maintained the concept of man's free will. Astrology was not deterministic for them. Brosseder found that 'Through judicious astrology, they claimed, an astrologer can only discern a man's inclination, but not predict his actual actions'.[36] The Wittenberg astrologers practice a different type of astrology than the astrology at the basis of Warburg's understanding of it. Brosseder also contrasts the situation in Germany with that in Italy, especially the magical, soul-oriented astrology espoused by Marsilio Ficino.[37] As Brosseder says, 'There are no hints in the books of the Wittenberg scholars showing that they adapted to Ficino's astrology'.[38] She continues,

> In the cold north on the shore of the Elbe, we do not feel any of the splendid magic of Italian art, in which the planets, transformed into pagan gods, traversed the vaults of ecclesiastical or noble buildings in opulently decorated celestial chariots. The Wittenberg print products were never adorned by emblems suggestive of paganism. No, Saturn was only an ethereal cluster and not the menacing god who devoured his offspring. With this naturalist soberness, Melancthon wanted to dispel the suspicion that he communicated with demons.[39]

This sentiment echoes the attitudes of practicing astrologers contemporary to Warburg.[40] Yet he didn't register any of this. His hunt for astrological demons sought justification in an image of the thirty degrees of Scorpio, which assigns different images as 'rulers' for each degree. These are known as parans. Warburg referred to them as 'hieroglyphics of fate' or 'Schicksalshieroglyphen'.[41] This term fits the images much better than 'demon' since some of the images depict towers, or rivers, and not living beings (such as animals, people, or monsters). As hieroglyphs, they require decoding. Warburg views them as rulers in an anthropomorphic sense rather than as emblems for the qualities of specific degrees of this sign, which can be understood in their correspondence with (and not causal determination of!) human nature.

The Devil in the Details

Warburg analyses a stunning example of one of these parans and the attendant celestial constellation, depicted as a devil on Luther's shoulder in a woodcut in the 1492 text *Weissagungen* (*Prophecies*) by Johannes Lichtenberger.[42] Warburg quotes a letter by Valerius Herberger capturing Luther's reaction to this image. Rather than dismiss the image entirely, Luther converts the prophetic interpretation of the images into a diagnostic one, which serves to reinforce the salience of the astrological imagery.

Popular interpretations of Lichtenberger's image suggested that the devil was a cohort of the monk. Combating this view, Luther interpreted the devil on his shoulder metaphorically as the Pope, the Kaiser, and the potentates (princes). Luther says, 'Aye, Doctor / Take a better look at the image / where is the devil sitting? / He is not sitting in the monk's heart / rather around his neck [...] but I mean he's sitting on my neck / through the Pope / the Kaiser and grand princes'.[43] Luther reinterpreted the image by performing a close reading – 'take a better look at the image'. The devil then becomes a diagnostic indicator of the burden that the Pope, the Kaiser and other elites place on his neck, as opposed to a prognostic depiction of the devil being Luther's ally in destroying Catholic faith. Luther did not dismiss the image as an unfit description of his situation; he embraces and celebrates it by inverting it. However, even though Luther thought that his interpretation of this star-based image defeats the message, it satisfied the range of possibilities given by such star knowledge.

The contemporary reception and impact of Warburg's *Heidnisch-antike Weissagung* monograph was not immediate. Fritz Saxl painstakingly tried to popularize Warburg's new book. Of all the reviews the book received, only two individuals offered criticism.[44] The practicing astrologer, Ludwig Rudolph, who eventually went on to be pivotal in the Hamburg School of astrology, criticized Warburg's deterministic stance: 'He who thinks that astrology preaches fatalism, errs. It will supply practical wisdom to him who understands it well. I am prepared to prove this at any time'.[45] Rudolph could see how Warburg arrived at a deterministic view, and countered that certain 'facts can only be ascertained by practice' of astrology.[46] Rudolph's letter reveals the contours of Warburg's exposure to astrology and his disconnect with the astrological revival happening around him.

The second major criticism of the work came from the scholar Carl Fr. Meinhof, who was upset with Warburg's account of Babylonian astrology. Saxl appears to have reacted to this extremely defensively:

Abb. 15. Die beiden Mönche aus der Ausgabe Lichtenbergers Mainz 1492
(Exemplar aus der Stadtbibliothek Hamburg).

Woodcut from Johannes Lichtenberger, *Weissagungen (Prophecies)* (1492).

[Carl Fr.] Meinhof's main criticism turned on Warburg's description of Babylon as the cradle of astrology. Whilst this was surely the case for the classical world, it was not the case for other continents, as exemplified by the system of astrology in Mexico. Saxl retorted that Warburg had not researched Babylonian astrology as such, had had only been interested in the '*Wanderung*', the *journey* of oriental astrology, of the processes being adapted to and adopted by new circumstances encountered. [Saxl said w]hether or not Luther believed in astrology and divination was 'very difficult' to ascertain. 'In order to characterize Luther fully, one would really have to say that it was not simply that he did not believe in all these things'.[47]

In this response to Meinhof, Saxl confirms Warburg's Eurocentric vision, as well as his lack of research into Babylonian astrology as such. This reaction dovetails with another of Saxl's admissions. According to McEwan, Saxl wrote to another reviewer that, 'he would not need to summarize the astrological contents, as Warburg used the astrological material only to explain the psychology of people in the Reformation'.[48] Warburg was not interested in astrological interpretation in and of itself, but as a means to another end.

Another interlude may shed light on Saxl and Warburg's defensive posturing. Warburg had been in contact with Franz Boll, a leading scholar and practitioner of astrology, requesting information about constellations and eclipses to provide evidence that would 'show an instance of survival of classical astrology among Luther's contemporaries which went so far as to change Luther's date of birth from 10th November 1483 to 22nd October 1484 – an example of retrospective prophecy and the power of belief in stars'.[49] On 13 September 1920, Saxl wrote back to Boll, stating (in McEwan's paraphrase),

Neither he nor Saxl, he wrote, could finish the article without Boll. They needed Boll's 'competent astrological view', as Saxl wrote, in one very important aspect: 'the link of Luther's nativity by Gauricus to the prophecy by Lichtenberger. Does Guaricus go back directly to Lichtenberger?' Saxl enclosed the copy of the Gauricus nativity, showing 'Saturn, Mercury, Jupiter, Venus and Sol all (in the ninth house) together with Scorpion, Mars in the second house in Aries' and the Lichtenberger text and raised the question of the position of Mars: 'He is in a ruling house. Can this be Aries? But above all, can Mars be ruler of this conjunction without even standing in conjunction with Jupiter and Saturn or to be on the ascendant (he is in the second house!)?

The answer to these questions is important for the whole history of the trajectory of astrological ideas'.[50]

Saxl's question about Mars strongly supports the view that he and Warburg were still unaware of the interpretive rules of classical astrology. According to traditional methods, Mars rules the conjunction because the conjunction is in Scorpio, one of the two signs ruled by Mars (the other being Aries). Regardless of Mars's zodiacal placement in the chart, it lords over any planets located in Scorpio. However, Saxl sought a direct link to explain how a planet can rule a conjunction if it isn't in a physical proximity with it. This evidence suggests that although Warburg and Saxl were interested in the symbolic meaning of the astrological images in their collection, they were not interested in learning the interpretational rules of astrology. Doing so would have both strengthened their own powers of analysis of those very images and simultaneously made this letter to Boll redundant.

Warburg's Hermeneutic Method

Warburg's hermeneutic – interpretative – method arose out of this examination of early modern astrological texts and images, yet his approach is deeply indebted to nineteenth-century anthropological practices and its emphases on stages of development and evolutionary thinking.[51] He saw the material he presented in his essay on Luther as the 'previously unread documents on the tragic history of the modern Europeans freedom of thought'.[52] Yet, the star knowledge brought to Europe from the Arab world in the twelfth and thirteenth centuries wasn't foisted upon them unwillingly. As Richard Woodfield has noted, 'the introduction of Arabic astrology into Western Europe heralded the *renovatio* of the science of astronomy'.[53] Warburg's insistence on viewing this trajectory in terms of overcoming superstition prevented him from recognizing the myriad positive legacies left by this cultural transfer. Bernd Roeck agrees that Warburg's Eurocentric vision sees the process of 'civilization' through a dialectical lens of overcoming 'primitive' states.[54] For all its claims to universality, it is a very Eurocentric universal. Warburg's efforts to liberate mankind from magic fear participates in ideologies of progress and conquest. Richard Woodfield has noted that:

Anthropology, as a discipline of understanding and self-understanding, has moved on since Warburg's day. It's also important to add that the world has changed since Warburg visited the Pueblo Indians: a multi-cultural sensitivity has led to an awareness of the process of demonization. Cultural difference is not the same as irrationality.[55]

Scholars since Warburg's time have gained an appreciation for cultural difference grounded in semiotics, and 'it is no longer a question of comprehensive explanations or universal development, but rather the problem of the *legibility*, or rather of *reading*, that now is foregrounded'.[56] Over time Warburg's early emphasis on an evolutionary causality shifted to a model based on a continual oscillation between poles of expression and orientation.

> ... the study of astrological imagery brought Warburg once more into contact with the basic questions of mankind, the emergence of rationality from magic fears. But it also suggested to him that evolutionism was not the answer to this permanent riddle. Every instrument of thought was double-edged, as it were. We always think in images and these images have their own power to enlighten us or to mislead us.[57]

Martin Luther demonstrated this symbolic charge – of what Ernst Gombrich has called the 'bipolarity of the image'[58] – in his reinterpretation of Lichtenberger's woodcut. Yet Warburg maintained the idea that celestial symbols are either to be interpreted as signs for scientific orientation or as magical demons. As Gombrich says, for Warburg, 'it was up to the individual who came into contact with this part of our heritage to decide whether to succumb to the primitive associations which turned these symbols into demons who ruled over human life – or to resist the temptation and instead turn to the energy derived from these cosmic symbols to the business of orientation'.[59]

If his work on Luther was a first attempt, Warburg's last, unfinished project, the *Mnemosyne Atlas*, presents a final iteration of his involvement with the history of the celestial imagination. Being an 'atlas', this project was expressly dedicated to the idea of orientation. In his opening speech to the exhibit of Warburg's *Mnemosyne* project in the Kunsthaus in Hamburg on 2 June 1994, Werner Hofmann uttered the most concise formulation of the hermeneutic praxis of the project: 'he thinks in intervals'.[60] Warburg had given an early draft of the work a title, 'Iconology of the Interval. Art historical material for a developmental psychology of the oscillation between a theory of causation based on images and one based on signs'.[61] Warburg cannot escape the temptation of a causal, explanatory principle. Yet, Hofmann notes an anti-horizontal-linear mode of reading Warburg's panels. Their arrangement challenges the common art museum experience. The images of the artworks are all photographs, no originals, which on one level, flattens them and strips them of any aura of 'the original' piece. However, they are nowhere close to establishing a closed-off and unified whole.[62] This scattered arrangement speaks perhaps to a shift in Warburg's concern with an evolution of images. In practice, the panels actually participate in a type of exhibition and thought process that defies linearity or even a tree-like or coral-like structure popular in depictions of evolutionary thought.[63] This three dimensional exhibition (the images are scattered and arranged in no particularly coherent order on the panels) speaks more to a genuine stellar arrangement, an actual *constellation* of images.

Conclusions

Aby Warburg is one of the most important historians of western astrology. In fact, it is difficult to imagine the modern discipline without him. He created a massive archival onion; peeling back the layers, one finds only more layers. The evolutionary impulse that gripped him on his journey to uncover a 'missing link' between the Middle Ages and the Renaissance gets sublimated into a form that models the subject it is trying to understand. Warburg confronted the spectator of the *Mnemosyne Atlas* with clusters of images. His library confronts the visitor with clusters of books, resisting more 'enlightened' classification systems – alphabetization or disciplinary compartmentalization by call number – even eschewing the idea of closed stacks in order to allow the visitor to aimlessly stumble through the collection and randomly find new material. In his scholarly work and his institutional design, Warburg created structures that enact an experience of the very subject he was trying to 'keep at bay'.[64]

In the end, Warburg proved himself to be a passionate student of *astrological images*, not astrological beliefs or practice. Although Warburg spent his life making connections between astrology and art, he never fully read what these artworks have to say because his preconceived notions of what they *should* represent blinded him to the possibilities of what they *could* represent. Martin Luther could give him a few words of advice, 'take a better look at the image'.[65] Warburg's legacy thus lies in the questions he asked rather than the answers he gave, and in the institute he built, which enables those questions to continue to be explored to this very day.

Notes

1. 'sehet nur das Bild ein wenig besser an', as quoted by Valerius Herberger, *Gloria Lutheri* (Leipzig: 1612), pp. 41–45, found in Aby Warburg, *Heidnisch-antike Weissagung in Wort und Bild zu Luthers Zeiten* (Heidelberg: C. Winter, 1920), p. 45.
2. Ron Chernow, *The Warburgs: The Twentieth Century Odyssey of a Remarkable Jewish Family* (New York: Random House, 1993), p. 283.
3. Ron Chernow, *The Warburgs*, p. 120.

4. Chernow, *The Warburgs*, p. 120.

5. Franz Boll, *Sphaera. Neue griechische Texte und untersuchungen zur geschichte der Sternbilder* (Leipzig: B. G. Teubner, 1903).

6. Bernd Roeck, 'Psychohistorie im Zeichen Saturns: Aby Warburgs Denksystem und die moderne Kulturgeschichte', in Wolfgang Hardtwig and Hans-Ulrich Wehler, eds, *Kulturgeschichte Heute* (Göttingen: Vandenhoeck & Ruprecht, 1996), p. 241 fn 52. 'Allerdings bemühte Warburg sich 1917 bei einem obskuren Astrologen gegen ein nicht unbetrachtliches Honorar um sein Horoskop'. Roeck also cites where one can find it: 'es ist im betreffenden Kästchen der berühmten Kartei des AWI noch erhalten', *ibid.*

7. Ernst H. Gombrich, *Aby Warburg: An Intellectual Biography* (London: The Warburg Institute, 1970), p. 204.

8. Fritz Saxl, 'Die Kulturwissenschaftliche Bibliothek Warburg in Hamburg', in L. Brauer, A. von Mendelssohn Bartholdy, A. Meyer-Abich, and J. Lemchke, eds, *Forschungsinstitute. Ihre Geschichte, Organisation und Ziele*, Vol. 2 (Hamburg: De Gruyter, 1930), p. 356. In: Michael Diers, Thomas Girst, Dorothea von Moltke, 'Warburg and the Warburgian Tradition of Cultural History', *New German Critique* 65 (Spring–Summer, 1995): pp. 59–73, here p. 71.

9. Saxl, 'Die Kulturwissenschaftliche Bibliothek Warburg in Hamburg', p. 356.

10. Gombrich, *Aby Warburg*, p. 22. The German quote reads: 'Als er dreizehn Jahre alt war, offerierte er mir sein Erstgeborenenrecht. Er als Ältester war bestimmt, in die Firma einzutreten. Ich wa[r] damals zwölf Jahre, noch nicht sehr überlegungsreif, und erklärte mich einverstanden, ihm das Erstgeborenenrecht abzukaufen. Er offerierte es mir aber nicht für ein Linsengericht, sondern verlangte von mir die Zusage, dass ich ihm immer alle Bücher kaufen würde, die er brauchte. Hiermit erklärte ich mich nach sehr kürzer Überlegung einverstanden. Ich sagte mir, dass schliesslich Schiller, Goethe, Lessing, vielleicht auch noch Klopstock von mir, wenn ich im Geschäft wäre, doch immer bezahlt werden könnten und gab ihm ahnungslos diesen, wie ich heute zugeben muss, sehr grossen Blankokredit. Die Liebe zum Lesen, zum Buch . . . war seine frühe grosse Leidenschaft'.

11. My emphasis. Saxl, *The History of Warburg's Library* (full ref?), in Gombrich, *Aby Warburg*, p. 327.

12. Saxl, *The History of Warburg's Library*, in Gombrich, *Aby Warburg*, p. 326.

13. Saxl, *The History of Warburg's Library*, in Gombrich, *Aby Warburg*, p. 26.

14. Saxl, *The History of Warburg's Library*, in Gombrich, *Aby Warburg*, p. 326. For more on Hamburg as the proper city for such an undertaking, see the recent dissertation by Emily Jane Levine, 'Culture, Commerce, and the City: Aby Warburg, Ernst Cassirer, and Erwin Panofsky in Hamburg, 1919–1933' (PhD dissertation, Stanford University, 2008).

15. Ron Chernow notes: 'By making books prohibitively expensive, Germany's inflation hurt many private scholars who subsisted on family inheritances. When Max and Fritz could no longer buy books, they turned to Paul and Felix, whose dollars enabled Saxl to continue buying books uninterrupted. This, in turn, helped to attract top scholars. Both American brothers found Aby's work rather arcane and probably supported it more from fraternal love than any great conviction of its ultimate worth. Ironically, despite Aby's contempt for Anglo-Saxon culture, it was American money that saved his library in the 1920s, then English money in the 1930s'. See: Chernow, *The Warburgs*, p. 256.

16. Gombrich, *Aby Warburg*, p. 130. Letter from 30 June 1900. German: 'Ich würde mich nicht einen Moment besinnen, meine Bibliothek dem Geschäft, der Firma geradezu auf's Conto zu setzen. Wenn ich nicht vorher abkratze, dann ist mein Buch nicht das schlechteste gewesen, was die Firma fertig gebracht hat. Lache nur nicht; ich

bin garnicht verblendet, im Gegenteil, ich bin eigentlich ein Narr, dass ich nicht mehr darauf bestehe, dass wir an uns zeigen, dass der Kapitalismus auch Denkarbeit auf breitester, nur ihm möglicher, Basis, leisten kann'.

17. Chernow, *The Warburgs*, p. 265.

18. Chernow, *The Warburgs*, p. 265.

19. Dorothea McEwan, 'Aby Warburg's (1866–1929) Dots and Lines. Mapping the Diffusion of Astrological Motifs in Art History,' *German Studies Review* 29, no. 2 (May 2006): p. 251.

20. Mark A. Russell, *Between Tradition and Modernity: Aby Warburg and the Public Purposes of Art in Hamburg, 1896–1918* (New York: Berghahn, 2007), p. 33.

21. Gombrich, *Aby Warburg*, p. 207.

22. See Nicholas Campion on the historical issues of chart rectification in 'Mythical Moments in the Rectification of History', in Noel Tyl, ed., *Astrology looks at History* (St Paul, MN: Llewellyn, 1995), pp. 25–64.

23. Warburg, *Heidnisch-antike Weissagung*, p. 21.

24. See Nicholas Campion and Liz Greene, eds, *Astrologies: Plurality and Diversity* (Ceredigion: Sophia Centre Press, 2011).

25. McEwan, 'Aby Warburg's (1866–1929) Dots and Lines', p. 248.

26. Warburg, *Heidnisch-antike Weissagung*, p. 5. English translation by Ernst Gombrich, *Aby Warburg*, p. 208.

27. Warburg, *Heidnisch-antike Weissagung*, p. 5. English translation by Ernst Gombrich, *Aby Warburg*, p. 208.

28. Warburg, *Heidnisch-antike Weissagung*, pp. 5–6. Emphasis Warburg's. English translation: Gombrich, *Aby Warburg*, p. 208.

29. Warburg, *Heidnisch-antike Weissagung* (1920), p. 24. Translation mine.

30. Warburg, *Heidnisch-antike Weissagung* (1920), p. 24. Translation mine

31. Jennifer L. Zahrt, 'The Astrological Imaginary in Early Twentieth–Century German Culture' (PhD dissertation, University of California, Berkeley, 2012).

32. Claudia Brosseder, 'The Writing in the Wittenberg Sky: Astrology in Sixteenth-Century Germany', *Journal of the History of Ideas* 66, no. 4 (Oct. 2005): pp. 557–76, here, p. 563.

33. Brosseder, 'The Writing in the Wittenberg Sky', p. 574.

34. Brosseder, 'The Writing in the Wittenberg Sky', p. 565.

35. Brosseder, 'The Writing in the Wittenberg Sky', p. 575.

36. Brosseder, 'The Writing in the Wittenberg Sky', p. 564.

37. Marsilio Ficino, *Three Books on Life*, ed. Carole C. Kaske and John R. Clark, Center for Medieval and Early Renaissance Studies (Binghamton, NY: State University of New York at Binghamton, 1989).

38. Brosseder, 'The Writing in the Wittenberg Sky', p. 564.

39. Brosseder, 'The Writing in the Wittenberg Sky', p. 564.

40. Zahrt, 'The Astrological Imaginary'.

41. Warburg, *Heidnisch-antike Weissagung*, p. 41. For a discussion of the parans, see Gombrich, *Aby Warburg*, pp. 197–98.

42. Jürgen G.H. Hoppmann, 'The Lichtenberger Prophecy and Melanchthon's Horoscope for Luther', *Culture and Cosmos* 1, no. 2 (Autumn/Winter 1997): pp. 49–59.

43. Valerius Herberger, *Gloria Lutheri* (Leipzig: 1612), pp. 41–45, found in Warburg, *Heidnisch-antike Weissagung*, p. 45. Translation mine. German original: 'Ey Herr Doctor / sehet nur das Bild ein wenig besser an / wo sitzt der Teuffel? / Er sitzt nicht dem Muenche im hertzen / sondern auff dem necken [...] aber ich meyne er sitzt mir auff dem nacken / durch Bapst / Keyser und grosse Potentaten'.

44. Dorothea McEwan, 'Making a Reception for Warburg: Fritz Saxl and Warburg's Book *Heidnisch-antike Weissagung in Wort und Bild zu Luthers Zeiten*', in Richard Woodfield, ed., *Art History as Cultural History: Warburg's Projects* (Amsterdam: G+B Arts, 2001), pp. 93–120.

45. McEwan, 'Making a Reception for Warburg', p. 109.

46. McEwan, 'Making a Reception for Warburg', p. 109.

47. McEwan, 'Making a Reception for Warburg', p. 110.

48. McEwan, 'Making a Reception for Warburg', p. 106.

49. McEwan, 'Making a Reception for Warburg', p. 96.

50. McEwan, 'Making a Reception for Warburg', p. 101. McEwan cites the letter as: [UB Heidelberg, Heid.Hs. 2109, F. Saxl to F. Boll, 13.09.1920.]

51. Sigrid Weigel, 'Aby Warburg's *Schlangenritual*: Reading Culture and Reading Written Texts', *New German Critique* 65 (Spring/Summer 1995): pp. 141–42. Ernst H. Gombrich, 'Aby Warburg und der Evolutionismus des 19. Jahrhunderts', in Robert Galitz and Brita Reimers, eds, *Aby M. Warburg: "ekstatische Nymphe ... trauernder Flussgott": Portrait eines Gelehrten* (Hamburg: Dölling und Galitz Verlag, 1995), pp. 52–73, here p. 52.

52. Warburg, *Heidnisch-antike Weissagung*, p. 70. The German reads: 'bisher ungelesene Urkunden zur tragischen Geschichte der Denkfreiheit des modernen Europäers'.

53. Richard Woodfield, 'Warburg's 'Method', in Woodfield, ed., *Art History as Cultural History*, p. 283.

54. Bernd Roeck, 'Psychohistorie im Zeichen Saturns: Aby Warburgs Denksystem und die moderne Kulturgeschichte', in Wolfgang Hardtwig and Hans-Ulrich Wehler, eds, *Kulturgeschichte Heute* (Göttingen: Vandenhoeck & Ruprecht, 1996), pp. 231–54, here pp. 236–37.

55. Woodfield, 'Warburg's 'Method', in Woodfield, ed., *Art History as Cultural History*, pp. 287–88.

56. Weigel, 'Aby Warburg's *Schlangenritual*', pp. 141–42.

57. Gombrich, *Aby Warburg*, p. 199.

58. Gombrich, *Aby Warburg*, p. 198.

59. Gombrich, *Aby Warburg*, p. 251.

60. Werner Hofmann, 'Der Mnemosyne-Atlas: Zu Warburgs Konstellationen', in Galitz and Reimers, *"ekstatische Nymphe ... trauernder Flussgott"*, pp. 172–83, here p. 174. Translation mine. German: 'Er denkt in Zwischenräumen'.

61. Matthew Rampley, 'Mimesis and Allegory', p. 132, in Woodfield, ed., *Art History as Cultural History*. Elsewhere the German reads, 'Ikologie des Zwischenraumes. Kunsthistorisches Material zu einer Entwicklungsphysiologie des Pendelganges zwischen bildhafter und zeichenmässiger Ursachensetzung', in Matthew Rampley, *The Remembrance of Things Past: On Aby M. Warburg and Walter Benjamin* (Wiesbaden: Harassowitz, 2000), p. 58.

62. Hofmann, 'Der Mnemosyne-Atlas: Zu Warburgs Konstellationen', p. 175.

63. Horst Bredekamp, *Les coraux de Darwin: Premiers modèles évolutionnistes et tradition de l'histoire naturelle* (Paris: Les Presses du réel, 2008).

64. Gombrich, *Aby Warburg*, p. 322.

65. See first note.

6

THE DAIMON IN TWENTIETH CENTURY PSYCHOLOGICAL ASTROLOGY

Alina Pelteacu

The notion of the daimon, as Gábor Betegh points out, is rather difficult to define.[1] Dorian Greenbaum pointed out that the term has 'bedevilled many a scholar and translator of Greek texts'.[2] In ancient Greece, the daimon was characterized as a sort of divine being that was circumscribed neither to a specific cult nor mythology nor by figurative representation.[3] The daimon was associated linguistically and mythologically with the ideas of destiny and divinity; what the daimon is distributing, then, would be the destiny, the lot of each person, but also the fate which is apportioned at a certain moment.[4] This imponderable aspect of the daimon was reflected by its assimilation with the notion of destiny on the one hand, but also with vengeance spirits, heroes, and the spirits of the dead on the other.[5]

In the fourth-century BCE *Derveni Papyrus,* the daimons were called 'assistants of the gods', and the anonymous author also presented the idea of a 'personal daimon' assigned to each soul.[6] For Heraclitus (c. early fifth-century BCE), the daimon was simultaneously guide, guardian, destiny, and fate as revealed through one's character: Man's character', he wrote, 'is his daimon'.[7]

The Daimon in Platonic Thought

It was the Greek philosopher Plato (428/427 or 424/423 – 348/347 BCE) who encapsulated the idea of the daimon most clearly as a liminal figure acting between gods and humans, and also as a personal guide.[8] This broader concept of the daimon had, in Platonic thought, essential philosophical importance in cosmology and theology as an element that ensured the unity of the cosmos.[9] Eventually, Plato, as E. R. Dodds (1893–1979) argued, transformed the idea of the daimon into a 'lofty spirit-guide', being identified with 'the element of pure reason in man', and in this guise, it developed into a respectable idea and was an element of continuity into medieval Christianity, as he wrote:

In that glorified dress, made morally and philosophically respectable,
he [the daimon] enjoyed a renewed lease of life in the pages of Stoics
and Neoplatonists, and even of mediaeval Christian writers.[10]

The daimon was embedded in Hellenistic theory and practice of astrology as a
way of integrating ideas of personal destiny into astrology.[11] Yet in the course of
history, the daimon has undergone periods of change and decline but also a revival,
often in connection with Plato's thought: hence, in the Renaissance, the daimon
was considered by Marsilio Ficino (1433–1499) and in the twentieth century by
C. G. Jung (1875–1961) and James Hillman (1926–2011). As Greenbaum writes,

> Astrology is linked to the bad daimon in the tenets of early Judaism
> and Christianity, held to be the creation of evil daimons who desire
> to deceive and corrupt mankind. Such entanglement plays a role in
> the demonisation of the daimon which rose to become the dominant
> paradigm by the Middle Ages. Still, the daimon has undergone periods
> of rehabilitation, e. g. in the Renaissance by Marsilio Ficino and in the
> twentieth century by Carl Jung and James Hillman.[12]

An analysis of some of Plato's key dialogues is helpful to draw out features of
the daimon. The *Timaeus* and the *Symposium* provide a consistent picture of
what Plato meant by the daimon as an intermediary between gods, goddesses,
and humans. The daimon Eros is an intermediary figure between man and
divinity, whose role is to arrange the passage from the sensible reality towards
the intelligible world, by stimulating the exercise of reason and encouraging
true knowledge.[13] The 'Myth of Er' in the *Republic* expanded on the notion
of the personal daimon as a personal guide connected with destiny, fate, and
character, the philosophical life, and the most elevated part of the soul, nous,
thus explaining the affinities of the human soul with the heavens.[14] As Plato put
it in the *Timaeus*:

> ... the most lordly kind of our soul, we must conceive of it in this wise:
> we declare that God has given to each of us, as his daemon, that kind
> of soul which is housed in the top of our body and which raises us
> seeing that we are not an earthly but a heavenly plant up from earth
> towards our kindred in the heaven.[15]

The contact with the divine world, the world of Forms or Archetypes, which
are the basis of all things in our world, was central to Plato's thinking: through

the daimon, which he connected with the higher part of the human soul, continual contact between the physical world and the divine realm is established through intellectual activity and as related to the planets' movements; thus the philosophical life is guided by one's daimon.[16]

The Location of the Daimon in Jung's Thinking

Plato's philosophical world view of life was significantly revised by the psychologist C. G. Jung (1875–1961). Jung's work was hugely influential on the way astrology developed in the twentieth century and, as Roy Willis and Patrick Curry argued, he created a significant place for spirituality at a time when scientific secularism was the leading ideology for modern Western people.[17] As a result, in psychological astrology, the birth-chart is seen both as a study of human personality and as a key for the human soul as the carrier of our divine spark in us.[18] For Jung, the daimon was equivalent to the unconscious:

> I prefer the term 'the unconscious', knowing that I might equally well speak of 'God' or 'daimon' if I wished to express myself in mythic language... A creative person has little power over his own life. He is not free. He is captive and driven by his daimon.[19]

In this sense, the daimon formed part of the process of communication between the soul and the divine, which was necessary for the success of the individuation process, which Jung, in turn, associated with the soul's journey through the planetary spheres in connection with human consciousness and the archetypal realm or Jung's term of the unconscious.[20] Individuation is a process that involves the unconscious content in a compensatory relationship with consciousness. Jung discovered that psyche is a self-regulating system: the regulating element situated in the unconscious compensates the conscious ego, or in other words, the ego is led by the unconscious towards its goal.[21] Consequently, the ego-self relationship is central to the individuation process.[22] Individuation itself was defined by Jung as follows:

> In general, it is the process by which individual beings are formed and differentiated [from other human beings]; in particular, it is the development of the psychological individual as a being distinct from the general, collective psychology. Individuation therefore is a process of differentiation, having for its goal the development of the individual personality.[23]

Jung recognized individuation as equivalent to alchemical work, through which *prima materia* (the underlying layer of existence) transforms into the philosopher's stone. And, for Jung, the *prima materia* and individuation are both represented by Mercurius. As Jung put it:

> Besides being the prima materia of the lowly beginning as well as the lapis as the highest goal, Mercurius is also the process which lies between, and the means by which it is effected.[24]

Mercurius' paradoxical nature reflects an important aspect of the self which is opposed to the figure of God in man, *Salvator Mundi*, the symbol of unity and consciousness. Mercurius owes its existence to the law of compensation, the process which the psyche balances itself.[25]

Whereas Plato identified the archetypes with geometrical forms, Jung personified them in a manner that enabled them to move into psychological reality.[26] Jung provided a new vision of the archetypes as a dynamic pattern of unique spiritual meaning, being active in nature as a whole, unrestricted by space-time limits, and manifesting through an individual's life as synchronistic experiences.[27] As Jung wrote:

> We conclude ... that we have to expect a factor in the psyche that is not subject to the laws of time and space ... [and] this factor is expected to manifest the qualities of time and spacelessness, i.e., 'eternity' and 'ubiquity.' Psychological experience knows of such a factor; it is what I call the archetype.[28]

And he continued: 'Archetypes are the most important basis for synchronistic events.'[29] This is vital for understanding that the individuation process cannot work without synchronous events triggering new awareness. Liz Greene pointed out that Jung considered these archetypes or patterns to be 'just as much outside as inside', at a personal level, symbolize unconscious complexes experienced as psychic compulsions.[30] They determine both character and fate (echoing Heraclitus's formula), being however amenable to conscious intervention through a developmental process initiated by the unconscious psyche.[31] Jung also identified his own daimon, which he named Philemon:[32]

> ...Philemon represented a force which was not myself. In my fantasies I held conversation with him, and he said things which I had not consciously thought... Psychologically, Philemon represented superior

insight. He was a mysterious figure to me. At times he seemed to me quite real, as if he were a living personality... and to me he was what Indians call a guru.[33]

In Jung's description of his guru one can recognize the characteristics of the personal daimon as an intermediary celestial being, but a living figure at the same time. Jung also claimed that he himself experimented with the encounter with the self: 'Through uniting with the self we reach the God... I have experienced it. It has happened thus in me'.[34] It is clear that the Platonic characteristics have become bound up with Jung's psychological language, and the comparisons between the two can be summarised as follows:

Plato	Jung
an intermediary entity	part of the collective unconscious / the realm of archetypes
one's destiny and fate	patterns / the individual's psychic complexes
one's personal guide	the regulating element situated in the unconscious compensating the conscious ego
one's character	the anthropomorphized archetypes / the 'persons' to whom we owe our entire personality
messenger between human and the divine	synchronistic experience
philosophical life	individuation

James Hillman: the Daimon, Archetypal Psychology and Individuation

A significant innovation in Jung's theories was made by the psychologist James Hillman (1926–2011). Hillman referred to his model as archetypal psychology, his concern being with what he called archetypal images.[35] Locating his theories in the Myth of Er, Hillman described the daimon as an imaginal figure accompanying each of us towards our purpose, identity, and fate:[36]

The soul of each of us is given a unique daimon before we are born, and it has selected an image or pattern that we live on earth. This soul-companion, the daimon, guides us here... The daimon remembers what is in your image and belongs to your pattern, and therefore your daimon is the carrier of your destiny.[37]

For Hillman the process of individuation is equivalent to 'the work of soul-making', or soul-deepening, which is a function of the personal daimon:

> The process of individuation or the work of soul-making is the long therapeutic labor of lifting repression from the inhumane aspects of human nature.[38]

> It is not my individuation, but the daimon's; not my fate that matters to the Gods, but how I care for the psychic persons entrusted to my stewardship during my life. It is not life that matters, but soul and how life is used to care for soul.[39]

Hillman's definition of the daimon as an 'individualized soul-image', Greene argued, involves not only environmental and genetic inheritance but also, the natal horoscope, as she wrote:

> … are all 'chosen' because they belong to the necessity of the daimon, who is both 'outside' the configuration of the horoscope and 'inside' because of the seminal moment of birth reflects the soul's own choice.[40]

Significantly, if the daimon is not in the birth chart, then neither is the Self.[41] In Hillman's view, the birth chart is consequently rather insufficient as a guide to individuation, and one must therefore engage with the daimon, with which, Hillman claimed, 'we are drawn together like threads into a *mythos*, a plot, until death do us part'.[42] Hillman, though, did not explain how his ideas can be used in practical astrology, his perspective on the individuation was given a practical voice by Greene's interpretation of what Hillman called the puer-senex dilemma in the horoscope.[43] For Jung, the puer is the archetype of the eternal youth and the senex the wise old man.

Hillman described the *puer eternus* as 'our angelic essence as a messenger of the divine, as divine message […] it is the call of a thing to the perfection of itself, the call of a person to his or her daimon, to be true to itself'.[44] He argued that is vital that the puer be recognized and valued, for it carries one's future and it is 'the futurity within every complex, its prospective meaning'. And to heal this archetypal split equals a turning to the soul because the puer must be devoted to anima. 'First psyche, then world'.[45]

To put this into context, Hillman argued that human beings are caught as manifestations of an archetypal split within the individual souls, identified as the senex-et-puer components of the ego. Thus, the ego must first undergo an archetypal therapy of its split root. These polarities – senex and puer – provide the archetype for the psychological foundation of the problem of history: the puer who transcends history is primordially perfect while the senex who is the image of history is perfected through time.[46] For Hillman, all polarities are subject to the primary division: conscious and unconscious. This primary division is given only as a potential within the archetype because theoretically is not divided into poles. It is a co-existing polarity and both poles of the archetype are necessary and equal. The archetype is ambivalent and paradoxical embracing both conscious and unconscious, an inherent opposition that splits into poles when enters ego-consciousness.[47]

So, the soul suffering and illness reflect the torn condition of the split archetype and to heal this means to reunite the polarities of ego which is senex-et-puer conceived as its order on the one hand and its impetus on the other.[48] And because these figures are in special relation, forming a two-headed archetype, there is no difference between the negative puer and negative senex. While negative senex results from this split archetype, the positive senex attitudes and behavior reflect its unity.[49] For both positive and negative senex the image is Saturn. The astrological view of personality is saturnine, while the psycho-dynamic view is mercurial. And the puer could be seen as a mercurial range of personalities.[50]

Hilman envisioned the re-approximation of the two halves of the archetype as 'the union of sames', whose primary image is given by the Renaissance maxim *Festina Lente* (make haste slowly), which describes an ego-ideal based on the two-faced archetype.[51] And this paragon may be achieved through one's individual history when the puer merges with the senex, and so the bipolar spirit becomes ambivalent. In Hillman's words 'The world of Saturn is pierced through with Mercurius…living from the principle which Jung circumscribed as synchronicity'.[52] This is the moment when the two faces of the archetype turned towards each other in a dialogue. Although Hillman did not deal with practical astrology, he has clearly identified a means of analysing the puer and the senex through the relationship between Mercury and Saturn, which then may point to a way of working with the Daimon.

Liz Greene's Astrology and Individuation

A key protagonist of psychological astrology has been the Jungian analyst Liz Greene, who linked the symbolic nature of astrology with that of myth while making connections between Jung's depth psychology and astrology.[53] Greene pointed out that although psychology and astrology use different languages and research methods and practices, the subject of their investigation is the same: the human psyche.[54] According to Greene, the astrological birth chart is a map of the individual's psyche, and comparable to a seed containing its basic potential and timetable for development. In her own words:

> A properly erected astrological birth chart is a symbolic map of the individual human psyche. This map is like a seed because it contains in microcosm the potentials existent within the individual and the periods of his life when these potentials are likely to be brought into actualisation.[55]

Like Jung and Hillman, Greene looks back to the Myth of Er. However, while Jung and Hillman's writings on astrology were very general, Greene is more specific and argues that the daimon involves not only environmental and genetic inheritance but also the natal horoscope. As she claimed:

> The individual's physical body, parents, and place and time of birth – in other words, not only environmental and genetic inheritance but also the natal horoscope – are all 'chosen' because they belong to the necessity of the daimon, who is both 'outside' the configuration of the horoscope and 'inside' because of the seminal moment of birth reflects the soul's own choice.[56]

The daimon, then is not contained within the birth chart, an idea reflected in similar claims that the Self is situated outside the chart.[57]

Greene held that analytical psychology, which attempts to explore the laws governing and regulating the psyche's activities, can benefit from what astrology has to offer through the study of planetary progressions and transits, and what they indicate about the individual's development.[58] In other words, astrology can provide psychology with a blueprint of all that potentially belongs to an individual: the kind of seed, the timing, and the patterns of growth to be considered. Psychology too can offer astrology a framework that makes its symbols understandable and appropriate for communication. This shared knowledge between the two becomes most evident and most universal when analysing human relationships.[59] As Greene put it:

> Relating is a fundamental aspect of life. It is archetypal, which means that it is an experience which permeates the basic structure not only of the human psyche but of the universe in its entirety.[60]

Greene maintained that relationships are also a path toward individual self-discovery. As she claimed: 'It would seem that through relating, we may find a path through which to bring alive again – or make conscious – the world of the heavens.'[61] And she added that 'perhaps the most important mechanism we possess that enables us to see into the psyche is that of projection'.[62] This assertion on the subject of relating is echoing Jung's words:

> Psychic projection is one of the commonest facts of psychology ...,
> and as a rule [we] deny that we are guilty of it. Everything that is
> unconscious in ourselves we discover in our neighbour, and we treat
> him accordingly. [63]

The problem Greene addressed was how to identify Jungian archetypes in the birth chart, of which prime examples are the puer, the eternal youth, and the senex, the wise old man.

Finding the puer in the chart is not a simple exercise but constitutes a kind of detective work where certain horoscope placements 'may have a flavour of a particular archetypal dilemma or story', and this way equates with the use of psychological material to enhance the astrological picture and to see,' a living dynamic at work in the chart, rather than a fragmented listing of character qualities'.[64] This dynamic work can be equated with the individuation process, which Greene considered, is a sacred work to be accomplished jointly by the individual and his or her daimon.

Embracing Jung's equation of individuation with the alchemical journey, and following Hillman's idea that the puer must be devoted to anima, Greene argues that the puer can learn compassion, without losing the essential spirit, through the medium of the soul.[65] The puer can then become an archetypal image.[66] Psychologically this means to conceptualise and turn experiences into patterns that are elusive, beautiful, and meaningful. [67]

Greene pointed to some of the astrological configurations that must be considered when analyzing a chart of the puer-senex dilemma which might give a 'home' to the puer in the birth horoscope.[68] The puer is particularly at home in a horoscope without much earth, particularly if air or fire are strongly emphasised.[69] Greene argued that Uranus provides a good home for the puer, being the airiest planet, as do Venus and Mercury, as both rule earthy signs as well as airy ones.[70] Aspects to Saturn are also important, mainly aspects to Sun and Jupiter. For example, Sun-Saturn contacts reveal the dilemma existing between the puer (the eternal youth) and the senex (the old man), and a difficult aspect between them will reflect a mythic conflict between the puer and the senex.[71]

Greene added that the relation between Sun and the zodiac sign Leo are linked with the themes of puer, as the experience of the divine child and his creative play.[72] In addition, the experience of Saturn reveals weaknesses in the ego's structure, while Pluto brings a feeling of fatality and the transformational qualities of transpersonal powers working in one's life.[73] Greene held that even though both planets bring suffering they don't crush the puer but rather humanize him.[74]

Greene argued that the most difficult aspect in analysing a horoscope is to consider the archetypal perspective, as the puer never enters the stage alone; he is a character in the play concerning the world he attempts to transcend, represented by 'the bodily realm of the mother', in order to reach 'the eternal spirit of the father'.[75] However, things are more complex as the spiritual father whom the puer is longing for has a shadow-side, an earthly dimension, which is the senex, and this dimension must be integrated by the puer in order to be truly united with God.[76] Translating astrologically Hillman's argument that the puer-senex polarity must be viewed also within the polarity of each end of the axis, Greene affirmed the importance of understanding that each planet or sign has a positive and negative dimension, and this is the case for the whole chart.[77]

According to this perspective, the puer is not relevant for every person in the same way, and this is why the astrologer/therapist must understand what the analysand has done with his/her chart and where certain astrological placements have fallen into the unconscious, and what might be necessary for balancing and integrating them in the individual's life, and eventually to follow the pattern and see where this energy will be directed by that person in the future.[78] This, of course, requires an understanding of astrological timing measures.

Greene adheres to the conventional astrological model in which the individual's development after birth is reflected by the motion of planets after birth, and symbolised by secondary progressions in which planetary positions for a certain number of days after represent the state of one's life the same number of years after birth.[79] Progressions are symbolic and synchronous with a certain psychic event, some constellation of a particular configuration of energy – the archetypes – in the unconscious. Thus, a progression reflects the need for inner recognition of an unexpressed quality and its integration into conscious awareness.[80]

While a progression is a symbolic movement and unrelated to the planet's physical position in the sky at any one time, a transit, by contrast, measures a planet's actual position in the zodiac on any date. According to Greene, both progressions and transits seem to operate alike, indicating that something is being constellated on a psychic level but not necessarily coincident with a physical event.[81] All transiting planets periodically return to the position they occupied at birth and, for Greene, the transit cycles of Saturn and Uranus are of significance for human relationships. Both of them occur for all individuals at about the same age (Saturn returns to its birth position typically after twenty-nine years and Uranus after approximately eighty-four years – and opposes its birth position after approximately forty-two years) and are said to coincide with periods of crisis, change of direction, and the building or breaking of relationships. Although these cycles symbolize collective patterns of growth for the entire humanity, the personal form such patterns will take depends on the individual.[82] Greene identified Saturn with the primitive side of human nature equivalent to Jung's concept of the shadow, which he had described as follows:

> The shadow is a moral problem that challenges the whole ego-personality, for no one can become conscious of the shadow without considerable moral effort. To become conscious of it involves recognising the dark aspects of the personality as present and real. This act is the essential condition for any kind of self-knowledge, and it therefore, as a rule, meets with considerable resistance. [83]

As the cycle of Saturn takes around twenty-nine years, it attains a critical relation to its initial position on an individual's birth chart every seven years approximately, forming 90° 'square' and 180° 'opposition' aspects to its birth position. In line with conventional astrological practice, Greene held that the nature of one's experience under the Saturn return will be indicated by the house, sign, and aspects of the planet on the birth chart.[84] However, she brought Jung into the equation, arguing that the completion of every cyclical Saturn return signals that 'the dark, undifferentiated and unconscious' side of the personality is activated.[85] Since the individual projects outside that which is unconscious within, the inner constellation of the shadow often comes with obstruction from other people, but handled properly, it can be an opportunity for great change and constructive self-realisation.[86]

Greene maintained, following Jung, that, difficult as it may be, the shadow must be integrated into one's life because the inner reality demands recognition.[87] So, the ego has the option to cooperate or to oppose the unconscious since the final choice is inherent in the seed (reflected in the horoscope); but the individual remains the only one accountable for the form this choice takes and the consciousness of its implications. As Jung put it:

> ... the integration of the shadow, or the realisation of the personal unconscious, marks the first stage of the analytical process, and ... without it a recognition of anima and animus is impossible. The shadow can be realised only through a relation to a partner, and anima

and animus only through a relation to a partner of the opposite sex, because only in such a relation do their projections become operative.[88]

Greene gave a practical voice to the use of psychological material to enhance the astrological picture and to see, as she claimed ' a living dynamic at work in the chart, rather than a fragmented listing of character qualities'.[89] This dynamic work can be equated with the individuation process, which Greene considered, as a sacred work done in co-participation by the individual and his daimon. As she wrote:

> The struggle towards individuation is not just a 'cure' for neurotic discomfort, but a sacred work done both for man and God. Ego and unconscious thus possess a strangely ambivalent relationship.[90]

Like Jung, Greene held that the individuation process, which engages the personal daimon, implies a psychodynamic relationship that is both transformative for the individual and its daimon. The underlying question, though, concerns the daimon's status as an important factor in the interpretation of a birth chart while not necessarily being present *in* the chart. Greene's references to the 'Self' and the mysterious ways in which growth is achieved, which cannot be read in a chart alone, are relevant and help to strengthen the argument that the daimon is indeed present in psychological astrology whether explicitly referenced a great deal or not.

Conclusions

In Platonic thought, the daimon can be an intermediary entity, a personal guide, a messenger between the human and the divine, and one's destiny, fate, and character. Jung adopted Plato's concept and located the daimon within the process of individuation, and Liz Greene then adapted both to the horoscope, which is then seen as a map of the individual's psyche, the dynamics of the personality including potential and character traits, and an understanding of the individual's psychological development over time, which is itself the individuation process. The inclusion of the daimon in modern psychological astrology, therefore, represents a renewed incorporation of Platonic cosmology in astrology, reinforcing modern astrology's relationship with the classical world.

Notes

1. Gábor Betegh, ed. and trans., *The Derveni Papyrus: Cosmology, Theology, and Interpretation* (Cambridge: Cambridge University Press, 2004), p. 86.

2. Dorian Gieseler Greenbaum, *The Daimon in Hellenistic Astrology: Origins and Influence* (Leiden-Boston: Brill, 2016), p. 1.

3. Andrei Timotin, *La démonologie platonicienne, histoire de la notion de daimôn de Platon aux derniers néoplatoniciens* (Leiden-Boston: Brill, 2012), p. 1.

4. Timotin, *La démonologie platonicienne*, p. 15.

5. See Homer, *The Odyssey*, trans. by Samuel Butler (London: A. C. Fifield, 1900) Book II, 134–135. For the daimon as vengeance spirit (referred to as the Erinyes); See Hésiode, *Théogonie, Les Travaux et les Jours, Le Bouclier*, trad. par Paul Mazon (Paris: Les Belles Lettres, 1928), *Travaux*, 121–126. For the posthumous title of daimon attributed to men of the Golden Age.

6. Betegh, *The Derveni Papyrus*, Col. 3, p. 9.

7. Heracleitus, para 247, in G. S. Kirk, J.E. Raven and M. Schofield, *The Presocratic Philosophers*, 2nd edition, (Cambridge: Cambridge University Press, 1983), p. 211; Stavros J. Baloyannis, 'The philosophy of Heracletus today', *Encephalos Journal*, Vol. 50, Issue 1 (January–March 2013), pp. 1–21 (p. 1), < http://www.encephalos.gr/pdf/50-1-01e.pdf>, [accessed 29 June 2018]; See James Hillman, *The Soul's Code: In Search of Character and Calling* (London: Bantam, 1997 [1996]), pp. 256–257. For Heraclitus' dictum *Ethos Anthropoi Daimon* – 'Character for man is daimon', Hillman offered a list of different interpretations as revealed by English translations, which understand daimon as guide, guardian, fate and destiny.

8. A. E. Taylor, *Plato: The Man and His Work* (London: Methuen, 1926), p. 1; Timotin, *La démonologie platonicienne*, p. 37.

9. Timotin, *La démonologie platonicienne*, pp. 330–331.

10. E. R. Dodds, *The Greeks and the Irrational* (Berkeley, CA: University of California Press, 1951 [1973]), p. 42.

11. Greenbaum, *The Daimon in Hellenistic Astrology*, pp. 2–3.

12. Greenbaum, *The Daimon in Hellenistic Astrology*, p. 10.

13. Plato, *Symposium*, Plato in Twelve Volumes, Vol. 9, trans. by Harold N. Fowler (Cambridge, MA: Harvard University Press; London: Heinemann, 1925), 202d–203a. Plato presented the daimon Eros as an intermediary figure between man and divinity, whose role is to arrange the passage from the sensible reality towards the intelligible world, by stimulating the exercise of reason and encouraging true knowledge.

14. Plato, *Republic*, Plato in Twelve Volumes, Vols.5 & 6, trans. by Paul Shorey (Cambridge, MA: Harvard University Press; London: Heinemann, 1969), Book X.617e, 620d–e.

15. Plato, *Timaeus*, Plato in Twelve Volumes, Vol. 9, trans. by W. R. M. Lamb, (Cambridge, MA: Harvard University Press; London: Heinemann, 1925), 90a–b.

16. Plato, *Republic* X. 613a.

17. See Patrick Curry and Roy Willis, *Astrology, Science and Culture: Pulling Down the Moon* (Oxford: Berg, 2004), p. 73.

18. See Lindsay Radermacher, 'The Role of Dialogue in Astrological Divination' (unpublished MPhilthesis, University of Kent, 2011), p. iv.

19. C. G. Jung, *Memories, Dreams, Reflections*, ed. by Aniela Jaffé, trans. by Richard and Clara Winston (New York: Random House, 1989), pp. 336–337, p. 357.

20. C. G. Jung, *Mysterium Coniunctionis*: *An Inquiry into the separation and synthesis of psychic opposites in alchemy*, Collected Works, Vol. 14, trans. by R. F. C. Hull

(Princeton, NJ: Princeton University Press, 1977), para. 308, p. 272.

21. C. G. Jung, *Modern man in search of a soul*, trans. by W. S. Dell and Cary F. Baynes (San Diego, New York, London: A Harvest Book Harcourt, Inc., 1933), p. 17.; C. G. Jung, 'The Relations between the Ego and the Unconscious' in *Two Essays on Analytical Psychology*, Collected Works, Vol. 7, 2nd edn, trans. by R. F. C. Hull (Princeton, NJ: Princeton University Press, 1966), para. 275, pp. 177–178.

22. Jung, Collected Works, Vol. 7, p. 110.

23. C. G. Jung., 'Definitions', *Psychological Types*, The Collected Works, Vol. 6, trans. R. F .C Hull (London: Routledge and Kegan Paul, 1971), pp. 408–86 (para 757).

24. C. G. Jung, *Alchemical Studies*, Collected Works, Vol. 13, trans. by R.F.C. Hull (London: Routledge, 1967), p. 235.

25. Jung, *Alchemical Studies*, p. 241, p. 245.

26. Plato, *Timaeus*, trans. R.G. Bury (Cambridge Mass., London: Harvard University Press, 1931), 52B-53C; Jung, *Alchemical Studies*, para. 299.

27. Robert Aziz, *C. G. Jung's Psychology of Religion and Synchronicity* (Albany, NY: State University of New York Press, 1990), pp. 57–58, p. 59. Aziz argued that the term synchronicity is used specifically to describe the acausal connecting principle in the space-time world of the archetype, while the synchronistic event takes place in the space-and time-bound macrophysical world of ego-consciousness.

28. C. G. Jung, 'Symbols and the Interpretation of Dreams' in *The Symbolic Life*, Collected Works, Vol. 18, trans. by R. F. C. Hull (Princeton: Princeton University Press, 1976), para. 523, p. 228.

29. Gerhard Adler and Aniela Jaffe, eds. *C. G. Jung Letters*, 2 vols. trans. by R. F. C. Hull (Princeton, N J: Princeton University Press, 1975), p. 289; See also C. G. Jung, 'Synchronicity an acausal connecting principle' in *The Structure and Dynamics of the Psyche*, Collected Works, Vol. 8, trans. by R. F. C. Hull (Princeton, NJ: Princeton University Press, 1975), para 942, p. 634. Jung used the term synchronicity to describe the acausal connecting principle in the space-time world of the archetype, while the synchronistic event takes place in the space–and time–bound macro-physical world of ego consciousness.

30. Liz Greene, *Jung's Studies in Astrology: Prophecy, Magic, and the Qualities of Time* (London and New York: Routledge, 2018), p. 28.

31. Greene, *Jung's Studies in Astrology*, p. 29.

32. C. G. Jung, *The Red Book: Liber Novus*, ed. by Sonu Shamdasani, trans. by Mark Kyburz, John Peck, and Sonu Shamdasani (New York & London: W. W. Norton, 2009), p. 359.

33. Jung, *Memories, Dreams, Reflections*, p. 183.

34. Jung, *Liber Novus*, p. 338.

35. C. G. Jung, *The Archetypes of the Collective Unconscious*, Collected Works, Vol. 9, Part I, trans. by R. F. C. Hull (London: Routledge, 1955), paras. 3, 4, pp. 3–4; James Hillman, *Re-Visioning Psychology* (New York: Harper & Row, 1975), p. 8.

36. James Hillman, *The Soul's Code: In Search of Character and Calling* (London: Bantam, 1997 [1996]), pp. 7–8.

37. Hillman, *The Soule's Code*, p. 8.

38. Hillman, *Re-Visioning Psychology*, p. 188.

39. Hillman, *Re-Visioning Psychology*, p. 175.

40. Greene, *Jung's Studies in Astrology*, p. 103.

41. Liz Greene, *The Astrology of Fate* (York Beach, ME: Weiser, 1984), p. 318; Liz Greene, *Relating: An Astrological Guide to Living with Others on a Small Planet*, 2nd edn (York Beach, ME: Weiser, 1978), p. 29.

42. James Hillman, *A Blue Fire*, ed. by Thomas Moore (London & New York: Routledge, 1990), p. 63.

43. James Hillman, 'Senex and Puer: An Aspect of the Historical and Psychological Present' in *Puer Papers,* ed. J. Hillman (Dallas: Spring Publications, 1979).

44. Hillman, 'Senex and Puer', p. 14.

45. Hillman, 'Senex and Puer', p. 16.

46. Hillman, 'Senex and Puer', p. 4, p. 13, p. 20.

47. Hillman, 'Senex and Puer', p. 5.

48. Hillman, 'Senex and Puer', p. 6.

49. Hillman, 'Senex and Puer', p. 12.

50. Hillman, 'Senex and Puer', p. 7.

51. Hillman, 'Senex and Puer', p. 19.

52. Hillman, 'Senex and Puer', p. 19.

53. See Nicholas Campion, *A History of Western Astrology,* Volume II: *The Medieval and Modern Worlds* (London: Bloomsbury, 2013 [2009]), p. 258; See also Laura Andrikopoulos, 'Myth, Enchantment&Psychological Astrology' (paper presented at the Annual Sophia Centre Conference, Bath, UK, 1-2 July 2017), <https://moodle.uwtsd.ac.uk/pluginfile.php/62783/mod_resource/content/1/Myth%20Enchantment%20and%20Psychological%20Astrology_Laura%20Andrikopoulos.pdf>, [accessed 21 June 2018].

54. Greene, *Relating*, p. 6.

55. Greene, *Relating*, p. 6.

56. Greene, *Jung's Studies in Astrology*, p. 103.

57. Greene, *The Astrology of Fate*, p. 318; Greene, *Relating*, p. 29.

58. Greene, *Relating*, p. 229.

59. Greene, *Relating*, p. 229.

60. Greene, *Relating*, p. 2.

61. Greene, *Relating*, p. 45.

62. Greene, *Relating*, p. 11.

63. Jung, *Modern man in search of a soul*, p. 142.

64. Liz Greene, *The Development of the Personality: Seminars in Psychological Astrology*, Vol. 1 (York Beach, ME: Weiser, 1987), p. 310.

65. Greene, *The Development of the Personality*, pp. 238–239.

66. Liz Greene and Howard Sasportas, *Dynamics of the unconscious: Seminars in Psychological Astrology,* Vol. 2 (York Beach, ME: Weiser, 1988), p. 292.

67. Greene, *The Development of the Personality,* pp. 269–270.

68. Greene, *The Development of the Personality,* p. 261.

69. Greene, *The Development of the Personality,* p. 261.

70. Greene, *The Development of the Personality,* p. 268, p. 265.

71. Greene, *The Development of the Personality,* p. 273.

72. Greene, *The Development of the Personality,* p. 272.

73. Greene, *The Development of the Personality,* p. 270.

74. Greene, *The Development of the Personality,* p. 270.

75. Greene, *The Development of the Personality,* p. 234.

76. Greene, *The Development of the Personality,* p. 234.

77. Greene, *The Development of the Personality,* p. 279.

78. Greene, *The Development of the Personality,* p. 310.

79. Greene, *Relating*, pp. 229–30.

80. Greene, *Relating*, pp. 235–36.

81. Greene, *Relating*, p. 240.

82. Greene, *Relating*, pp. 240–241.

83. C. G. Jung, *Aion: Research into the Phenomenology of the Self*, Collected Works, Vol. 9, Part II, trans. by R. F. C. Hull (London: Routledge & Kegan Paul, 1959), p. 8.

84. Greene, *Relating*, p. 244.

85. Greene, Relating, p. 241.

86. Greene, *Relating*, pp. 242–243.

87. Greene, *Relating*, p. 245.

88. Jung, *Aion*, p. 22.

89. Greene, *The Development of the Personality*, p. 310.

90. Greene, *The Astrology of Fate*, p. 256; Greene and Sasportas, *Dynamics of the unconscious*, p. 254.

7

THE NATURE OF THE SOUL WITHIN CONTEMPORARY WESTERN ASTROLOGY

Jayne Logan

In many forms of modern western astrology, the soul is viewed as a unique vehicle and container of all the individual's experiences, and its karmic history, both good and bad, creates an imprint reflected by the personality. But, as Bernadette Brady concluded, any interpretation by the astrologer depends on their individual perspective and beliefs, which includes their notions about fate and free will.[1] She argues that, when a birth chart is used to talk of the person's journey through life, there is an acceptance of 'the presence of some form of fate or destiny', noting that, 'The question of what is, and what is not written for a life lies at the heart of astrology, as one can only read what is destined for an individual, free will by definition being unreadable'.[2]

Brady argues that, once the existence of fate is acknowledged, the concept of free will is automatically drawn in.[3] The implications of belief in fate were considered by Liz Greene, who suggested that, when the individual feels a loss of control and a sense of powerlessness, they are unable to make a choice or decide on a course of action to affect their own outcome.[4] Nicholas Campion adds that all types of astrology start with some idea of fate or destiny, where people believe they have 'a lack of control over their lives but then set out to create choice, negotiate with nature, and enter into a dialogue with time'.[5] In her ethnographic work Brady also found that the desire to seek control over one's life is a major reason why people adopt astrology.[6] Campion extends the debate, pointing out that, in the contemporary West, astrology is part of the mix that often leads the individual to seek options and answers in some form of counselling or psychotherapy, and that such discussions are often connected to debates about soul.[7] This, of course, raises another question, which is what soul actually is. The psychologist James Hillman says the soul, 'refers to the deepening of experiences' [...] [and] the imaginative possibility in our natures'.[8] Brian Clark, a notable psychological astrologer, associates the soul with 'the breath of life' and as an animating power: paraphrasing the classical Stoic view he suggests it 'animates the natal chart'.[9]

The Soul in Western Astrology

The importance of the soul in western astrology is firmly based in such classical works as Claudius Ptolemy's *Tetrabiblos*, one of the central texts of medieval and Renaissance astrology. In Book III Ptolemy wrote that:

> Of the qualities of the soul, those which concern the reason and the mind are apprehended by means of the condition of Mercury observed on the particular occasion; and the qualities of the sensory and the rational part are discovered from one of the luminaries which is the more corporal, that is, the moon, and from the planets which are configured with her in her separations and applications.[10]

In other words, soul is expressed through mind, emotion and body: one's ability to reason corresponds to Mercury's constantly shifting, dynamic relationships with the other planets, and one's emotional and physical condition to the Moon's similar relationships. The astrological notion of soul inherited by Ptolemy was largely based on a combination of Plato and Aristotle's ideas, with additional Stoic influences.[11] Plato described how the soul originated in the stars and incarnated in the physical body at birth, and could express itself through the physical body, the emotions and the mind.[12] In Platonic cosmology the essence of the individual is the soul, not the body, and the soul itself incarnates through multiple lives. Aristotle rejected reincarnation but likewise saw the soul as an animating force, operating through the body, feelings and intellect.[13] Inherent in these ideas, as later applied to astrology, are notions of the birth horoscope as a description of the soul's current incarnation and the individual's purpose and destiny. In Platonic cosmology the soul was regarded as both manifest in matter and transcendent, surviving physical death to be born again, a notion which collided with Christianity's requirement for a once-only incarnation and a soul which was answerable only to God in medieval astrology. The solution to this problem in medieval astrology was simple: the soul was specifically excluded from astral influences (the concept of planets as physical influences was central to Aristotelian cosmology), which were reserved for the body alone.[14] The planets influence the body, and the body may then influence the soul, but the planets cannot influence the soul, which is therefore not a matter for astrology. The soul made a slight return to astrology in the Renaissance thanks to the revival of Neoplatonism, as epitomised by Marsilio Ficino.[15] But, in general, the soul played no part in western astrology until the nineteenth century.

The Soul in Modern Western Astrology

From the late nineteenth century the notion of the soul's journey in modern western astrology has been underpinned by the theories of karma and reincarnation, concepts imported into the west from India via Theosophy.[16] Karma, as Robert Solomon describes it, is 'the "residue" of action with every act having a relative consequence'; thus, karma is the aggregation of every experience the soul has had so far.[17] Martin Gansten argues that, in the process of its translation from India to the West, karma acquired an evolutionary and purposeful character which was then adapted to astrology.[18] For Theosophists, individual destiny as an expression of karma can be described by the horoscope and, with the knowledge gained, an opportunity is created for the individual to actively engage with karmic circumstances to improve the experience of current and future incarnations. The concept of karma and the practice of astrology are inextricably linked, as A.R. Wadia observes, but in his view there is an obvious danger, which he sees as fatalism.[19] However, as Gansten observed, there is both a descriptive part of astrology which may recognise fate, and a prescriptive side which may assert the individual's freedom to act.

Influenced by such notions, a number of astrologers, including Alan Leo (1860–1917) and Dane Rudhyar (1895–1985), established the foundation for a series of theories and practices which encompass spiritual and personal development, self-knowledge, and evolutionary consciousness. Leo declared:

> Today my whole belief in the science of the stars stands or falls with Karma and Reincarnation, and I have no hesitation in saying that without these ancient teachings, Natal Astrology has no permanent value. The law which gives to one soul a nativity of good environment in which refinement, opportunity, and sound moral training are uppermost; and to another poverty, disease, and immoral training, is manifestly unjust to say the least, apart from its being without any apparent purpose.[20]

Alice Bailey, who was also deeply influenced by Theosophy, wrote about 'that intelligent will which links the [...] spirit with [...] the personality, functioning through a physical vehicle'.[21] Such ideas have been explicitly developed through the School of Evolutionary Astrology, founded by Jeffrey Wolf Green (originally as the 'Pluto School' in 1994). Green argues that 'the Soul is an immutable consciousness that has its own individuality or identity that remains intact from life to life'.[22] In his book *Pluto: The Evolutionary Journey of the Soul*, he argued that, in each lifetime, the 'Soul manifests a personality that has a subjective consciousness and unconsciousness', and each personality relates directly to the evolutionary necessities of the soul.[23] Each personality allows the soul to, 'experience life in particular ways in order to grow and evolve' and that 'each personality created is directly linked to the past evolutionary and karmic history of the soul'.[24] The evolutionary astrologer and therapist Mark Jones, who is influenced in turn by Green, suggests that 'the deep self is the true nature of psyche or soul' and 'the essence of the human being'.[25] Alan Oken, who is also deeply influenced by Bailey, argues that the soul 'is a collector of experiences [...] synthesizing the growth achieved, lessons learned, and lessons [still] to be learned from past lives'.[26] The theoretical movement of the soul from one life to another underpins the idea of reincarnation and, as Stephen Arroyo notes, it is inseparable from karma: one cannot be considered without the other.[27]

Among the Indian texts influential on western astrologers, including Jeffrey Wolf Green himself, is Paramahansa Yogananda's *Autobiography of a Yogi*. Yogananda reflected on the teachings of his guru, emphasising the purpose of reincarnation, indicating that 'you cannot work out your past karma without worldly experiences'.[28] Connecting karma and reincarnation with astrology, he claimed that, 'a child is born on that day and at that hour when the celestial rays are in mathematical harmony with his individual karma'.[29] Yogananda both reflects the inseparable nature of karma and reincarnation and infers a purpose and a plan to exactly when a child is born, and an incarnation begins. Oken refers to these points in time as '"appropriate" and karmically induced moments'.[30] Jeffrey Green argued that every soul, or every life, is unique and the reasons people come to astrology as either student or client, are as varied as the individuals themselves. Similarly, Mark Jones argues that the horoscope represents 'a unique being, with specific karma, and a specific set of issues and concerns' that underlie the purpose of the consultation.[31]

Robert Solomon suggests that life changing moments such as birth, marriage, financial crisis, war, natural disaster, and death are often perceived to relate to fate in connection with karma.[32] For Green, events such as these cause people to feel stress and confusion, often triggering those big life questions such as 'Why me?', 'Why this?', 'Why now?'.[33] He observes that while not everyone cares about karma, or about understanding themselves, 'they still want to know what they should be doing' and he attributes to Jung his claim that the 'prime role of the counsellor is to validate objectively the subjective reality of the client'.[34] The notion of karma or karmic influence then provides a potential answer to life's problems, offering the individual an explanation of their experience in life and a way to make sense of the challenges they face.

Understanding how one may have arrived in the circumstances of their life is just part of the picture relating to the '*Why?*' questions. Wadia also pondered the next step, at least partially. He considered that while the influence of karma determines the circumstances of one's life, and the qualities of that life are reflected in the horoscope, it is up to the individual 'to build [their] new karma within the limits of [their] environment'.[35] The notion of the individual contributing to, or influencing, an outcome leads to the contemplation of free will. Equipped with new self-knowledge or understanding raises a logical question, 'what can I do now?'.

Gansten argues that karma allows for the interplay of fate and free will, drawing on the prescriptive aspects of astrology and how the astrologer might practically apply these ideas relative to Soul.[36] From the perspective of the Soul-oriented practitioner, this is a task picked up by Mark Jones, who considers the natal chart to be a symbolic representation of karma.[37] He then uses the horoscope to understand the hidden forces driving both the personality and the Soul to gain an understanding of what circumstances may have existed in a prior life, in addition to the conditions in the current life.[38] From a therapeutic point of view, he notes that, without understanding the origin of a problem, it is not possible to begin to heal it and, by combining prior-life material with traditional astrological understanding, there is a significant dimension added to the work of healing.[39] In his practice, Jones aims to help the client 'identify and transform powerful internal conflicts [...] while acknowledging [the human] regenerative capacity for spiritual healing and soul evolution'.[40] In his book *The Soul Speaks*, he refers to the spiritual understanding of karma, stating 'there is no fate – there is only the expression of who you are'.[41] In effect, he is suggesting the individual is a product of all the incarnational experiences absorbed and assimilated by the Soul over many lifetimes. He refers to a passage from Yogananda's *Autobiography* where he describes the horoscope as 'a challenging portrait, revealing [the individual's] unalterable path and its probable future results'.[42] From Jones' point of view this unalterable path represents, at least in part, 'the deepest intentions of the Soul', symbolized in the horoscope by the planet Pluto (its placement and aspects), 'and the variety of prior life egos manifested by the soul in order to express' these intentions (reflected by the South Node of the Moon).[43] He argues that in the chart, from an evolutionary perspective, Pluto together with the nodal axis of the Moon (which indicates where its apparent path through the sky intersects with the Sun's) offers a picture of the individual's past orientation as well as their evolutionary intention.[44] In his view the location of Pluto in any horoscope 'provides the baseline understanding – the context – for the entire birth chart', offering an indication of the 'central evolutionary concerns stemming from deep within the soul'.[45] This characterizes the core psychological realizations from past events, those with the highest intensity which have significantly affected development of the self.[46] He asserts that the 'idea of intensity is of central importance: as the innermost psyche measures prior experience by impact not by duration'.[47] It is this intensity that reflects what has mattered most to the deep self of the individual and has markedly influenced the current life experience.[48] Jones refers to symbolic representations, arguing that 'the reality of the deep self is multi-dimensional [and] includes all past experience as well as potential for the future': it therefore includes memories or events from early childhood, life in the womb, or prior lives.[49]

Psychological Astrology

Reincarnation is sometimes considered literally, but at other times seems to be more metaphorical. In his paper 'A Critical Review of Reincarnational Astrology', Glenn Perry argued that, as Brady had concluded, the astrologer's own world view conditions their interpretative model, writing that 'past life claims in astrology [...] reflect the metaphysical convictions of the practitioner'.[50] To this end he is cautious about the use of karma and reincarnation and expresses ethical concerns about practicing astrologers who use definitive statements about an individual's past lives and suggests the importance of acknowledging the speculative nature of what he terms 'reincarnational astrology'.[51] He added that 'Astrology [...] is more than a belief system; it is a service and a product'.[52] In other words, the point is to work for the client. [53] To consider the astrologer's approach in this respect we might refer to Rudhyar's view on the purpose of astrology which he said,

> ... is not so much to tell us what we will meet on our road, as it is to suggest how to meet it – and the basic reason for the meeting. Which quality in us, which type of strength is needed to go through any specific phase of our total unfoldment as an individual person.[54]

From Rudhyar's perspective, two primary functions are identified. First, the delineation of factors associated with soul; and second, the practical application of those factors. His perspective infers that what underpins the astrologer's work is their particular approach to the horoscope, and the individual's current needs and phase of development. Stephen Arroyo, who is deeply influenced by Rudhyar, embraces this view and clearly states his belief that 'the individual's experience is foremost'.[55] Arroyo followed Rudhyar's humanistic approach to astrology, placing the interests and concerns of the individual at the centre of astrological interpretation, and refers to the birth-chart as 'a whole, unified, living symbol', representing the individual as a 'living unit of divine potential'.[56] In this worldview, everything and everyone is connected, each material object and living being co-existing as part of a much greater whole.[57] Arroyo argues that the individual arrives in this incarnation with a primary life pattern revealed symbolically through the natal chart, indicating the soul's present fate or karma.[58] In his book *Astrology, Karma & Transformation*, he talks about 'the deeper meanings, the inner dimensions, and the growth-oriented experiential level of interpretation'.[59] Arroyo considers that 'almost any factor [in the chart] can be regarded as karmic' and those karmic patterns reveal the conditions the individual will meet to 'provide the exact spiritual lessons' they must work with in this incarnation.[60] From his perspective, astrology provides a map of the individual's challenges, talents, attachments, behaviours and mental tendencies, making it possible for them to face their destiny in a constructive and beneficial way.[61] He considers astrology 'as a tool for spiritual and psychological growth'.[62] In his view, it is one's attitude towards events that determines the outcome of their experiences, the results of which are realized by either self-growth or some degree of suffering.[63] Each individual therefore has the power to choose their attitude and commit to acquiring self-knowledge which, as Arroyo suggests, will assist them in 'becoming a more illuminated soul'.[64]

Arroyo's approach focuses on the urge toward self-transformation, dispensing with the negative references that might be associated with fate.[65] He also contends that the ultimate purpose for the individual soul is not to achieve any particular freedom in this life, and that the current incarnation is only a necessary part of the soul's journey towards illumination. From his point of view, a person's attitude towards their experience is the crucial factor in determining whether they will grow by meeting difficult experiences and learning the intended lessons.[66] Although Arroyo considers the chart from a holistic perspective, he considers the planet Saturn, noting that it is often referred to as the 'Lord of Karma', since its position and aspects within the horoscope often reveal where the individual meets their most specific and focused challenges, resulting in frustration and grief.[67] Although the whole horoscope reveals the individual's karma, Saturn has a special role, as emphasised by Liz Greene. In her book *Saturn*, Greene suggests that this planet indicates certain challenges which do not seem connected with any personal flaw or fault on the part of the individual, they just seem to happen.[68] Saturn, as 'Lord of Karma', she suggests, provides the avenue for each person to gain 'eventual freedom through self-understanding'.[69] She goes on to say that free will must be earned through a path of self-discovery, a course of action which is not generally contemplated until circumstances reach a point where it is too painful to remain static; so, one must 'consider their own character and behaviour for the purpose of pursuing self-knowledge to initiate change'.[70] Liz Greene offers her perspective on the astrologer's view of fate, based on her experience, both as a psychologist and an astrologer. In her book, *The Astrology of Fate*, she argues that something definitely exists,

> whether one calls it fate, Providence, natural law, karma or the unconscious – that retaliates when its boundaries are transgressed or when it receives no respect or effort at relationship, and which seems to possess a kind of "absolute knowledge" not only of what the individual needs, but of what he is going to need for his unfolding in life.[71]

She goes on to say that she does not pretend to know what 'it' is, although she is open to calling it fate and considers that if it was better understood, 'we might be of far greater assistance to our clients' as well as ourselves.[72] In other words, the astrologer's proper function is to help the client. In Jones' view the goal of 'astrological counselling is to help generate the energy required by the individual to resist the gravitational pull of the past', symbolized by Pluto in the chart.[73] He is also adamant that one must remain grounded in the material reality of the individual.[74] Consultation with the client must be a two-way dialogue to provide contextual relevance and to ensure the focus is on the individual not the astrologer or astrological technique. As Christina Rose observed, 'the act of interpreting a birth chart is only of limited value unless the client can be involved in that process' and then guided in ways where that information is useful and can be practically applied.[75] Arroyo is similarly concerned, identifying the astrologer as someone who is looked upon as a helpful guide or counsellor.[76] He believes that it is the quality of the work and the level of consciousness that matters most, suggesting that astrology is not 'something self-contained and isolated' but instead must be seen within the helping professions as part of counselling.[77] Further, he notes that without application to an individual or a specific situation, the full potential of astrology cannot be realized.[78]

For the astrologers I have discussed, some commonalities are apparent: first, each of them has an explicit interest in the well-being of their clients; second, they each have a less rigid view of the concept of fate, allowing them flexibility to facilitate the spiritual evolution and psychological development of their clients on a case-by-case basis; third, they each refer to the presence of karmic influence symbolically represented in the horoscope; and finally, they consider astrology as a tool in their practice, which they seem to strongly align under the label of 'the helping professions'. Additionally, underlying each practice is either the acceptance or openness to the notion of the soul's teleological nature, as evidenced by references to evolutionary intent and an onward journey.

And finally, as to the question of whether the soul itself is described in the horoscope, and what the implications are, opinions differ. Mark Jones says that 'people are not bound by Astrology', the natal chart is 'simply a reflection of what has occurred for the individual up to this point, and therefore what potentialities might manifest beyond this point', both for the individual life and the continuing journey of the soul.[79] Arroyo's perspective adds to this, indicating that the horoscope is a map to assist the individual on their road of self-discovery and self-realization.[80] The higher purpose of astrology, he says, 'is not to try and change one's destiny, but rather to fulfil it through growing in awareness'.[81]

In conclusion, whether defined as 'immutable consciousness', 'intelligent will', the 'breath of life', or 'the essence of the human being', in particular strands of psychological astrology, the idea of soul provides a conceptual thread running through psychological and soul-based astrology, stringing together a collection of beads representing memories, experiences, events, circumstances, and opportunities, all common to the individual's lived experience. If, as some astrologers have suggested, the soul is a container of all its experiences, then the entire narrative of that story forms the basis of the astrologer's work. Whether psychological or spiritual, the evolution of the soul is linked to the individual in the current incarnation through an expression of its unique personality, as Jeff Green suggested. We might then consider that the astrologer is a co-facilitator in the soul's onward journey, as Rudhyar suggested, helping the individual to meet the challenges on the road and to find a way forward. With this in mind, the notion of seeking control in one's life and the idea of negotiating with fate becomes, instead, a process of participation to create and broaden the scope of meaningful choices. Ultimately, in some forms of modern psychological astrology the soul is considered both a facilitator and enabler, since tasked with certain experiences it must, in the usual course of life, interact with other souls. It is not operating within a solitary remit and as it engages in any karmic or life event there will be implications extending beyond its own karmic history, including the connection with the astrologer.

Notes

1. Bernadette Brady, *A Place in Chaos* (Bournemouth: The Wessex Astrologer, 2006), p. 111.
2. Brady, *A Place in Chaos*, p. 111.
3. Brady, *A Place in Chaos*, p. 111.

4.   Liz Greene, *The Astrology of Fate* (Newburyport, MA: Red Wheel/Weiser LLC, 1987), p. 2.

5.   Nicholas Campion, *Astrology in World Religions* (New York: New York University Press, 2012), p. 16.

6.   Bernadette Brady, 'Theories of Fate Among Present Day Astrologers' (unpublished doctoral thesis, University of Wales Trinity Saint David, 2011), p. 290.

7.   Campion, *Astrology in World Religions*, p. 17.

8.   James Hillman, *Re-Visioning Psychology* (New York: Harper & Rowe, 1975), p. xvi.

9.   Brian Clark, *From the Moment We Met* (Stanley, AUS: Astro*Synthesis, 2018), p. 7; also see Diogenes Laertius, 'Zeno' in *Lives of Eminent Philosophers*, trans R.D. Hicks (London: William Heinemann, 1925), vol. 2, pp. 110-263, VII 156-7.

10.   Claudius Ptolemy, *Tetrabiblos*, trans. F.E. Robbins (Cambridge, MA: Harvard University Press, 1940), III.13.

11.   Hendrick Lorenz, 'Ancient Theories of Soul', in Edward N. Zalta , ed., *The Stanford Encyclopedia of Philosophy* (Summer 2009 Edition), at https://plato.stanford.edu/entries/ancient-soul/ (accessed 23 August 2021). Nicholas Campion, 'Astronomy and Psyche in the Classical World: Plato, Aristotle, Zeno, Ptolemy', *Journal of Cosmology* 9 (2010): pp. 2179–86; Nicholas Campion, 'Astronomy and the Soul', in Anna-Teresa Tymieniecka and Atilla Grandpierre, eds, *Astronomy and Civilisation in the New Enlightenment*, Analecta Husserliana (The Yearbook of Phenomenological Research), Vol. CVII (Heidelberg: Springer, 2011), pp. 249–57.

12.   Plato, *Phaedrus*, trans. H.N. Fowler (Cambridge, MA, and London: Harvard University Press, 1914), 246A, 253 C-D; Plato, *Republic*, 2 Vols, trans. Paul Shorey (Cambridge, MA, and London: Harvard University Press, 1937), X, 611 D, 612 A; Plato, *Timaeus*, trans. R.G. Bury (Cambridge, MA, and London: Harvard University Press, 1931), 41D-E.

13.   Aristotle, *On the Soul*, trans. W.S. Hett (Cambridge, MA, and London: Harvard University Press, 1936).

14.   Thomas Aquinas, *Summa Contra Gentiles*, 4 Vols, trans. Vernon J. Bourke (Notre Dame, IN: University of Notre Dame Press, 1975), III.84.14; John North, 'Celestial Influence – the Major Premiss of Astrology', in *Stars, Minds and Fate: Essays in Ancient and Medieval Cosmology* (London: The Hambledon Press, 1989), pp. 243–98.

15.   Marsilio Ficino, *Meditations on the Soul* (Rochester, VT: Inner Traditions, 1996).

16.   H.P. Blavatsky, *The Key to Theosophy* (1889; London: Theosophical Publishing House, 1987), pp. 33-34, pp. 46–47.

17.   Robert C. Solomon, 'On Fate and Fatalism', *Philosophy East and West* 53, no. 4 (October 2003): p. 451.

18.   Martin Gansten, 'Reshaping Karma: an Indic Metaphysical Paradigm in Traditional and Modern Astrology', in Nicholas Campion, ed., *Cosmologies* (Lampeter: Sophia Centre Press, 2010), pp. 52–68. See also Martin Gansten, 'Patterns of Destiny' (unpublished doctoral thesis, Lund University, 2003), pp. 4–6.

19.   A.R. Wadia, 'Philosophical Implications of the Doctrine of Karma', *Philosophy East and West* 15, no. 2 (1965): p. 151.

20.   Alan Leo, *Esoteric Astrology: A Study in Human Nature*, (1913; London: Modern Astrology, 1925), p. vii.

21.   Alice Bailey, *A Treatise on Cosmic Fire* (1925; New York: Lucis Publishing Company, 2012), p. 46.

22.   Jeffrey Wolf Green, *Pluto: Volume 1: The Evolutionary Journey of the Soul* (Bournemouth: The Wessex Astrologer, 2011), p. 1.

23.   Green, *Pluto*, p. 1.

24. Green, *Pluto*, p. 1.

25. Mark Jones, *Healing the Soul* (Portland, OR: Raven Dreams Press, 2011), p. 10; Mark Jones, *The Soul Speaks* (Portland, OR: Raven Dreams Press, 2015), p. 16, p. 29.

26. Alan Oken, *Alan Oken's Complete Astrology-The Classic Guide to Modern Astrology* (1980; 1988; Berwick, ME: Ibis Press, 2006), p. xvi.

27. Stephen Arroyo, *Astrology, Karma & Transformation* (1978; Sebastopol, CA: CRCS Publications, 1992), p. 4.

28. Paramahansa Yogananda, *Autobiography of a Yogi* (1946; 1988; Los Angeles, CA: Self Realization Fellowship, 2012), p. 39.

29. Yogananda, *Autobiography of a Yogi*, p. 39.

30. Alan Oken, *Soul Centered Astrology: A key to Your Expanding Self* (Lake Worth, FL: Ibis Press, 2008), p. 88.

31. Jones, *Healing the Soul*, p. 21.

32. Solomon, 'Fate and Fatalism', p. 451.

33. Green, *Pluto*, p. 2.

34. Green, *Pluto*, p. 3.

35. Wadia, 'Implications of Karma', pp. 150–51.

36. Gansten, 'Reshaping Karma', p. 53.

37. Jones, *Healing the Soul*, p. 13.

38. Jones, *Healing the Soul*, back cover.

39. Mark Jones, 'About Evolutionary Astrology', at https://www.plutoschool.com/about/evolutionary-astrology [accessed 26 July 2020]; Jones, *Healing the Soul,* p. 11.

40. Jones, *Healing the Soul*, back cover.

41. Jones, *The Soul Speaks*, p. 28.

42. Yogananda, *Autobiography of a Yogi*, p. 182.

43. Jones, 'About Evolutionary Astrology'.

44. Jones, *Healing the Soul*, p. 97.

45. Jones, *Healing the Soul*, p. 23.

46. Jones, *Healing the Soul*, p. 24.

47. Jones, *Healing the Soul*, p. 10.

48. Jones, *Healing the Soul*, p. 10.

49. Jones, *Healing the Soul*, p. 10.

50. Glenn Perry, 'A Critical Review of Reincarnational Astrology', at <http://aaperry.com/ reincarnational-astrology/> (accessed 3 January 2019).

51. Glenn Perry, 'Reincarnational Astrology', p. 2.

52. Perry, 'Reincarnational Astrology'.

53. Campion, *Astrology in World Religions*, p. 17.

54. Dane Rudhyar, *Person Centered Astrology* (Santa Fe, NM: Aurora Press, 1981), p. 9.

55. Arroyo, *Karma & Transformation*, p. 256.

56. Arroyo, *Karma & Transformation*, p. xi.; James R. Lewis, *The Astrology Book: The Encyclopedia of Heavenly Influences* (Detroit, MI: Visible Ink Press, 2003), p. 558.

57. Lewis, *Astrology Book*, p. 558.

58. Arroyo, *Karma & Transformation*, p. 7.

59. Arroyo, *Karma & Transformation*, p. x.

60. Arroyo, *Karma & Transformation*, p. 9.

61. Arroyo, *Karma & Transformation*, p. 3, p. 9.

62. Arroyo, *Karma & Transformation*, p. 256.

63. Arroyo, *Karma & Transformation*, p. 8.

64. Arroyo, *Karma & Transformation*, p. 8.

65. Arroyo, *Karma & Transformation*, p. 256.

66. Arroyo, *Karma & Transformation*, p. 7.

67. Arroyo, *Karma & Transformation*, p. 9.

68. Liz Greene, *Saturn: A New Look at an Old Devil* (1977; Newburyport, MA: Red Wheel/Wiser LLC, 2011), pp. 10–11.

69. Greene, *Saturn,* pp. 10–11.

70. Greene, *Saturn,* pp. 10–11.

71. Greene, *Fate,* p. 8.

72. Greene, *Fate,* p. 8.

73. Jones, *Healing the Soul,* pp. 23–26.

74. Jones, *Healing the Soul,* p. 14.

75. Christina Rose, *Astrological Counselling: A basic guide to astrological themes in person-to-person relationships* (Wellingborough: Aquarian Press, 1982), p. 15.

76. Arroyo, *Karma & Transformation,* p. 239.

77. Arroyo, *Karma & Transformation,* pp. 241–42.

78. Arroyo, *Karma & Transformation,* pp. 241–42.

79. Jones, 'About Evolutionary Astrology'.

80. Arroyo, *Karma & Transformation,* p. 246.

81. Arroyo, *Karma & Transformation,* p. 246.

8

CHARLES CARTER, MARGARET HONE AND PSYCHOLOGICAL ASTROLOGY

Laura Andrikopoulos

The rise of psychology and psychoanalysis in the twentieth-century forms the backdrop to the claim that the twentieth century brought a new form of Western astrology, one which has been labelled 'psychological astrology'.[1] Roy Willis and Patrick Curry, as well as Nicholas Campion, agree that this branch stemmed from both the work of the Theosophist and astrological reformer Alan Leo (1860–1917) at the beginning of the twentieth century, along with the influence of the psychologist Carl Gustav Jung (1875–1961), and that it was developed by a series of astrologers in the English-speaking world including Charles Carter (1887–1968), Dane Rudhyar (1895–1985), Liz Greene (1946–) and Stephen Arroyo (1946–).[2] Margaret Hone (1892–1969) has also been identified as a key twentieth-century psychological reformer, particularly by Alison Bird and Bernadette Brady.[3]

Of all these astrologers I will address Charles Carter and Margaret Hone, both of whom were prominent in British astrology. Charles Carter was one of the founders of the Faculty of Astrological Studies (FAS) in 1948 in London, one of the most established and influential private schools of astrology in the English-speaking world, becoming its first Principal; Margaret Hone, another of the four co-founders, also later became its Principal between 1954 and 1959.[4] As such, it is natural to consider their work together. Both post-date the reformation of Alan Leo whilst pre-dating the heyday of psychological astrology from the 1970s to the 1990s, in which it was common to interpret astrological birth-charts in a fully psychological manner.[5] This chapter will examine Carter and Hone's work, considering how and why the work of each adopts psychology and the depth psychology of Carl Jung, before considering the extent to which their interpretations may be considered psychological.

Adopting Psychology

Psychology may broadly be defined as a means of explaining the human mind and related behaviour: in other words, it prioritises the inner life.[6] Psychological astrology then fuses astrology with psychology as an explanation for human mental processes and behaviour. Charles Carter's approach to astrology was partly psychological in the sense that he did not always assert that astrology dealt with the inner life. He saw astrology as a practical science, which, he wrote, 'studies certain predispositions or tendencies in human life, which are sometimes indicated so clearly that they become virtual certainties'.[7] He was clear that astrology does not involve any form of psychism, by which he meant psychic ability or mediumship; for Carter, astrology belonged in the realm of science in the broadest sense, either being a causative science or a science of correspondences.[8]

One of Carter's first books was *An Encyclopaedia of Psychological Astrology*, a mixture of significations for both character and disease which was first published in 1924, and was still being reprinted in 1976.[9] Some of the interpretations address psychological concerns, attributing them to astrological factors. For example, in his discussion of the problem of an explosive manner, Carter claimed this is due to 'Mars-Uranus afflictions, or to afflictions in fixed signs, especially if Mercury or the Moon be affected'.[10] (afflicted at this time meant the square or opposition aspect approximately 90 and 180 degrees respectively between two planets as observed from the Earth). There is psychology here of a rather deterministic kind, suggesting that the horoscope still implies fate, but simply of a psychological kind, so that if the individual has such a Mars-Uranus aspect, they will have an explosive temper and there is little they can do about it.

Whilst Carter did not spend a great deal of time discussing psychology in his astrology books, there are occasional glimpses of his awareness of its importance. In a particularly clear passage, when he had been considering whether the astrological aspects (precise distances between planets, usually measured in the zodiac) have either an inner or an outer meaning, he stated:

> I find that the only satisfying belief is, that environment is a reflection of the Inner, either as it is or was, so that, though an aspect may seem quite foreign to our character and only appropriate to our external conditions, in reality both correspond.[11]

This is a very important statement. Carter turned to an inner, or psychological, perspective for philosophical reasons, having recognised that psychology plays a vital role in how the environment is experienced. It is only natural that what was previously thought in astrology to correspond to a mixture of both character and circumstance, might in fact relate back to character at the root and in the new version the external reflected the internal rather than being in a reciprocal relationship with it. Significantly, the individual has the freedom to make a difference, as can be seen in a late musing on how to deal with the planet Saturn:

> A good response to Saturn... is one of the best features that a map can display. So long as conscientious work, prudence, punctuality, common-sense, and temperate and well-controlled habits have any worth, so long will Saturn, rightly understood and interpreted in our lives, be a planet of the utmost value.[12]

Thus, the individual is actually able to choose how to respond to Saturn and embrace the positive qualities of the planet, thereby making the most out of it: the 'response to Saturn' is therefore located in the domain of the psychological.

Margaret Hone, Carter's successor as the Principal of the Faculty of Astrological Studies, was keen to stress that astrology is derived from a conception of the universe working as a whole: it is, she wrote, 'a unique system of interpretation of the correlation of planetary action in human experience'.[13] She added that it had been suggested that a more modern name for astrology is 'The Cosmic Correlation Theory'.[14] She rejected the idea of actually changing the name but approved of the idea underlying it, and asserted that astrologers should make use of statistics to show the validity of the correlations.[15] She was acutely aware, however, of wider cultural and legal problems in light of astrology's continuing reputation as 'fortune-telling' and the associated Witchcraft Act of 1735 and the Vagrancy Act of 1824.[16] She offered some pragmatic advice to the astrological practitioner:

> The entire basis of astrology rests on the premise that the 'pattern' of a person correlates with the planetary pattern of his birth-moment. The pattern will, at times, exteriorise as 'events'. The accuracy of these, which can be checked in earlier life, gives the astrologer the belief that tendencies deduced from calculations of future dates may be expected to eventuate as certain types of happenings in later life.

> Until these Acts are altered, the astrologer is advised to preface all his remarks with a statement which shows that he realises the position, and conforms with the law of his country in making it plain that he is not dogmatically stating that events will happen, but that, from his point of view, the likelihood is that tendencies of a certain nature may bring about results of that nature.[17]

The introduction of the emphasis on 'likelihood' and 'tendency' addressed two concerns. On the one hand they reflected a philosophical viewpoint, that astrological symbols take a variety of expression and therefore no particular event can be forecast from one particular symbolic pattern. On the other hand, they are absolutely necessary to avoid any charge of fortune-telling and of predicting the future. Encapsulating her view of astrology as a means of reading the quality of a moment of time, Hone appealed to a phrase from Carl Jung:

> A great phrase was moulded by C. G. Jung, the psychologist, when he wrote: 'Whatever is born, or done, in this moment of time, has the qualities of this moment of time'. Here is the secret of astrology. It lies in the understanding of TIME, and time guards its secrets.[18]

For Margaret Hone, if modern astrology was to be bound up with psychology, then fortune telling in the sense of simple prediction is no longer an option: that the individual's behaviour and outer life events are linked to the inner awareness of their psyche means that precise events cannot be predicted:

> In modern times, with the growth of psychology, it is found that the astrological natal chart is the key to those deeper urges and drives which are the very core of a man and which give the clue to the understanding of the psyche as a whole. It is realised that the quality of certain *trends and periods* in a life may be assessed by the chart, but that to attempt to make a shot at foretelling actual events is only likely to bring disbelief on what is an interpretative and deductive art, *not a system of fortune-telling*. It is true that precise prediction is sometimes successful, but who can say how much of this is due to the astrologer's innate intuition or even to flashes of precognition?[19]

Hone's adoption of psychology, whilst beginning with an awareness of the legal risks associated with an astrology that focuses on event prediction, developed into an embrace of a psychological perspective on the birth-chart for philosophical reasons.

Intimations of Depth Psychology

Depth psychology and psychoanalysis both include the idea of the unconscious in their model and treatment of the psyche.[20] Jung's own depth psychology rests on a model that emphasises the interplay between the conscious and unconscious parts of the psyche, with the resulting tension producing a process he called

Individuation, which is a psychological journey:

> In general, it is the process by which individual beings are formed and differentiated; in particular, it is the development of the psychological *individual* as a being distinct from the general, collective psychology. Individuation therefore is a process of *differentiation*, having for its goal the development of the individual personality.[22]

Intimations of depth psychology may be glimpsed within Carter's philosophical presentation of astrology. By 1954 he had inserted an entry into the latest edition of his *Encyclopaedia of Psychological Astrology* for 'Inferiority Complex'. He himself noted he had been obliged to include it by the tide of cultural change, writing that 'this term is so commonly used nowadays that it calls for special mention'.[23] Carter claimed that feeling inferior could be a particular problem should there be a bad Saturn in the horoscope and possibly also due to problems with Neptune; he stated that 'astrological treatment would take the form of endeavouring to stimulate the normal action of the positive planets, by meditating on their significance and purpose'.[24] That is, the individual is able to influence their fate through conscious reflection on their psychological tendencies, thereby changing the expression of the planetary pattern in their horoscope. He also added entries on 'Introversion and Extroversion', terms which Jung had made popular in his book *Psychological Types*.[25] Other additions were 'ego' and 'unconscious'. For example, in discussing the signs of the zodiac Carter related them to the ego's journey: under Taurus he wrote:

> the ego has veritably discovered the wonders and delights of the external world, beginning with its own body.[26]

Such a conception of the signs, as part of the ego's unfolding journey through the zodiac and houses (the term in astrology used to denote how a chart is made up of areas signifying different areas of a person's being or life), foreshadows later work in psychological astrology, such as that of Howard Sasportas, co-founder of the Centre for Psychological Astrology, writing in the 1980s and 1990s, in which the individual is imagined as on a journey.[27] Carter himself was aware of the idea of the unconscious, and occasionally brought this into his discussion. When writing of the astrological aspects (the term used for the angular relationships between planets and other points in a horoscope), he stated:

In judging these matters it is necessary to remember that we see but a part of each individual, and only a little even of ourselves. The great ocean of the unconscious underlies the conscious, as the visible iceberg but a fraction of the whole.[28]

He also referred to the unconscious as part of his interpretation of the opposition aspect:

The Opposition is a passive configuration. It tends to make the native an instrument in the hands of others, either conscious or unconscious.[29]

Carter's forays into psychoanalytic thought, though, are dispersed throughout his work and not presented as an integrated whole. Margaret Hone, however, took the psychoanalytic influence a stage further in her assertion that whereas previously astrology had focused on physical events, it should now focus on the inner motivation of human beings. She saw this as the most important factor in producing a modern form of astrology:

Whereas, in even more material days than the present, astrology was used in relation to purely physical happenings, it is now realised that many happenings in a man's life are concurrent with certain psychological states, which in turn spring from an inner motivation. It is the study of man, from this point of view, which is perhaps the strongest trend in MODERN ASTROLOGY.[30]

For Hone, being modern is equivalent to being psychological, and advances in psychological understanding cannot be ignored. If the things which happen to human beings often relate to inner, psychological factors rather than to an external fate, then it is vital that astrology moves to a more psychological focus. Hone took the growing awareness of psychology in society and overtly expressed it in a new conception of planetary influence:

It may be true that the planets do have this direct effect on human beings... from the point of view of psychology, a more modern expression of the same truth is that each planet seems to represent in the person, a certain drive or urge in the unconscious. He is subject to its compulsion but the more he becomes consciously aware of it, the better he can deal with it, for the sake of attaining his own self-understanding and his resultant ability to become a happy member of society.[31]

The planets are now redefined as unconscious drives and urges. The astrological pattern for each individual is then seen as part of the deeply unconscious layer of his, her or their psyche. The expression of this pattern may still appear as fate, unless the individual becomes conscious of the operation of the pattern, and of each planet. This, then, is the task of modern astrology: to develop psychological awareness in order to free the individual from fate, achieved through the autonomous effort of the individual to become more conscious. Such a conception is not necessarily related to the wider notion of one's place in the cosmos or the destiny of the soul. It does, however, have a beneficial impact on society, with Hone having claimed that an increase in self-understanding is important to producing happy members of society. The avoidance of fate as the crucial rationale for the practice of astrology came through Hone's understanding of the main lesson of depth psychology:

> The great lesson of modern "depth psychology" is that neuroses and psychoses arise from those things in ourselves which we refuse to face and accept. If suppressed, they remain in the unconscious but break out in some other form to hurt us.[32]

Astrology thus becomes a means of mitigating the hurtful outbreaks of unconscious activity that stem from being unaware. It becomes a tool for the modern individual to take charge of their life and fate through increased psychological self-understanding.

Astrological Interpretations

For Hone, the understanding of the psyche as conscious and unconscious meant that outward behaviour stems from inner processes, 'it is then realised', she wrote, 'that outward behaviour is the result of inner urges and that it is therefore natural that the same astrological significator applies to both'.[33] This understanding led to a psychological form of interpretation. For example, a progression (a term used for a method of forecasting which moves planets through the zodiac from their position at the birth of the individual by one day for every year of life) of the Sun to Saturn in the second house (associated with finances) of the natal chart might then mean something as follows:

> For two years, this person will be driven to try to compensate for a lack which he feels. It is intolerable to him to feel inferior and mean-spirited because, through financial stress, he cannot show himself as the big-hearted, generous person he wishes to be.[34]

Whilst this interpretation does show awareness of psychological understanding such as ideas of compensation, a sense of lack, and feeling inferior, it does not offer a truly dynamic means of the individual dealing with the particular movement. Instead, they simply experience these feelings for two years. Although Hone embraced Jung's work in theory, there is no significant integration of it into her astrological interpretations.which contained a combination of psychological and non-psychological factors. For example, she stated that the Sun placed in the seventh house of the horoscope (associated with relationships and marriage) indicated a 'successful marriage', apparently regardless of one's inner processes.[35] Elswhere, though, she did point to the importance of inner processes. For example, the Sun placed in the twelfth house indicated, 'a secluded start to life and an ability to use the unconscious side of the psyche'.[36] The twelfth house itself represents the unconscious.[37] There is always a certain determinism in circumstances to which the indivdual must respond. For example, the movement of the planet Saturn over the position of Venus in the natal chart is seen as 'a limitation or denial of love or happiness'.[38]

In general, Hone's new astrological system was based around reducing each planetary meaning to a few psychological keywords, to enable a student to easily learn and understand astrological interpretation, asserting that this is a 'new method of teaching'.[39] An example of this method may be seen in the keywords for the planet Mars, whose 'true meanings' were given as combative, constructive and courageous, whereas its negative meanings, arising from 'overstress or misuse' were a tendency to be aggressive, angry, cruel and destructive.[40] The crux is that Mars, even though it can also symbolise an outer event, always possesses psychological meanings and may take either positive or negative expression. It is this psychological meaning that is always present, lying behind any event.

Conclusion

Charles Carter and Margaret Hone were both important to the development of psychological astrology. Their careers as astrologers overlapped, both being founders of the Faculty of Astrological Studies, and both claim that astrology is broadly a science and generally reject any form of psychism. Their embrace of psychology stems in the main from philosophical reasons, as they both recognised that the developing science of psychology had demonstrated that what happens to a person is intimately related to their character and psychological dynamics. The spectre of prosecution for fortune-telling is, however, also a factor, and is addressed explicitly by Hone.

Charles Carter's works evidence some psychological terms being adopted, such as 'Inferiority Complex', 'Introversion', 'Unconscious' and 'Ego', although Hone's work demonstrated an increased level of integration as she argued the planets were drives and urges in the unconscious. Both discussed what they saw as an important tenet of depth psychology: that suppressed parts of the personality erupt into outer events and fate. As such the astrologer has the key task of helping an individual come to greater awareness of hidden parts of the personality, thereby helping the individual attain a greater level of freedom of what appears to be fate.

In their interpretations, both Carter and Hone oscillate between greater and lesser degrees of psychological sophistication. Deterministic interpretations are found in both, as are tantalising glimpses of ideas that would go on to become the standard, such as one end of an astrological opposition likely operating as unconscious. Carter and Hone's work may be seen as on the cusp of the depth psychology revolution in astrology, and offers glimpses into what would later become dominant narratives for interpreting astrological birth-charts.

Notes

1.   Patrick Curry and Roy Willis, *Astrology, Science and Culture* (Oxford: Berg, 2004), p. 72.
2.   Curry and Willis, *Astrology, Science and Culture*, p. 72; Nicholas Campion, 'Prophecy, Cosmology and the New Age Movement: The extent and nature of contemporary belief in astrology', PhD thesis (Bath Spa University, 2004), p. 111, pp. 117–18.
3.   Alison Bird, 'Astrology in Education: An Ethnography' (PhD thesis, University of Sussex, 2006), p. 123; Bernadette Brady, 'Theories of Fate among Present-day Astrologers' (PhD thesis, University of Wales: Trinity Saint David, 2011), p.169.
4.   See www.charlescarter.co.uk (accessed 30 May 2021); Margaret Hone, *The Modern Textbook of Astrology* (London: LN Fowler, 1951).
5.   See, for example, Liz Greene and Howard Sasportas, *Dynamics of the Unconscious* (York Beach, ME: Weiser, 1988); Darby Costello, *The Astrological Moon* (London: CPA Press, 1996).
6.   Thomas Hardy Leahey, *A History of Psychology, Sixth Edition* (New Delhi: Pearson, 2013), p. 113.
7.   Charles Carter, *The Principles of Astrology* (London: Theosophical Publishing House, 1963), p. 13.
8.   Carter, *Principles of Astrology*, p. 14.
9.   Carter, *Encyclopaedia of Psychological Astrology*.
10.   Carter, *Encyclopaedia of Psychological Astrology*, p. 70.
11.   Carter, *Astrological Aspects* (London: Ascella, 1930), p. 12.
12.   Carter, *Essays on the Foundations of Astrology* (London: Theosophical Publishing House, 1978), p. 37.

13. Hone, *The Modern Textbook of Astrology* (London: LN Fowler, 1951), p. 16.

14. Hone, *The Modern Textbook of Astrology* (London: LN Fowler, 1951), p. 16.

15. Hone, *Modern Textbook*, p. vii.

16. Hone, *Modern Textbook*, p.15.

17. Hone, *Modern Textbook*, p.15.

18. Hone, *Modern Textbook*, p. 17; Carl Gustav Jung, 'Richard Wilhelm: In Memoriam', in Collected Works, vol.15 *The Spirit in Man, Art and Literature* (London: Routledge, 1966), p.56. See also Carl Gustav Jung, *Letters Volume 2 1951-1961*, trans. R.F.C. Hull (Hove, Sussex: Routledge, 2011), p. 176.

19. Hone, *Modern Textbook*, p. 287.

20. Peter Homans, *Jung in Context: Modernity and the Making of a Psychology*, Second Edition (London: University of Chicago Press, 1995), p.xv.

21. Carl Gustav Jung, *The Archetypes and the Collective Unconscious, Second Edition*, trans. R.F.C. Hull (London: Routledge, 1990), pp. 288–89.

22. C. G. Jung., 'Definitions', *Psychological Types,* The Collected Works, Vol. 6, trans. R. F .C Hull (London: Routledge and Kegan Paul, 1971), para 757.

23. Charles Carter, *An Encyclopaedia of Psychological Astrology* (London: Theosophical Publishing House, 1963), p. 107.

24. Carter, *Encyclopaedia of Psychological Astrology*, p. 108.

25. Carl Gustav Jung, *Psychological Types*, trans. H.G. Baynes (London: Routledge, 1991), p. 148.

26. Carter, *Foundations of Astrology*, p. 112.

27. See Howard Sasportas, *The Twelve Houses* (London: Thorsons, 1985).

28. Carter, *Astrological Aspects*, p. 12.

29. Carter, *Astrological Aspects*, p. 9.

30. Hone, *Modern Textbook*, p. 17.

31. Hone, *Modern Textbook*, pp. 19–20.

32. Hone, *Modern Textbook*, p. 262.

33. Hone, *Modern Textbook*, p. 299.

34. Hone, *Modern Textbook*, p. 299.

35. Hone, *Modern Textbook*, p. 150.

36. Hone, *Modern Textbook*, p. 151.

37. Hone, *Modern Textbook*, p..95.

38. Hone, *Modern Textbook*, p. 246.

39. Hone, *Modern Textbook*, p. 21.

40. Hone, *Modern Textbook*, p. 29.

9

THE DEVELOPMENT OF THE HOROSCOPE COLUMN
AND ITS RELATIONSHIP WITH WOMEN'S MEDIA

Kim Farnell

Introduction

This chapter examines the origins of the modern astrological horoscope column, which became a widespread and familiar feature of the print media in the twentieth century. All commentators until now, such as Nicholas Campion, have placed it in the 1930s.[1] However, my research indicates that the true date is earlier and needs to be understood in the context of women's magazines.

According to Campion, the definition of a horoscope column is that it comprises:

> Twelve paragraphs, one for each of the approximate thirty-day periods when the sun occupies each of the signs of the zodiac... These 'horoscopes' are based on brief readings for individuals born with the sun in the respective signs of the zodiac and consisting of a combination of generalised advice and prediction.[2]

In modern astrology, horoscope columns tend to be seen as women's fare and readers are often described as 'obsessed' with reading them.[3] This is in contrast to the male 'avid' football fan (for example) who might be equally as eager to read the latest match results.[4] Numerous polls have indicated that more women say they believe in astrology than men.[5] Similarly, Shoshanah Feher notes that women are 'overrepresented in astrological communities' and that Nicholas Campion that 'Ninety per cent of the students at the average astrology class are female, and while glossy magazines aimed at women all carry astrology columns, none aimed at men carry them'.[6]

Accepted Origins of the Horoscope Column

The accepted heritage of the horoscope column is that it emerged 24 August 1930 when R.H. Naylor wrote a column for the *Sunday Express* about the new-born Princess Margaret.[7] Along with the analysis of the Princess's birth chart, Naylor added general political predictions and comments based on readers' dates of birth. A flood of appreciative letters persuaded the editor of the *Sunday Express* to commission a feature, 'Were You Born in September?', for the following Sunday. This too was well received and Naylor began to write a series of articles entitled 'What the stars foretell for this week' from October 1930. Its positive reception led to further astrological features and the idea was adopted by most of the press.[8]

The *Sunday Express'* rival *The People* featured a column written by Edward Lyndoe, emulating Naylor's format, from 1 October 1933.[9] The *Sunday Dispatch* sought the services of William J. Tucker whose column first appeared in September 1936.[10] One by one, all the national press took up similar features. And at this point in the story it is usually noted that women's magazines adopted the horoscope column as a regular feature, for example, 'By 1940 an astrology column with personal forecasts was appearing in every mass-circulation Sunday newspaper, in most women's magazines'.[11]

Naylor himself did not use the twelve-sign format we are familiar with today until he wrote an eight-page pull-out for *Prediction* magazine in January 1936.[12] The twelve-sign format that indicated the signs rather than simply referring to dates appears to have first appeared in the US magazine *Your Destiny* in 1932, an earlier date than generally given.[13] For example, Nicholas Campion states that the first such column appeared in *American Astrology* in 1933.[14] However, I contend that the horoscope column developed earlier than Campion and others have suggested.

Newspaper Origins

Horoscope columns have featured in the press since the late nineteenth century, albeit in a different form.[15] For example, from February 1894 the *Boston Post* carried a column that had originated in its sister paper the *Sunday Post*. It was advertised as written by a woman astrologer, illustrating how such columns occupied women's space in papers from an early date. The content was general in nature without reference to zodiac signs.[16]

> Monday—In the early morning the predominating influence is beneficial, and unless those operating In thy nativity forbid, thou mayest transact and undertake matters of importance, such as writing, signing contracts, executing important documents, etc., favorable for seeking employment, dealing with the scientific, literary and educational classes; later in the day the influences are less favorable... [17]

That such columns were regular features in the press is attested by the satirical content that appears from time to time. For example, in 1895 the *Scranton Tribune* carried 'Told by the Stars', a 'daily horoscope' by 'Ajacchus' (jackass).[18] This was a regular column that continued until at least 1902.[19]

> A child born on this day will be handsome at times, but will look sweetest when photographed in a Kirmess costume. A girl will possess an amiable disposition during the ice cream season...[20]

Also from 1895, offers of free horoscopes began to appear alongside astrology columns to attract readers:

> Every Saturday in this column, we will give the correct horoscopes of all persons who will send us the minute, hour, day and year on which they were born. Astrology is a fascinating study, and the Courier-Journal will tell your past and future free of charge.[21]

By 1901 columns regularly appeared that carried predictions for the upcoming week, often also citing the relevant planetary ruler of the day.[22] The earliest column I have so far found that uses the heading 'daily horoscope' occurred in the *Buffalo Times* in 1907.[23]

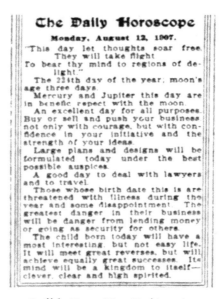

Figure 1: *Buffalo Times* (New York) 11 August 1907

This column ran until November 1926 and it is an example of astrological columns originating from the McClure syndicate, the main suppliers of unattributed astrology press columns. McClure horoscopes changed little in content over the next few years and can generally be identified by the tagline 'The stars incline, but do not compel'.[24]

Attributed columns were primarily written by (or at least, credited to) women and increased in number during the 1920s, focusing around those who had their birthday on the date under consideration. For example, Doris Blake's columns appeared in New York's *Daily News* until 1923; the following example is from 1922.[25]

If your birthday is today you are
PRACTICAL
You are intensely interested in the practical things of life. You have to fight this side of your nature to get the best out of life. Even when you marry it will be done after a practical, common sense deliberation in which romance does not have to be dominant. You are inclined to melancholy at times, as too much of the practical and not enough of the lighter vein will eventually make one.

Figure 2: *Daily News* (New York) 2 January 1922

The earliest twelve-sign column I have so far found in US newspapers appears in the *Clinton Times-Tribune* of 10 January 1935.[26]

Although my search has so far focused on US newspapers, similar columns appeared in the British press.[27] However, the twelve-sign format we are familiar with today wasn't a given when horoscope columns became more popular. For example, Adrienne Arden's column in the *Sunday Mirror* provides an example of an alternative format whereby the seven-division grouping is according to the zodiac sign's planetary ruler, rather than the sign itself.[28] This means that five of the divisions cover two zodiac signs, with 'Sun Subjects' and 'Moon Subjects' covering the zodiac signs of Leo and Cancer respectively.

The majority of horoscope columns in both US and UK newspapers were placed in the women's section of the paper, next to items perceived to be of

DAILY ASTROLOGICAL GUIDE

Forecast for Friday, January 11

ARIES– for those born March 21 to April 19.

Commencing 10:45 a., m., ruler Mars. Energetic but confused. Your position is good today, but you endanger it.

TAURUS for those born April 20 to May 21.

Commencing 10:45 a., m., ruler Venus. Keep everything to yourself today, and act as little as possible. You are feeling your power, but this is not a time to impress it.

GEMINI for those born May 21 to June 21.

Commencing 10:45 a., m., ruler Mercury. Yesterday's energies produce today's nervousness. Friends are irritating. Don't believe anything you hear.

Figure 3: *Clinton Times-Tribune* (Oklahoma), 10 January 1935

What the Stars Say

Seven-Day Forecast By Adrienne Arden

SUN SUBJECTS

(All Birthdays July 22-August 21)

HOME life should be highly stimulating this week, if you can get over the difficult patch which you may experience to-day.

There is a chance of some new work or interest materialising within the next day or two. You also seem to have an opportunity presented to you to test out an impression or plan which you have been turning over in your mind.

Wednesday is likely to be an eventful day so far as your daily occupation is concerned.

You should be able to make wonderful progress with any job you have in hand then.

Relationships with the opposite sex will call for more than the average amount of tact.

MOON SUBJECTS

(All Birthdays June 21-July 21)

IF you are puzzled by any problem in your personal or business affairs, or if you are seeking fresh fields of endeavour, reserve your full fire for Tuesday this week.

You should then be able to make headway at a better pace. Self-confidence will be strong by mid-week, and you can expect a good deal of co-operation from friends and close associates.

The end of the week emphasises your health —don't make too many demands on your nervous system. Remember that unnecessary anxieties fritter away your strength.

JUPITER SUBJECTS

(All Birthdays November 22-December 20 and February 19-March 20)

PERSONAL relationships tend to loom large in the week that is opening for you. Possibly you will meet some old friends. At any rate the stress is laid on companionship, which should be entertaining and helpful.

By mid-week there is a difficult patch in the business outlook. You will need to exercise a little additional care and understanding to navigate this successfully.

Home interests to-day should be dealt with quietly; too much display or domination would lead to immediate upsets

THIS WEEK'S BIRTHDAYS

Much happiness is gained through friends by readers whose anniversaries fall to-day and Tuesday. It will not be easy, however, to increase the weekly income.

Birthdays to-morrow and Thursday show advance gained from unexpected sources. Monday's subjects, however, will find it more difficult to choose their own methods. Fate seems to take a hand and over-rule their destinies.

Wednesday anniversaries mark a year of tremendous activity.

For Friday's birthdays there is a great deal of change and new possibilities.

Plenty of thrills and enjoyment are in store for the fortunate readers who have their birthday on Saturday. For the unattached there is almost certainly a romance.

MARS SUBJECTS

(All Birthdays March 21-April 20 and October 23-November 22)

SOME important news reaches you, and you are very much interested in the new situation to which it refers.

Something may happen which will exasperate you, but you must keep your own counsel, as no good would come of hasty words just now.

For trying out new plans and also for important interviews select Wednesday.

An opportunity occurs later which would allow you to strengthen your position.

Readers whose business brings them into direct touch with the public should have an extremely favourable spell.

MERCURY SUBJECTS

(All Birthdays May 21-June 20 and August 22-September 22)

DON'T expect too much to come from aggressive tactics this week. However strong your attempts are to get going with anything like the speed you would wish they seem to be fated to misfire.

Home and friendship ties are important. Where feelings run high make some concession—it should be worth the sacrifice.

This is not a "peak week" for any of your interests. In almost all your undertakings your best policy would be to pursue your way quietly. You will be tempted to skip the details of your work, but these are the very things that, if handled badly at this time, would trip you up.

SATURN AND URANUS SUBJECTS

(All Birthdays December 21-January 19 and January 20-February 18)

YOUR private affairs gain a definite ascendancy.

You find yourself directing great interest to domestic, friendship or family ties. It is a highly propitious time for both entertaining and visiting friends.

The outlook connected with your daily tasks is a stirring one. It looks as though you will be kept very busy to cope with the demands that are made on you.

VENUS SUBJECTS

(All Birthdays April 21-May 20 and September 23-October 22)

YOUR creative abilities are strongly accentuated. Try making new things, beginning new undertakings. People will be both interested and interesting.

There is scarcely any element of dullness in your immediate prospects.

The most difficult period comes about mid-week, when there will probably be a clash of opinions.

Romantic interests are also emphasised, but it is towards the week-end that they reach their highest point.

Figure 4: *Sunday Mirror* (London), 14 March 1937

interest to women readers (for example, fashion) and attributed (when by-lined) to a woman astrologer.[29] In other words, horoscope columns were seen as being part of a woman's world from an early stage. Therefore, it was natural to associate them with women's media in general.

Women's Magazines

The history of women's magazines has been well documented (most notably in Cynthia White's book *Women's Magazines*).[30] However, only recently has detailed attention been paid to their content. In her thesis, 'Domestic Culture in Woman's Weekly, 1918-1958', Eleanor Reed examines the content of *Woman's Weekly* in detail to ascertain its readers' interests and aspirations, pointing out the inclusion of astrology in *Woman's Weekly* from 1928 and discussing horoscopes' mass popularity in the 1930s being related to the prospect of war.[31] Reed also points out that cosmology appears to have been especially popular amongst working-class women in interwar Britain.[32] This is supported by the amount of space allocated to horoscopes in different magazines aimed towards different audiences surveyed by Reed, who notes that a lack of interest in horoscope columns is associated with aspirations to lower-middle-class culture.[33] The wordage and placement of horoscope columns in women's magazines could potentially be highly revealing in terms of the importance and credibility or otherwise placed on such content by the magazine and warrants further examination.

It is clear that astrological columns had long been a feature of women's magazines before they were ubiquitous in newspapers, although they didn't follow the twelve sign format. For example, *Peg's Paper*, one of the first women's magazines aimed at working-class women, included horoscopes from 1928.

Far from being vague and woolly, these early columns often used very specific astrological language.

> Mercury the messenger is affected by Mars... tempers will be very touchy today and there will be many misunderstandings, think well before making any decisions from 7pm to 8pm... If you were born near the 26 February or August some deceit threatens, avoid going on the water today.[34]

Peg's Paper featured a number of psychic columnists in the late 1930s, including agony aunt Madame Sunya, who answered readers' questions about their (mostly romantic) futures, clairvoyant Nell St John Montague, who considered the influence of semi-precious stones over readers' love lives, and Gypsy Holmes,

Figure 5: *Peg's Paper*, 16 September 1924

who explored the significance of names. Other publications, such as *Woman's Weekly,* devoted only a quarter of a page to considering horoscopes.[35]

The introduction of colour weeklies in the 1930s, along with the continuing high sales of penny weeklies, meant that for the first time women's magazines reached a mass audience.[36] By the 1930s, a third of British women worked outside the home and the growing number of women working in offices and factories had created a new market for magazines which was met by the launch of numerous titles.[37] It has commonly been noted that magazine reading is a collective practice for young women, a practice that does not apply to young men.[38] This practice extends into adulthood, and the horoscope column provided ideal material for such shared reading practices along with the problem page. It is notable that, both in newspapers and women's magazines, the horoscope column is commonly placed next to the problem page, and on some occasions there is an overlap of content.

Three titles led the pack: *Woman's Own* (1932), *Woman's Illustrated* (1936) and *Woman* (1937), although older titles such as *Woman's Weekly* (1911) remained popular and adapted to the new formats.[39] *Woman*, for example, was launched in June 1937 and within a year was selling 500,000 copies a week.[40] In addition, sales figures for women's magazines vastly understate their readership and therefore potentially their influence. Jonathan Bignell points out that it is commonly accepted that women's magazines are read not only by their purchaser but by between five and fifteen other readers as well.[41] All of these magazines carried horoscope columns.

Figure 6: *Peg's Paper,* 26 December 1936

Astrology, along with clairvoyance, palmistry and card reading were featured regularly in early 1930s women's magazines as a sales point. For example, *Lucky Star* on 7 September 1935 offered a free fortune teller's ring, the column 'Confessions of a Hollywood Fortune Teller' written by Nell St John Montague, and a clairvoyant's problem page.[42] *Miracle* magazine in February 1935 offered a free zodiac necklace.[43]

Figure 7: *Lucky Star,* 7 September 1935

Some titles didn't carry a column, such as *Good Housekeeping* which denounced them as 'indefinite and vague' in 1939.[44] Those magazines that did sometimes squeezed the columns into a half page between advertisements and part of a story, and sometimes made a feature of them.[45]

Figure 8: *Betty's Paper*, 6 April 1933

Personality and character were often linked during the era when advertising and editorial was adopting a psychological approach. For example, a 1924 advertisement in *Home Chat* used language that would be familiar to modern-day horoscope readers to describe a beauty product:

> Girls! Here is a chance to get to know yourselves. What are your powers – what are your weaknesses? For what position in life does your personality fit you?... Think what it would mean to know! – you would understand yourself better... You would be equipped with a knowledge of your gifts and an explanation of your failures. You would cultivate Character – and with it Beauty.[46]

This psychological tone that became increasingly widespread during the period created a space in which popular astrology and the horoscope column fitted perfectly.[47] The language change can be seen as part of a bigger trend, but the adjustment of the base content of newspaper horoscope columns from focusing on (for example) business matters and offering instruction to family matters and relationship issues focused on emotions may be related to the content of columns in women's magazines and warrants further investigation. For example, a typical 1928 column in the New York *Daily News* states:

> The first half of today can be disastrous for those who insist on saying just what they think. Avoid extremes of conduct and hasty conclusions.[48]

In the 1930s, the same publication carried the following:

> Keep a strict check on your emotions today, don't do anything foolish, and all will be as well as could be expected. Be especially on guard against the self-indulgent type of error. Socially poor in evening.[49]
> Tomorrow. Keep your emotions valuable by keeping them friendly. Avoid anger.[50]

The reverse also took place. As astrology became big business, rather than filler for women's pages, women astrology columnists in women's magazines were replaced by famous male astrologers from the national press – for example, Edward Lyndoe became the astrologer for *Woman* a few months after its launch in October 1937.[51]

Little attention has been paid to the development of the horoscope column and its relationship with women's media. The horoscope column has been frequently described as rubbish and women's rubbish at that.

> Anyone with any sense knows that this newspaper horoscope rubbish is only for mugs to read.[52]

> When the Astrological Association came into being, I urged that it was the moment for serious astrologers to declare loudly and insistently their opposition to the rubbish in the tabloids and women's magazines.[53]

> Astrology which still persists to-day in the women's magazines, so that anyone who is sufficiently credulous (and what woman is not?) may consult the stars...[54]

Figure 9. *Woman*, 19 October 1937

It is also associated with a low-class audience. A recent shift has led to associating horoscope columns with the LBGTQ community, but the dismissive tone remains the same.[55]

Conclusion

Until now it has been universally assumed that the origins of the modern horoscope column lie in the 1930s. However, it now appears that they began a good forty years earlier, in the mid-1890s, most notably in the American press, where such columns are common. Newspaper astrology columns then increased in frequency in the 1920s at the same time as they became common in women's magazines. The relationship between women's media and the changing language of modern popular astrology is clearly significant and there is an emerging story which could seriously illuminate our understanding of early twentieth century social relations.

Notes

1. Nicholas Campion, *Astrology and Popular Religion in the Modern West* (London: Ashgate, 2012), p. 76.
2. Nicholas Campion, 'Prophecy, Cosmology and the New Age Movement: The Extent and Nature of Contemporary Belief in Astrology' (unpublished doctoral thesis, Bath Spa University College, 2004), p. 132.
3. See, for example, Daisy Buchanan, 'Why so many intelligent, educated women are obsessed with reading horoscopes', *The Telegraph* (1 January 2015), at https://www.telegraph.co.uk/women/womens-life/11319415/Horoscopes-Why-educated-women-are-obsessed-with-star-signs.html (accessed 10 December 2019).
4. See, for example, *footyfacts*, at http://www.footballstatisticsresults.co.uk/ (accessed 10 December 2019), which is dedicated to the 'avid' football fan.
5. Chava Gourarie, 'Why are horoscopes and media a match?', *Columbia Journalism Review,* 3 March 2016, at https://www.cjr.org/analysis/horoscopes_astrology.php (accessed 10 December 2019).
6. Tracy Thornton, 'Ideas of Order: The Meaning and Appeal of Contemporary Astrological Belief' (unpublished MA thesis, University of Oregon, 2016), quotes Shoshanah Feher, 'Who Holds the Cards? Women and New Age Astrology', in James R. Lewis and J. Gordon Melton, eds, *Perspectives on the New Age* (Albany, NY: State University of New York, 1992); Nicholas Campion, *A History of Western Astrology Volume II* (London: Bloomsbury, 2009), p. 279.
7. Campion, 'Prophecy, Cosmology and the New Age Movement', p. 142.
8. Chelsea Rischel, 'Princess Margaret's Role in the Creation of the Modern Horoscope, *Independent,* 19 February 2021, at https://www.independent.co.uk/life-style/royal-family/princess-margaret-astrology-horoscope-zodiac-b1804806.html (accessed 17 July 2021); Rae Orion, *Astrology for Dummies* (London: Wiley, 2001), p. 55; Claudia Baldoli, Andrew Knapp and Richard Overy, *Bombing, States and Peoples in Western Europe 1940-1945* (London: Bloomsbury Academic, 2011), p. 160.
9. The *People* (London)*,* 1 October 1933, p. 16.
10. Ellic Howe, *Astrology and the Third Reich* (Wellingborough: Aquarian Press, 1984), p. 69,
11. Geoffrey Dean and Arthur Mather, 'Sun Sign Columns', *Astrology and Science*, at https://www.astrology-and-science.com/S-hist2.htm (accessed 9 January 2020).
12. *Prediction* (London), January 1936.
13. *Your Destiny* (New York), January 1932.
14. Nicholas Campion, *Astrology and Popular Religion in the Modern West* (London: Ashgate, 2012), p. 76.
15. For example, *Boston Post* (Boston, Massachusetts), 21 January 1894; *St. Louis Globe-Democrat* (St. Louis, Missouri), 31 January 1894; *Topeka Daily Capital* (Topeka, Kansas), 2 February 1894; *Lake Charles Commercial* (Lake Charles, Louisiana), 3 February 1894; *Pittsburgh Post-Gazette* (Pittsburgh, Pennsylvania), 1 May 1894; *Nashville Banner* (Nashville, Tennessee), 5 January 1895; *Los Angeles Evening Express* (Los Angeles, California), 7 December 1895; *Courier-Journal* (Louisville, Kentucky), 9 February 1895; *Inter Ocean* (Chicago, Illinois), 21 March 1897.
16. *Boston Post* (Boston, Massachusetts), 25 February 1894, p. 23.
17. *Boston Post* (Boston, Massachusetts), 25 February 1894, p. 23.
18. For example, the earliest so far found, *Scranton Tribune* (Scranton, Pennsylvania), 11 March 1895, p. 4.
19. For example, *Scranton Tribune* (Scranton, Pennsylvania), 7 June 1902, p. 4.

20. *Scranton Tribune* (Scranton, Pennsylvania), 15 March 1895, p. 4.

21. *Courier Journal* (Louisville, Kentucky), 2 February 1895, p. 10.

22. For example, 'What the stars predict', *Cincinnati Enquirer* (Cincinnati, Ohio), 7 April 1901, p. 29.

23. *Buffalo Times* (Buffalo, New York), August 1907, p. 2.

24. For example, *News Tribune* (Tacoma, Washington), 29 February 1908; *Harrisburg Telegraph* (Harrisburg, Pennsylvania), 1 January 1913; *MC Times Recorder* (Zanesville, Ohio), 28 February 1913; *Sacramento Star* (Sacramento, California), 10 March 10, 1913; *Buffalo Times* (Buffalo, New York), 3 January 1920; *Akron Evening Times* (Akron, Ohio), 7 January 1920; *San Bernardino County Sun* (San Bernardino, California), 11 January 1922; *Fort Wayne Sentinel* (Fort Wayne, Indiana), 25 January 1922.

25. *Daily News* (New York), 2 January 1922, p. 33.

26. The *Clinton Times-Tribune* (Oklahoma, Illinois), 10 January 1935.

27. For example, the *Halifax Evening Courier*, 1 March 1927; *Dundee Courier*, 12 September 1929; *Leicester Chronicle*, 29 August 1931.

28. Adrienne Arden, 'What the Stars Say', *Sunday Mirror*, 14 March 1937, p, 34.

29. Non-bylined and without acknowledgement to a syndicate columns appeared in *Lincoln Star* (Lincoln, Nebraska), 9 February 1920; *Sioux City Journal* (Sioux City, Iowa), 1 January 1921; *Miami News* (Miami, Florida), 17 January 1927 [on the women's page]. Non-bylined columns appeared on the women's page in the *Chicago Tribune* (Chicago, Illinois), 2 December 1921; *Dayton Herald* (Dayton, Ohio), 8 April 1922; *Times Union* (Brooklyn, New York), 27 November 1921; *Evening Star* (Washington, District of Columbia), 2 November 1926; and the *Evening Star* (Washington, District of Columbia), 1 January 1927. McClure horoscopes appeared in the *Vancouver Sun* (Vancouver, British Columbia), 1 January 1920 and see note 20 above. News Syndicate horoscopes appeared in the *Daily News* (New York, New York), 6 Oct 1929. Columns credited to women include those by Elsa Allen, *Brooklyn Daily Eagle* (Brooklyn, New York), 23 April 1922, and the *San Francisco Examiner* 26 February p. 24; by Genevieve Kemble, *Dayton Daily News* (Dayton, Ohio), 29 Apr 1920; *Dayton Herald* (Dayton, Ohio), 1 January 1925 and *Arizona Daily Star* (Tucson, Arizona), 2 February 1923 [on the women's page]; Doris Blake (Antoinette Connelly), in the WP *Daily News* (New York, New York), 31 October 1921 [on the women's page]; and Mary Blake, in the *Miami News* (Miami, Florida), 25 July 1925, and the *Missoulian* (Missoula, Montana), 24 January 1928. During this period, I have found no horoscope columns bylined with a male name.

30. Cynthia White, *Women's Magazines, 1693–1968* (London: Michael Joseph, 1970).

31. Eleanor Reed, 'Domestic Culture in *Woman's Weekly*, 1918-1958' (unpublished doctoral thesis, University of Roehampton, 2018).

32. Reed, 'Domestic Culture in *Woman's Weekly*, 1918-1958', p. 150.

33. Reed, 'Domestic Culture in *Woman's Weekly*, 1918-1958', p. 346.

34. *Red Star Weekly*, 13 July 1932.

35. Reed, 'Domestic Culture in *Woman's Weekly*, 1918-1958', p. 150.

36. Fiona Hackney, 'They Opened up a Whole New World': Feminine Modernity and Women's Magazines, 1919-1939' (unpublished doctoral thesis, Goldsmith's College, University of London, 2010), p. 187.

37. 'British Labour Statistics Historical Abstract 1886-1968: Table 109', quoted on Office of National Statistics, at https://www.ons.gov.uk/aboutus/transparencyandgovernance/freedomofinformationfoi/annualpercentageofemployedwomenintheuk (accessed 17 July 2021); and Cynthia White, *Women's Magazines, 1693–1968* (London: Michael Joseph, 1970).

38. For example, see Mary Jane Kehily, 'More Sugar? Teenage magazines, gender displays and sexual learning', *European Journal of Cultural Studies* 2, no. 1 (1999): pp. 65–89, at http://www.brown.uk.com/brownlibrary/SUG.htm (accessed 9 January 2020).

39. Hackney, 'They Opened up a Whole New World'.

40. 'Magforum', at http://www.magforum.com/womens_weekly_magazines.html (accessed 10 December 2010).

41. Jonathan Bignell, *Media Semiotics: An Introduction* (Manchester: Manchester University Press, 1997), p. 58.

42. *Lucky Star,* 7 September 1935.

43. *Miracle,* 16 February 1935.

44. St. John Irvine, 'Tell Your Fortune, Lady?' *Good Housekeeping,* February 1939, p. 20.

45. Reed, 'Domestic Culture in *Woman's Weekly,* 1918-1958', p. 151.

46. Hackney, 'They Opened up a Whole New World', quotes *Home Chat,* 3 May 1924, p. 131.

47. Hackney, 'They Opened up a Whole New World', quotes *Home Chat,* 3 May 1924, p. 131.

48. *Daily News* (New York, New York), 25 June 1928, p. 6.

49. *Daily News* (New York, New York), 2 January 1932, p. 210.

50. *Daily News* (New York, New York), 1 January 1934, p. 28.

51. *Woman's Own,* 9 October 1937.

52. Bradford Observer (Bradford), 29 September 1938, p. 3.

53. Dennis Elwell, *Astrological Journal,* January 1991, pp. 6–16, quoted at Dean and Mather, 'Sun Sign Columns'.

54. *Chelmsford Chronicle* (Chelmsford), 1 December 1950, p. 3.

55. Hannah Ewens, 'Why Straight Men Hate Astrology So Much, *Vice,* 2018, at https://www.vice.com/en/article/qvq87p/why-straight-men-hate-astrology-so-much (accessed February 2021).

10

SPATIO-TEMPORAL REPRESENTATIONS AND THE
LANGUAGE OF ASTROLOGY

Crystal Eves

The word 'astrology' is an umbrella term encompassing many different traditions of looking to the sky for information about life on Earth. Claire Chandler offers the following definition:

> Astrology is a rich, sophisticated, symbolic language that can be used to explore a wide variety of areas: it is the study of the nature of time as measured by the motions of the planets.[1]

Chandler's definition reflects a linguistic understanding of astrology, one that Nicholas Campion has found to be a common characterization among students and practitioners of the craft.[2] Whether astrology has a right to claim this characterization when evaluated by linguistic standards is the initial aim of my research. My second aim is to explore the lived-experience of a select group of highly experienced and active Canadian astrologers in order to learn how they mentally represent time. The rationale for this exploration extends from the findings of the psycholinguistic researcher Lera Boroditsky and her colleagues, whose work has demonstrated that distinct language knowledge and usage can correlate with distinct time conceptualization and processing.[3]

The Study of Astrology and its Adherents

Astrology, its practice and practitioners, has been studied academically from many angles. Early studies sought to understand who adhered to this ancient practice, and labelled the astrological adherent as both marginalised and potentially susceptible to authoritarian rule.[4] Subsequent studies contradicted such assertions of marginality, instead characterizing keenly interested adherents as predominantly female, well-educated and employing astrology in order to navigate uncertain times.[5] Recent research has also examined the philosophical and religious beliefs held by students and practitioners of astrology, their notions

145

of fate, and the lived experience of learning the craft.[6] The act of reading an astrological chart has been characterised as a conversation with the divine, and chart delineation has been likened to a creative experience.[7] Other studies have explored astrology's representation on the Internet, its defence against polemics, and its truth claims have also been studied.[8] Whereas much of the previous research focused on investigating those who engage with astrology, why they reach for it, and what occurs in the process, my study aims to add something novel, by looking at whether engagement with astrology, by what Radermacher calls 'attentive astrologers, those who practice intensively', correlates with conceptualizations that occur outside of the practice of the craft; specifically, how time is represented in the mind. [9]

Time and Astrology

As far back as the Greek classical period, time was being discussed in relation to planetary movements.[10] In the modern day, the concept of time remains interwoven with the field of astrology. Notable to this study are: the concept of spiral development over time, exemplified by, but not limited to, the ideas of Dane Rudhyar (1895–1985); and the notion of qualitative time, suggested by Carl Jung (1875–1961) and rooted in the Greek concept of *kairos* all of which will be discussed at more length below.[11]

Spiral development over time

References to spirals abound in astrological writing. Astrologers Max Heindel (1865–1919), Alan Leo (1860–1917), A.T. Mann, Jinni Meyer and Joanne Wickenburg, have all written about the importance of spirals in astrology.[12]

Dane Rudhyar, who, according to Patrick Curry, was one of three people who 'most influentially developed the psychological "school" of astrology', puts forth ideas that overlay spirals with personal growth.[13] Rudhyar's view, according to Bernadette Brady, was that, 'each person moved toward a sense of personal wholeness via a spiral path of repeating cycles'.[14] Rudhyar felt that personal development was cyclical, stating, 'Life is a process and every process is cyclic'.[15] As he explained in personal correspondence, 'Cyclic development is not in terms of circles, but of spirals'.[16] For Rudhyar, 'Astrology is a study of cyclic processes', and 'The study of cycles is a study of time'.[17] Given these comments, as well as others such as, 'Astrology, as we know it, deals essentially with the measuring of time', it is easy to infer that Rudhyar is saying time itself is spiral in nature. [18] Whether Rudhyar intended this conflation of spiral development with time being spiral is uncertain. What *is* certain is that this understanding is a natural conclusion for astrologers to reach. Brady says that the 'notion of emergent spiral time' derived from Rudhyar, is a notion that 'was evident' in the responses she obtained from astrologers in her own research.[19] In semantic terms, it should be noted that a spiral can either be a two-dimensional curved line moving increasingly away or toward a point, or a three- dimensional helix or coil.[20] It is therefore important, when speaking of spirals, to clarify the reference.

Time as kairos

The Canadian psychoanalyst and sociologist Elliott Jaques (1917–2003) adopts the classical Greek division of time into two types: *chronos* – ordinary clock time – and *kairos* , 'seasonal time, the time of episodes with a beginning, middle and an end'.[21] When the Greek physician Hippocrates (ca. 460–ca. 370 BCE) said, 'Every kairos is a chronos, but not every chronos is a kairos', he was, as Sipiora and Baumlin wrote, capturing the idea that only certain times are thematically opportune or appropriate, in otherwords, can be seen as *kairos*.[22]

The notion of certain times being specifically opportune for some purpose has been connected to astrology since Mesopotamian times.[23] Carl Jung, who studied astrology, presents a version of this theory when he writes, 'It is not the apparent positions of the stars which work, but rather the times which are measured or determined by arbitrarily named stellar positions. Time thus proves to be a stream of energy filled with qualities'.[24] Jung later changed his thinking, saying 'Qualitative time. This is a notion I used formerly but I have replaced it with the idea of synchronicity'.[25] Despite this retraction, the concept of *qualitative time* persists in astrological literature, as is evidenced when Charles and Suzi Harvey stated, 'Astrology… deals with the ever-changing qualities of time'.[26] Not all astrologers feel that this is the proper use of Jung's concepts: Maggie Hyde for example.[27] Nevertheless, it is the case that astrologers will consider certain periods of astrologically-determined time to be thematically meaningful, or as Brady says, 'embedded with a quality', adding that astrologers will consider 'the future time' as *Kairos* – containing this type of embedded quality.[28]

I am therefore highlighting two ways in which time has been considered within astrology. The first is spiral development and growth over time, illustrated by the work of Dane Rudhyar and others. The second is *kairos*, time that is thematically encoded, appropriate, or opportune for some specific purpose. Should either of these models of time be present in the time conceptualizations of my sample group, then it would constitute a potential link between astrological concepts and the mental representations of time within this sample of astrologers.

Psycholinguistics and Time

Psycholinguistics is the study of 'the mental and neural processes as well as the behavior associated with language'.[29] One area of research covered by the field of psycholinguistics is the concept of Linguistic Relativity, which has roots in the Sapir-Whorf hypothesis, a theory which proposes that, 'the words and structures of a language can affect how the speakers of that language conceptualize or think about the world'.[30] Although Linguistic Relativity is regarded with scepticism by linguists such as Geoffrey Pullum, psycholinguistic research since the turn of the twenty-first century, particularly that out of the lab of Lera Boroditsky, has renewed interest in the idea that language interplays with how individuals conceptualize and process time.[31]

The time-related experiments of Boroditsky and her colleagues rest upon earlier widely accepted research noting the tendency of humans to use spatial metaphors when referencing the concept of time.[32] In 1973, Clark made the following observations:

> English descriptions of time appear to be based on a spatial metaphor in which time is viewed as a single dimensional, asymmetric continuum, running horizontally from front to back through the speaker. Furthermore, there appear to be two (not incompatible) movement metaphors:
>
> (1) The moving-time metaphor views events as moving forward (pastward) past a stationary ego, and
>
> (2) The moving-ego metaphor views the speaker as moving forward (futureward) past stationary events.[33]

A challenge to the unidimensional feature of Clark's model was put forth by psycholinguist Casasanto, who, noting that English speakers sometimes say they have 'oceans of time', asks, 'But is time necessarily conceptualized in terms of unidimensional space?'[34] Casasanto's objection, however, has limited validity as his example refers to quantities of time and Clark's model refers to passage of time. That one is correctly speaking to the issue of passage of time and not some other measure of time, is an important distinction that was carefully considered in the weighing of the results of this study.

Boroditsky and her colleagues have explored various ways in which language has a bearing on the processing and representation of time. Notably, in *Remembrances of Times East*, Boroditsky and Gaby documented an instance where distinct language knowledge correlated with a distinct mental representation of time.[35] Also of note, Lai and Boroditsky found that the time conceptualizations and temporal reasoning for bilingual speakers can be influenced by both known languages.[36] This is relevant because all interviewees in this study are English speakers who engage in the 'language' of astrology; should astrology be considered a language, one might expect that English language metaphors of time might comingle with astrological time metaphors.

Astrology as a Language

Studies have shown that high percentages of astrological practitioners consider their craft to be a language.[37] This characterization was also made by William Lilly, the renowned seventeenth-century astrologer, and by prominent twentieth and twenty-first century astrologers such as Liz Greene, Bernadette Brady, Dane Rudhyar, and Mike Harding.[38] That astrology is optimally characterized as a language, or has language features, is also the opinion of academics such as Ann Geneva, Alison Bird and Lindsay Radermacher.[39]

If astrology is a language, as many astrologers believe, it is not an alphabetic one because its graphic symbols, *glyphs,* do not correspond to sounds.[40] Instead, astrology's *glyphs* represent entire ideas which, according to Maria Mateus, makes them ideographic in nature.[41] An ideograph is 'a graphical symbol that represents an idea'.[42] Without direct correspondence to sound, ideographic languages are not spoken, and must be verbalized through a translation into a spoken language. It is the translation of astrology's ideographic symbols into meaningful interpretations that Bird believes to be astrology's linguistic feature. She says, 'the astrological enterprise of discerning meanings in the glyphs and symbols of a geocentric sky-map and translating these into everyday words is unarguably linguistically oriented'.[43] That astrology is often referred to as a language seems fitting considering that the word astrology stems from the root astro-logos and means: the word of the stars, or the logic of the stars.[44] Although many have characterized astrology's symbol system as a language, it does not necessarily follow that it satisfies the linguistic criteria to be considered so – those criteria are presented below.

Criteria for Language

According to Fasold and Connor-Linton, 'A precise definition of language is not easy to provide'.[45] One definition of language offered by Finegan and Besnier states that language is, 'A set of elements and a system for combining them into patterned sentences that can be used to accomplish specific tasks in specific contexts'.[46] A modification on that definition, by Fasold and Connor-Linton, defines language as 'a finite system of elements and principles that make it possible for speakers to construct sentences to do particular communicative jobs'.[47] In lieu of a definition of language, many linguists refer to Charles Hockett's (1916–2000) design features for human language.[48] A linguist anthropologist, Hockett listed thirteen characteristics of human language. Over time, Hockett's list has been trimmed to six necessary requirements for language. This trimmed list, compiled by Matthew Traxler, is presented here:

1. Semanticity – ability to communicate meaning either through the language's individual units or in longer expressions.

2. Arbitrariness – there is not necessarily a relationship between the actual object represented and the symbol used to represent it. That is to say, one word could just as easily be used to mean the same thing as another word.

3. Discreteness – components of the language are organized into a set of distinct categories with clear boundaries between the categories.

4. Displacement – the ability to communicate information about events not immediately in view.

5. Duality of Patterning – that we can simultaneously perceive language stimuli in multiple ways. One can perceive the symbol, for example, and then also perceive the meaning.

6. Generativity – a large number of messages can be created from a finite number of language symbols.[49]

According to Traxler, 'Language scientists agree that all of the preceding characterize human language'.[50] Satisfying these criteria is, therefore, required for a symbol system to be considered a human language. Whether it is sufficient is harder to determine because, as linguist Julie Sedivy mentions, it remains unknown which 'are the optional versus the obligatory aspects of language'.[51] According to Finegan, one feature of naturally occurring human language is that it is 'acquired without explicit learning'.[52] This does not apply, however, to written language, which must be learned explicitly. Finegan states, 'In every society, every ordinarily healthy human being knows how to speak; writing on the other hand, is an advanced technology, even a luxury, and it is not a luxury possessed by everyone'.[53] As there is no clear and agree-upon definition of language, all of the criteria presented above will serve as the linguistic standard by which the astrological symbol system will be evaluated.

Methodology

My own research took place in two phases. First, I evaluated astrology's symbol system in order to determine whether it might properly be considered a language by linguistic standards. In the absence of a strict and universally agreed definition of language, I evaluated astrology's symbol system against Traxler's essential short-list of Hockett's human language features. I considered known definitions for language and Finegan's ideas about implicit and explicit language learning were taken into account, while acknowledging that astrology's symbol system is ideographic in nature. Second, I conducted ethnographic research, interviewing seasoned Canadian astrologers who are actively engaged with astrology's symbol system, in order to gain insight into how they conceptualize time. My intention was to evaluate the resulting interviews against psycholinguistic findings regarding the interplay of mental representation and language. I distributed a call for interview volunteers to 138 email addresses in the June 2019 electronic newsletter of Astrology Toronto, a Canadian astrology organization headquartered in Toronto, Ontario, specifying that interviewees should have a minimum of five years' experience with astrology, and ongoing engagement with it. Thirty-minute telephone interviews were conducted with candidates who met the experience and engagement requirements, and were recorded, transcribed and coded for themes. One interview was provided in written form rather than verbally.

The interview questions included background and engagement information and specifically asked interviewees to describe their mental representation of how time passes; they were asked to visualize in their minds how they would represent the passage of time, and then asked to describe that picture. If the interviewee needed clarification of the question, they were provided the conventional example for English-speakers of time as a straight line.[54] This prompt was utilized to not unduly influence the interviewee to offer a representation other than that which would be normally expected in an English-speaking population. If they described time as a continuum or flow, they were asked to clarify whether in their model, future time moves toward them, or they move toward future time, these being Clark's standard metaphors of 'moving-time' or 'moving-ego'.[55]

Findings: Part One – Language Evaluation

Modern astrology has a codified system for reading the heavens, and employs symbols called *glyphs* to represent relevant features of the sky both real and calculated. These symbols have meanings and rules of application, can speak to almost any situation, and are used to communicate information. Whether this constitutes language by linguistic standards is explored below. As mentioned earlier, there are six language features present in all human language, for which there is consensus among linguists.[56] It follows that should astrology's symbol system *not* contain one of the preceding features then it may *not* be considered a human language. All six are considered in turn.

1. *Semanticity* – astrology's system does indeed convey meaning. The *glyphs* of its system represent sky features and relationships between them and, according to Brad Kochunas, the questions of what, how, and where, can be addressed using the elements of astrology.[57] That meaning is not only conveyed, but at potentially very deep levels, is expressed when Kochunas writes that, 'Astrology provides a framework for imagining a profound intimacy between ourselves and our environment'.[58]

2. *Arbitrariness* – astrology's symbols could very easily be represented by other symbols. For example, Pluto has two *glyphs* that are commonly used in contemporary Western astrology, each being equally valid in the system (♇and ⯓).[59] It does not matter which symbol is used to point to the concept of Pluto, they are both understood to mean 'Pluto'. Both Campion and Greene have pointed out that astrological symbols could be seen as embodying the qualities of that which they represent.[60] This fact may have presented a challenge to the notion of arbitrariness within the system, were it not for the existence of obvious counter-examples of dual representations such as for Pluto (shown above) and for the planet Uranus (♅ & ⛢).[61] The presence of these dual *glyphs* suggests that, even if the system has features that require specific *glyphs* only (i.e., may not and could not be represented by any other symbol), this requirement does not apply to the entire *glyph* system and arbitrariness is maintained. Furthermore, the English language has words that are expressly imitative of the sound they represent (onomatopoeic words) which might be considered somewhat analogous to any astrological *glyphs* that symbolically embody the astrological feature they represent.[62] Onomatopoeia exists in English and does not negate its satisfaction of the criterion of arbitrariness in that language, nor would the existence of embodied symbols for some features of the astrological system do the same.

3. *Discreteness* – each of the *glyphs* in astrology point to something specific, either a celestial feature (like a planet or asteroid) or a calculated sky feature (like angles between planets, or points in the

moon's orbit called nodes).[63] Illustrating discreteness: the symbol for a 180° angle between planets, ☍, called an opposition, is never considered to be the symbol for a 0° angle, ☌ , called a conjunction. The *glyphs* represent discrete concepts.

4. *Displacement* – the astrological system, through its rules and *glyphs*, is capable of making comments about cycles and situations in the present, the past, or the future, as evidenced by astrologers Marion March and Joan McEvers when they write, 'Through astrology you can always see yesterday, today and tomorrow'.[64] Astrologers use various techniques (such as secondary progression, solar arc direction and transits) to discuss future and current events, and March and McEvers write that, by working these techniques backward, one can also use the chart to discuss the past.[65] This ability to address issues and circumstances that are not in the present moment satisfies the criterion of displacement. In contrast to, for example, an animal barking, which is considered a vocal response to present moment circumstances.

5. *Duality of Patterning* – astrology's *glyphs* have duality of patterning in that one can perceive the symbol as a drawing on a page, while simultaneously considering it as meaning some sky feature (for example, the Moon), *and* considering what that sky feature symbolizes in the astrological system (the Moon, for example, symbolizing emotions).[66]

6. *Generativity* – astrology has the capacity to combine its *glyphs* in a variety of ways to yield completely different messages. For example, the *glyph* combination (♇ □ ☉), representing Pluto at a 90° angle (square) to the Sun, has a different meaning than the *glyph* combination (♇ △ ☉) representing Pluto at a 120° angle (trine) to the Sun. Both of these *glyph* combination meanings would then be modified if, to that combination, another planet and angle were added. For example, Pluto square to the Sun, with the Sun trine to Venus, (♇ □ ☉ △ ♀), would be interpreted in a slightly different way than Pluto square to the Sun without that Venus addition. Brady says that through, 'planets, aspects, houses and signs' a "million or so stories" can be told.[67] The possible combinations, and therefore the interpreted meanings, are almost endless, and as such the requirement of generativity is satisfied.

These characteristics are required for a symbol system to be considered a language and astrology's symbol system meets each one. However, that linguists find these characteristics necessary, does not mean they are sufficient. What can be said is that astrology's symbol system cannot be disqualified as a language on the basis of these criteria; an evaluation of other comments on features that frame language is also required.

When evaluating astrology in relation to Finegan's comments that spoken 'language rules are... acquired without explicit learning', astrology's system appears to fall short.[68] Humans do not simply come to know astrology; it must be studied to be learned. However, since astrology is ideographic, only appearing in written form until translated, its acquisition can only be compared to written language learning. Such a comparison reveals that astrology is learned exactly as other *written* languages: explicitly.[69] That astrology is not a spoken language does not disqualify it from being considered a language, as other non-vocal languages (for example, sign language) exist.[70]

Although astrology can 'speak' of all manner of human activity as it relates to the sky, it cannot express intention or directives such as, 'I will be right back' or 'Pass me the hammer'. For this reason, astrology has limited application, meant to be used in the specific context of interpreting sky elements in relation to human concerns. Wide application, however, is not a requirement of language. Finegan and Besnier's definition for language requires that it have 'A set of elements and a system for combining them' and that the application is to 'specific tasks in specific contexts.'[71] Similarly, Fasold and Connor-Linton's definition requires language to perform 'particular communicative jobs.'[72] Limited application is allowed.

Given the preceding evaluation, it can be seen that when compared to various linguistic criteria – several known definitions and a short list of Hockett's features of language compiled by Traxler – astrology's symbol system stands up quite well.[73] Although, in contrast to spoken languages, it must be taught explicitly to be learned, as an ideographic system (a written system) this is in keeping with how humans learn written languages. Where astrology is most unlike spoken human languages is in the fact that it cannot be used in applications that require direct communication between individuals; in this sense, it has limited application, but it does perform specific communicative functions in those limited contexts, and this falls within the guidelines of two definitions offered for language by Finegan and Besnier, and also Fasold and Connor-Linton.[74] Historians, researchers, astrological students, and practitioners would seem to be characterising astrology acceptably when they characterize it as a language. Furthermore, when considered as a language, astrology is best described as a limited-application ideographic language. On this basis, it follows that the findings from the ethnographic research presented here might be justifiably contextualized within a psycholinguistic understanding of language and time.

Findings: Part Two – Ethnographic Research Results and Discussion

From my call for volunteers, I interviewed nine astrologers who satisfied the screening criteria, generating 110 pages of transcribed information.

Experience and Engagement

All my respondents were Canadian and English-speaking. The sample had thirty-one years of experience on average with a median of twenty-five years. Active engagement time (consulting, discussing, learning, reading, teaching, writing, researching, erecting or examining charts) averaged 18.7 weekly hours, with a median of twenty hours across the nine respondents. I intended to sample astrologers who were very experienced and sufficiently engaged on an ongoing basis to retain fluency in the concepts of astrology. This sample more than satisfied those criteria.

References to Language

During the interviews, over half of the respondents, when being asked about their background with astrology, spontaneously made reference to it as a language which reflected the tendency found by Campion for astrologers to regard their craft in this manner.[75] A sampling of such comments follows:

'[Astrology] really spoke to me as living... it was a living literature', and 'I think astrology is more of a language and a language art than a science... I think it's our first language'.[76]

'I knew I was connected to that language'.[77]

'[Astrology] gave me a language to be able to recognize [patterns and solutions]'.[78]

'I feel like I have access to and proficiency in a language that is so full of wisdom'.[79]

'This language of astrology really started to embed itself in my head'.[80]

Conceptualization of time – standard model

All respondents in this study were English-speaking and as such the expectation was that they would express the standard time metaphors for English speakers: time represented as a straight line with the future in front of them, going in only one direction.[81] This was not the result. Instead, the interviewees described a variety of non-standard conceptualizations.

Astrological symbolism and concepts

The spatio-temporal representations provided by the sample were replete with astrological symbolism, frequently mentioning planetary cycles, zodiacs and charts. Time was often described as occupying three-dimensional space, sometimes as spherical. Ideas associated with the astrologer Dane Rudhyar featured prominently, both his concept of the spiral nature of cycles and his idea that astrology is a study of time as well as a study of personal growth. The concept of thematic *kairos* was also prevalent, indicating that much of the sample felt that time was not a neutral entity, but instead contained themes, mostly related to astrological cycles.

Spiral Time

Two of the astrologers conceptualized time as a spiral. The first stated that she felt time was a spiral moving in an upward counter-clockwise direction stating, 'I see time as a spiral, not as just a cycling over and over again, but as a spiral. Each round takes us to a different level'.[82] In terms of a single year of time she said, 'it would be like a cylinder going around and up, like one of those DNA drawings maybe'.[83] As DNA is represented as a double-helix, this would indicate that she was referring to a 3-dimensional spiral. Another astrologer also conceptualized time as a spiral, saying time 'would be a spiral' that 'goes clockwise, I would think'.[84] When asked to clarify, she mentioned that this was a helix (3-dimensional) spiral that could be oriented up and down or in any direction. This same astrologer felt that a smaller span of time, such as a year, would be represented as the standard river metaphor, which corresponds to the *moving-ego* sense of Clark's traditional model.[85]

Time as Growth

A few interviewees had time conceptualizations that were organized around the principle of growth, sometimes directly related to planetary cycles. One interviewee felt that time unfolded like the growth in nature, like the 'progression from a seed to a flower, or a seed to a tree, like very slow unfurling of growth from something tiny, literally a seed, slowly, slowly growing to its full potential… '.[86] When asked how she conceptualized a year generally, this interviewee had a difficult time with that concept, as she felt, 'there is no general', each year having a specific set of themes that were 'unfurling'.[87] In this response we get time as personal growth in the long-term conceptualization of time (the plant growing to its potential) combined with thematic time, described earlier as *kairos,* in the short-term.

Another respondent represented time as a coloured path of 'rectangles' representing periods of planetary cycles that develop in front of her, that 'are slightly curved, and form a circle which is complete at the end of my life'.[88] That time develops in front of her and eventually curves to bend back toward her, is a three-dimensional conception of the time as a river metaphor in the *moving-time* sense. This representation expresses both personal growth and *kairos* time.

Time as kairos

In a more unusual representation, one astrologer felt that time passed in a series of circular cycles, 'like a bunch of clocks on the wall ticking away' and that those clocks would represent astrological concepts.[89] In mentioning this, she said that this view was 'from an astrological perspective, which is my perspective'.[90] When characterizing a year, she said it, 'would probably, specifically look like January to December and I probably visualize some kind of a chart with the planets. That's how I would see a year'.[91] That each clock in this image represents an astrological concept or theme, speaks directly to the idea of *kairos,* in this case where the themes are the symbolized meanings of the astrological cycles.

Time as Spherical

One interviewee felt that time expanded outward from the self, wherein the present feels concrete and the future feels, 'almost like an aura all around you, kind of growing'. She described shorter time spans in the more regular way as being spatially ahead of her, and that she steps into it in a *moving-ego* sense.[92] Here we get a mixed metaphor with a traditional spatial time representation in the short-term and a more unconventional spherical representation in the long-term.

Another astrologer conceptualized time as 'events circling around me... like a galaxy going around... almost like an orbit'.[93] These circling events were not on one orbital axis, they would be 'above me, below me, beside me, circling'.[94] Within this representation the future would be directly in front of her spatially. In this representation, the events that orbit around her represent *kairos* time as Jaques defines it.[95] The future, however, is seen as being spatially in front of her in Clark's *moving-ego* sense.[96] Time, therefore, flows in a stream in front of her and she can move forward to experience it, but once she has done so, time moves into a thematic spherical representation that orbits around her as *kairos* episodes.

Curvilinear three-dimensional time

One surprising finding is that the time conceptualizations were often curvilinear as opposed to Clark's linear time.[97] The majority of conceptualizations were also described as existing in three-dimensional space. There were two helix spirals, several spheres, a band around a sphere, and a block of overlapping rectangles that circled back to the self. This is highly non-standard and contrary to normal spatio-temporal representations for English-speakers.[98] The implications of these results are discussed below.

Discussion

The main finding of the ethnographic research is that, for this sample, fluency in astrology did correlate with time conceptualizations that seemed informed by astrological concepts, and were non-standard by linguistic models for an English-speaking sample. These findings were consistent with a Linguistic Relativity understanding that postulates that language can affect how one conceptualizes the world.[99] They are also consistent with the research of Boroditsky and colleagues documenting that distinct language knowledge can lead to distinct spatio-temporal representation.[100]

All of the interviewees used astrological symbolism or concepts in either their long-term or short-term representation of time; some used this symbolism for both. When astrology is considered as a language, the fact that its symbolism, metaphors and concepts informed the astrologers' mental representations of time is in keeping with psycholinguistic research that finds that the concepts and metaphors built into one's language have some bearing on how one mentally represents the concept of time.

Representations of spirals and personal growth themes were prevalent and seemed to reflect astrological concepts exemplified by the work of Dane Rudhyar. This prevalence of influence is consistent with Rudhyar's status as being highly influential within Western astrology.[101] Many of the astrologers included *kairos* features in their representations. This is in keeping with Brady's comments that astrologers often see the future time as imbued with *kairos*.[102]

One of the most interesting contrasts to linguistic theory is the predominance of three-dimensional time representation within the sample. This is highly unconventional, as the standard expectation for English speakers, informed by Clark's understanding, is that time is represented spatially as unidirectional and on one axis.[103] It was noted earlier that, when Casasanto questioned Clark's model by presenting counter-examples that were neither unidirectional nor on one axis (such as, 'oceans of time'), he was not speaking of passage of time but rather of quantities of time.[104] It therefore bears asking: were the astrologers with their three-dimensional time conceptualizations actually referring to their spatial representation of time-passing, as was queried, or something else? A case-by-case consideration of the non-standard conceptualizations was performed and, being potentially over-cautious, five of the samples were removed from the psycholinguistic comparison.

As an ideographic language, astrology requires translation to one's spoken language, which for this sample was English. This necessarily produced a commingling of English language time metaphors with any effect presenting from knowledge of astrology. Of the representations that were deemed most comparable to psycholinguistics, all contained some element of the standard English spatio-temporal metaphor. This is understandable given the constraints of the astrological language and the work of Lai and Boroditsky, which found that, for bilingual individuals, time metaphors from one's first language can influence time metaphors in one's second language.[105] As Lai and Boroditsky further demonstrated, that influence can also go in the other direction (second language time conceptualization, influencing the first language time conceptualization), which is fortunate for this study as it means that concepts from astrological understanding (second language) can influence the English language metaphors (first language). Had this not been the case, the astrological concepts may not have had the opportunity to present themselves in an interview conducted in English.

The overall results of my study are consistent with psycholinguistic research that supports Linguistic Relativity. All of the responses that were deemed comparable to psycholinguistic models contained elements that could be regarded as informed by astrological concepts, or the astrological language. In fact, all respondents (nine) included some astrological themes or elements either in the long or short-term representations of time. Furthermore, the comparable conceptualisations contained distinct time representations that would not be anticipated by standard models for English-speakers. As exploratory, qualitative research, however, the results of this study are only indicative of this particular, rather small, sample.

Summary

In summary, I found that astrology has grounds to be considered a language and, in this limited sample, knowledge of that language led to distinct time conceptualizations that reflected the concepts of astrology, and presented in non-standard ways not predicted by conventional linguistic models for English-speaking samples. Being qualitative research, these results are not generalizable; however, my findings are intriguing as they have shown, at least for this small sample, that long and on-going engagement with astrology correlates with differences in the way time is conceived compared to standard English-speaking populations.

Notes

1.   Claire Chandler, 'What Is Astrology?', www.clairechandler.com/astrology/what-is-astrology [page no longer active] cited in Frances Clynes, 'An Examination of the Impact of the Internet on Modern Western Astrology' (PhD thesis, University of Wales Trinity Saint David, 2015), p. 126.

2.   Nicholas Campion, 'Prophecy, Cosmology and the New Age Movement: The Extent and Nature of Contemporary Belief in Astrology' (PhD thesis, University of the West of England, 2004), p. 248.

3.   Lera Boroditsky, 'How Languages Construct Time', in Stanislaus Dehaene and Elizabeth Brannon, eds, *Space, time and number in the brain: Searching for the foundations of mathematical thought* (London: Academic Press, 2011), pp. 333–41; Lera Boroditsky and A. Gaby, 'Remembrances of Times East: Absolute Spatial Representations of Time in an Australian Aboriginal Community', *Psychological Science* 11 (2010): pp. 1635–39, p. 1635.

4.   Theodor Adorno, 'The Stars Down to Earth', in Stephen Crook, ed., *The Stars Down to Earth and Other Essays on the Irrational in Culture*, Ebook edn (1953; London: Taylor & Francis, 2002), p. 121; Robert Wuthnow, 'Astrology and Marginality', *Journal for the Scientific Study of Religion* 15, no. 2 (1976): pp. 157–68.

5.   G.A. Tyson, 'People Who consult Astrologers: A Profile', *Personality and Individual Differences* 3 (1981): pp. 119–26, p. 119; Shoshanah Feher, 'Who Looks to the Stars? Astrology and Its Constituency', *Journal for the Scientific Study of Religion* 31, no. 1 (1992): pp. 88–93, p. 91; Bridget Costello, 'Astrology in Action: Culture and Status in Unsettled Lives' (PhD dissertation, University of Pennsylvania, 2006), p. ii.

6.   Nicholas Campion, 'Prophecy, Cosmology and the New Age Movement: The Extent and Nature of Contemporary Belief in Astrology' (PhD dissertation, Bath Spa University College, 2004); Bernadette Brady, 'Theories of Fate Among Present-day Astrologers' (PhD dissertation, University of Wales Trinity Saint David, 2012); Alison Bird, 'Astrology in Education: An Ethnography' (PhD dissertation, University of Sussex, 2006).

7.   Lindsay Radermacher, 'The Role of Dialogue in Astrological Divination' (MA thesis, University of Kent at Canterbury, 2011); Darrelyn Gunzburg, 'How Do Astrologers Read Charts?', in Nicholas Campion and Liz Greene, eds, *Astrologies: Plurality and Diversity* (Ceredigion: Sophia Centre Press, 2011), pp. 181–200.

8.   Frances Clynes, 'An Examination of the Impact of the Internet on Modern Western Astrology' (PhD dissertation, University of Wales Trinity Saint David, 2015); Teri Gee, 'Strategies of Defending Astrology: A Continuing Tradition' (PhD dissertation, University of Toronto, 2012); Garry Phillipson, 'Astrology and truth: a context in contemporary epistemology' (PhD dissertation, University of Wales Trinity Saint David, 2019).

9.   Radermacher, 'The Role of Dialogue in Astrological Divination', p. 128.

10. Plato, Timaeus trans. R.G. Bury and W.R.M. Lamb (Cambridge, MA: Harvard University Press; London, William Heinemann Ltd., 1931), 38c.

11. Roderick Main, *Jung on Synchronicity and the Paranormal* (Princeton, NJ: Princeton University Press, 1997) p. 80; Carl Jung, 'Letter to B. Baur (January 29, 1934)', in *Letters Vol I*, trans. R.F.C. Hull, eds G. Adler and A. Jaffe (Princeton, NJ: Princeton University Press, 1973), pp. 138–39, cited in Roderick Main, *Jung on Synchronicity and the Paranormal* (Princeton, NJ: Princeton University Press, 1997), p. 80; Elliott Jaques, *The Form of Time* (New York: Crane Russak, London: Heinemann, 1982), p. 14.

12. Max Heindel, *Simplified Scientific Astrology*, 5ᵗʰ edn (Oceanside, CA: Fellowship Press, 1919), p. 26; Alan Leo, *Esoteric Astrology* (1913; Rochester, NY: Destiny Books, 1989), p. 29; Alan Leo, *Practical Astrology* (1933; Pomeroy, WA: Health Research, 1966), p. 201; A.T. Mann. *The Round Art of Astrology—an illustrated guide to theory and* practice (London: Paper Tiger, 1979; London: Vega Books, 2003), p. 113; Jinni Meyer and Joanne Wickenburg, *The Spiral of Life* (Seattle, WA: Search, 1974).

13. Patrick Curry and Roy Willis, *Astrology, Science and Culture: Pulling Down the Moon* (Oxford and New York: Berg, 2004), p. 72.

14. Brady, 'Theories of Fate Among Present-day Astrologers', p. 130.

15. Dane Rudhyar, *The Pulse of Life: New Dynamics in Astrology* (The Hague: Servire, 1963), p. 20.

16. A letter written by Dane Rudhyar to Lelard Miller on 13 December, 1976, p. 1. Re-quoted from Deniz Ertan, *Dane Rudhyar: his music, thought, and art*, p.120, cited in Brady, 'Theories of Fate Among Present-day Astrologers', p. 129;

17. Rudhyar, *The Pulse of Life: New Dynamics in Astrology*, p.2 0.

18. Rudhyar, *The Pulse of Life: New Dynamics in Astrology*, p. 20; Dane Rudhyar, *The Lunation Cycle: A Key to the Understanding of Personality* (The Hague: Servire, 1967), p. 11; Dane Rudhyar, 'The Clock of your Inner Life', *Horoscope Magazine* (August 1967), p. 1, at www.khaldea.com/rudhyar/astroarticles/clockofyourinnerlife.php (accessed 18 July 2021).

19. Bernadette Brady, 'Theories of Fate Among Present-day Astrologers', p. 228.

20. Collins Gage *Canadian Paperback Dictionary New Edition* (Toronto: Thomson-Nelson, 2006), p. 828.

21. Elliott Jaques, *The Form of Time* (New York: Crane Russak; London: Heinemann, 1982), p. 14.

22. Phillip Sipiora and James S. Baumlin, *Rhetoric and Kairos: Essays in History, Theory and Praxis* (New York: State University of New York Press, 2002), pp. 97–99. See also John E. Smith, 'TIME, TIMES, AND THE 'RIGHT TIME'; "CHRONOS" AND "KAIROS"', *The Monist*, Vol. 53, No. 1, Philosophy of History (January, 1969), pp. 1-13.

23. Nicholas Campion, *A History of Western Astrology* Vol. 1 (London: Continuum Books, 2008), p. 63.

24. Roderick Main, *Jung on Synchronicity and the Paranormal* (Princeton, NJ: Princeton University Press, 1997), p. 80; Jung, 'Letter to B. Baur (January 29, 1934)', pp. 138–39.

25. Carl Jung, 'Letter to Andre Barbault (May 26, 1954)', in *Letters Vol 2*, trans. R.F.C. Hull, eds G. Adler and A. Jaffe, (New York: Routledge, 1976), p. 176, cited in Roderick Main, *Jung on Synchronicity and the Paranormal* (Princeton, NJ: Princeton University Press, 1997), p. 88

26. Charles Harvey and Suzi Harvey, *Principles of Astrology: The only introduction you'll ever need* (Toronto: Harper Collins, 2013; Ebook edition, Thorsons, 1999], p. 7.

27. Maggie Hyde, *Jung and Astrology* (London: The Aquarian Press, 1992), p. 163; Brady, 'Theories of Fate Among Present-day Astrologers', p. 156.

28. Brady, 'Theories of Fate Among Present-day Astrologers', p. 156.

29. Matthew J. Traxler, *Introduction to Psycholinguistics: Understanding Language Science* (Chichester: John Wiley & Sons Ltd., 2012), p .2.

30. Julie Sedivy, *Language in Mind: An Introduction to Psycholinguistics* (Sunderland, MA: Sinauer Associates, Inc, 2014), p. 498.

31. Geoffrey Pullum, 'The great Eskimo vocabulary hoax', *Natural Language and Linguistic Theory* 7 (1989): pp. 275–81.

32. Boroditsky and Gaby, 'Remembrances of Times East: Absolute Spatial Representations of Time in an Australian Aboriginal Community', p. 1635.

33. H. Clark, 'Space, Time, Semantics and the Child', in T.E. Moore, ed., *Cognitive Development and the Acquisition of Language* (New York: Academic Press, 1973), p. 52.

34. D. Casasanto, L. Boroditsky et al., 'How deep are effects of language on thought? Time estimation in speakers of English, Indonesian, Greek and Spanish', *Proceedings of the 26ᵗʰ Annual Conference of Cognitive Science Society* 26, no. 25 (2004): pp. 575–80, p. 576.

35. Boroditsky and Gaby, 'Remembrances of Times East: Absolute Spatial Representations of Time in an Australian Aboriginal Community', pp. 1635–39.

36. V.T. Lai and Lera Boroditsky, 'The immediate and chronic influence of spatio-temporal metaphors on the mental representations of time in English, Mandarin and Mandarin-English', *Frontiers in Psychology* 4 (2013): p. 142.

37. Campion, 'Prophecy, Cosmology and the New Age Movement: the Extent and Nature of Contemporary Belief in Astrology', p. 248.

38. William Lilly, *England's Propheticall Merline*, 1644 (sic throughout), p. 135. Cited in Ann Geneva, *Astrology and the Seventeenth Century Mind: William Lilly and the Language of the Stars* (Manchester: Manchester University Press, 1995), p. 175; Liz Greene in Darrelyn Gunzburg and Liz Greene, 'An Interview with Liz Greene', *The Mountain Astrologer* 119 (February/March 2005): pp. 48–49, cited in Radermacher, 'The Role of Dialogue in Astrological Divination', p. 167; Bernadette Brady, *Predictive Astrology: The Eagle and the Lark* (San Francisco, CA: Weiser Books, 1999), Kobo edn, Chapter 1, p. 1; Dane Rudhyar, *The Astrology of Personality: A Re-Formulation of Astrological Concepts and Ideals, in Terms of Contemporary Psychology and Philosophy*, 3ʳᵈ edn (1936; Garden City, NJ: Double Day, 1970), p. xi; Mike Harding, in Garry Phillipson, *Astrology in the Year Zero* (London: Flare Publications,2000), p. 97.

39. Geneva, *Astrology and the Seventeenth Century Mind*, p. xv; Bird, 'Astrology in Education: An Ethnography, p, 2; Radermacher, 'The Role of Dialogue in Astrological Divination', p. 162.

40. Edward Finegan, *Language: Its Structure and Use* (1989, 1994; Boston, MA: Heinle & Heinle, 1999), p. 430.

41. Maria Mateus, in private email conversation 6 November 2014

42 https://www.historyofvisualcommunication.com/02-ideograms (accessed 13 April 2019).

43. Bird, 'Astrology in Education: An Ethnography', p. 2.

44. Nicholas Campion, *A History of Western Astrology Vol 1*, p. x.

45. Ralph Fasold and Jeff Conner-Linton, *An Introduction to Language and Linguistics*, 2nd edn (Cambridge: Cambridge University Press, 2014), p. 1.

46. Edward Finegan and Niko Besnier, *Language: Its Structure and Use* (San Diego, CA: Harcourt Brace Jovanovich, 1989); Finegan, *Language: Its Structure and Use*, p. 11.

47. Fasold and Conner-Linton, *An Introduction to Language and Linguistics*, p. 1.

48. Charles F. Hockett, 'The Origin of Speech', *Scientific American* 203 (1960): pp. 88–111.

49. Matthew Traxler, *Introduction to Psycholinguistics: Understanding Language Science* (Chichester: Wiley-Blackwell, 2012). p. 3.

50. Traxler, *Introduction to Psycholinguistics*, p. 3.

51. Sedivy, *Language in Mind: An Introduction to Psycholinguistics*, p. 50.

52. Finegan, *Language: Its Structure and Use*, p. 11.

53. Finegan, *Language: Its Structure and Use*, p. 427.

54. Interviewee #1 and Interviewee #5,

55. Clark, 'Space, Time, Semantics and the Child', p. 52.

56. Traxler, *Introduction to Psycholinguistics*, p. 3

57. Brad Kochunas, *Astrological Imagination: Where Psych and Cosmos Meet* (New York: iUniverse, 2008), pp. xvi–xxi.

58. Kochunas, *Astrological Imagination*, p. xvi

59. L. Blake Finley, 'Planetary Glyph Symbolism including the Transneptunians', *The Uranian Institute* (April 2002), at http://www.uranian-institute.org/bfglyphs.htm (accessed 14 August 2019).

60. Nicholas Campion, 'Is Astrology a Symbolic Language?', in Nicholas Campion and Liz Greene, eds, *Sky and Symbol* (Ceredigion: Sophia Centre Press, 2013), pp. 9–20; Liz Greene, 'Signs, Signatures and Symbols: the Language of Heaven', in Nicholas Campion and Liz Greene, eds, *Astrologies: Plurality and Diversity in the History of Astrology*, (Ceredigion: Sophia Centre Press, 2011), pp. 17–46.

61. The Tiny Totem Blog, 2014, at https://thetinytotem.blogspot.com/2014/06/the-planets-in-astrology.html#:~:text=There%20are%20two%20glyphs%20for%20Uranus.%20The%201st%2C,matter%2C%20on%20top%20of%20the%20circle%20of%20spirit. (accessed 1 June 2021).

62. https://www.merriam-webster.com/dictionary/onomatopoeia (accessed 1 June 2021).

63. NCGR Board of Examiners, under direction of Bruce Scofield, *Education Curriculum and Study Guide for Certification Testing* (Washington, 2015), pp. 16–28

64. Marion March and Joan McEvers, *The Only Way to Learn About Tomorrow* (San Diego, CA: ACS Publications, 1988), p. xxiii.

65. March and McEvers, *The Only Way to Learn About Tomorrow*, p. xxiii, p. 50, p. 56.

66. NCGR Board of Examiners, under direction of Bruce Scofield, *Education Curriculum and Study Guide for Certification Testing*, p. 17.

67. Bernadette Brady, *Predictive Astrology: The Eagle and the Lark*, Ch. 1, p. 2.

68. Finegan, *Language: Its Structure and Use*, p. 11.

69. Finegan, *Language: Its Structure and Use*, p. 427.

70. Traxler, *Introduction to Psycholinguistics,* p. 3.

71. Finegan and Besnier, *Language: Its Structure and Use*; Finegan, *Language: Its Structure and Use*, p. 11.

72. Fasold and Conner-Linton, *An Introduction to Language and Linguistics*, p. 1.

73. Traxler, *Introduction to Psycholinguistics*, p. 3.

74. Finegan and Besnier, *Language: Its Structure and Use*; Finegan, *Language: Its Structure and Use*, p. 11; Fasold and Conner-Linton, *An Introduction to Language and Linguistics*, p. 1.

75. Campion, 'Prophecy, Cosmology and the New Age Movement: The Extent and Nature of Contemporary Belief in Astrology', p. 248.

76. Interviewee #1, pp. 1–3.

77. Interviewee #6, p. 1.

78. Interviewee #2, p. 3.

79. Interviewee #5, p. 4–6.

80. Interviewee #8, p. 2.

81. Clark, 'Space, Time, Semantics and the Child', p. 52.

82. Interviewee #1, p. 5.

83. Interviewee #1, p. 5.

84. Interviewee #3, p. 4.

85. Clark, 'Space, Time, Semantics and the Child', p. 52.

86. Interviewee #5, p. 7.

87. Interviewee #5, p. 8.

88. Interviewee #4, private email 12 June 2019.

89. Interviewee #6, p. 5–7.

90. Interviewee #6, p. 5.

91. Interviewee #6, p. 6.

92. Interviewee #2, p. 6.

93. Interviewee #7, p. 3–4.

94. Interviewee #7, p. 4.

95. Jaques, *The Form of Time*, p 14.

96. Clark, 'Space, Time, Semantics and the Child', p. 52.

97. Clark, 'Space, Time, Semantics and the Child', p. 52.

98. Clark, 'Space, Time, Semantics and the Child', p. 52.

99. Sedivy, *Language in Mind: An Introduction to Psycholinguistics*, p. 498.

100. Boroditsky and Gaby, 'Remembrances of Times East: Absolute Spatial Representations of Time in an Australian Aboriginal Community', pp. 1635–39.

101. Curry and Willis, *Astrology, Science and Culture: Pulling Down the Moon*, p. 72.; Nicholas Campion, *A History of Western Astrology, Volume II: the Medieval and Modern Worlds* (London: Continuum International Publishing Group, 2009), p. 262.

102. Brady, 'Theories of Fate Among Present-day Astrologers', p. 156.

103. Clark, 'Space, Time, Semantics and the Child', p. 52.

104. Casasanto, Boroditsky et al., 'How deep are effects of language on thought? Time estimation in speakers of English, Indonesian, Greek and Spanish', p. 576.

105. Lai and Boroditsky, 'The immediate and chronic influence of spatio-temporal metaphors on the mental representations of time in English, Mandarin and Mandarin-English', p. 142.

11

PANPSYCHISM AND ASTROLOGY

Garry Phillipson

Consciousness is a conundrum. It is the most immediate and intimate fact of life, yet its nature and provenance resist scientific and philosophical analysis, and it is sometimes characterised (as will be seen presently) as lacking any basis in reality. Astrology is also a conundrum, not least because public belief in it remains strong despite it regularly being denounced in the name of science as lacking any basis in reality.[1] This is a discussion paper and as such it raises more questions than it answers. I will consider panpsychism – the view, briefly, that consciousness is present throughout the cosmos. This is a view admitted by its supporters and detractors alike initially to appear 'absurd' and 'crazy'.[2] In particular I will consider the possibility that, in a panpsychic universe, meaningful interaction might occur between an individual and the cosmos in which they live.

Astrology will be taken as – so to speak – a test case for such meaningful interaction. When astrology is criticised in the name of science, this is typically on the basis of two issues. One is the lack of an explanation, in terms of Newtonian physics, for how it would work – how planets would affect life on Earth; the other is the lack of statistical evidence in terms of replicable correspondences between astrological factors and events in the world.[3] In this paper I will ask whether both types of criticism may be obviated by panpsychism. I will consider parallels between astrology and divinatory practices, and will discuss astrology itself as a form of divination. I believe there are also parallels with some alternative therapies that presuppose deep involvement between mind and body, the human and the cosmic – acupuncture, for instance.[4] My hope is that readers with no direct interest in astrology *per se* may, on this basis, still find interest in this paper.

The following section introduces the 'hard problem of consciousness' – which poses a dilemma for philosophy and for science because it seems as if it could imply a panpsychic reality. After this I will briefly discuss panpsychism and the related idea of animism – with particular reference to historic instances of animism being considered relevant to astrology. To lend perspective to these concepts, I will then turn to mind-body dualism and the idea sometimes seen to follow from it – epiphenomenalism, the idea that mind is a secondary effect of physical processes. Panpsychism might either support or undermine astrology, an issue which will be considered under the heading 'The celestial body problem'. This will be built upon by considering a panpsychic model of astrology proposed by David Hamblin, followed by my critique, which will consider parallels between astrology and mathematics via the anthropic principle.

The 'Hard Problem of Consciousness'

The current interest in panpsychism derives to a significant extent from David Chalmers' formulation of the 'hard problem of consciousness': 'It is widely agreed that experience arises from a physical basis, but we have no good explanation of why and how it so arises. Why should physical processing give rise to a rich inner life at all?'[5] In this, Chalmers added his voice to a chorus of similar sentiments echoing down the centuries, from thinkers such as Gottfried Leibniz, T. H. Huxley and William James.[6] Each remarked that there is no known way in which physical events in the brain could generate consciousness. The conclusion drawn by Thomas Nagel was that:

> unless we are prepared to accept... that the appearance of mental properties in complex systems has no causal explanation at all, we must take the current epistemological emergence of the mental as a reason to believe that the [physical] constituents have properties of which we are not aware, and which do necessitate these results.[7]

Either consciousness arises in a way that is miraculous (or at least unexplained), or – the panpsychic position – it is already somehow latent before it emerges in forms we recognise. Astrology has its own version of the 'hard problem'. The craft is 'the practice of relating the heavenly bodies to lives and events on earth, and the tradition that has thus been generated', as the historian and philosopher of astrology Patrick Curry put it.[8] An explanation of how there could be a meaningful connection between horoscopic factors such as the principal celestial bodies of the Solar System and events on Earth, has proved as intractable as an explanation of how the firing of neurons in the brain could generate consciousness.[9]

Panpsychism

Panpsychism stalks through the thought of many philosophers and scientists. Illustrations of this tendency include the contention of Alfred North Whitehead

(1861–1947) that '[t]he world is not merely physical, and nor is it merely mental'; and that of Arthur Eddington (1882–1944), that the knowledge of physics, 'is only an empty shell... It is knowledge of structural form, and not knowledge of content. All through the physical world runs that unknown content, which must surely be the stuff of our consciousness'.[10] The definition of the term 'panpsychism' is not free of controversy, but representative formulations from David Skrbina are that 'all things have a mind, or a mind-like quality', and that '[a]ll objects, or systems of objects, possess a singular inner experience of the world around them'.[11] I will not dig down into the nuances of the definitional disputes here – these are introduced by Skrbina in his book, as is the history of panpsychism in western philosophy, which I will also pass over in order to focus on this paper's idiosyncratic trajectory.[12]

Francesco Patrizi of Cherso (1529–1597) is widely credited with first using the term 'panpsychism' in a work published in 1591.[13] He wrote of 'participation' between different levels of being in the cosmos.[14] In the same work, he praised Plotinus, Marsilio Ficino and Pico della Mirandola for their understanding of astrology, and included a translation of the *Hermetica* as the final section of the book.[15] Patrizi thus looked more to Neoplatonism than the science that was beginning to take shape in his lifetime, leading his contemporary Johannes Kepler to characterise him as 'lucidly insane'.[16]

Animism

'Animism' is a term which has been associated with both panpsychism and astrology. Skrbina described the term as:

> most commonly used in a primitive, pre-scientific sense in which objects have "spirits" – e.g. the "spirit of the tree" inhabiting an oak... This dualistic and highly anthropocentric nature characterizes animism and distinguishes it from philosophical panpsychism... Animism thus is taken as having little if any philosophical standing.[17]

This unsympathetic evaluation corresponds with the intentions of Edward Burnett Tylor (1832–1917), who introduced the term to anthropology. For Tylor the term was innately pejorative. He used 'animism', in this weaponised sense, to dismiss astrology, remarking that 'one of its fundamental conceptions, namely, that of the souls or animating intelligences of the celestial bodies, is rooted in the depths of savage life'.[18] In similar vein, Franz Cumont (1868–1947), in his influential study of astrology's early history, wrote that in Babylon circa the fifth century BCE, 'Numerous traces are found of a primitive 'animism' which regarded as divinities animals, plants, and stones, as well as wind, rain, and storm, and believed them to have mysterious relations with mankind'.[19]

The view of animism as a crucial part of the cosmology in which astrology prospered has been accepted by some influential twentieth century western astrologers. Thus Marc Edmund Jones (1888–1980) wrote of 'the survivals of a primitive animism in astrological practice', and Dane Rudhyar (1895–1985) wrote of 'The Animistic Stage' in human development as host to the beginnings of astrology.[20]

The dismissive definition of 'animism' is open to challenge. For example, the professor of religious studies Graham Harvey argued that, 'Far from being a primitive, simplistic and irrational misunderstanding of the nature of life, animism has much to contribute to significant debates taking place in particular academic disciplines'.[21] He advocated a 'new animism', characterised by 'a concern with knowing how to behave appropriately towards persons, not all of whom are human'.[22]

When someone wishes to dismiss panpsychism from further consideration, a popular tactic is to allege that it would entail beliefs that would fit Tylor's definition of 'animism' – for instance that rocks are conscious – a position often taken to be sufficiently absurd as to require no rebuttal.[23] I will presently review an astrological argument whereby the celestial bodies – which might be characterised as large rocks – are conscious.[24] First it will be useful to delve into the philosophy of mind-body dualism in order to clarify what has long been the received wisdom regarding mind, body, and the relationship (or lack thereof) between them.

Dualism

Mind-body dualism – specifically as formulated by Rene Descartes – would have proscribed animism, had the term existed in his day. Thus he asserted that 'there are no powers in stones and plants that are so mysterious, and no marvels attributed to sympathetic and antipathetic influences... In short, there is nothing in the whole of nature...' which could not be explained in terms of 'principles which are known to all and admitted by all, namely the shape, size, position and motion of particles of matter'.[25] Whilst he also wrote of mind and soul, these had no place in the physical world: 'The only principles which I accept, or require, in physics are those of geometry and pure mathematics; these principles explain all natural phenomena...'[26] On this point Descartes echoed Galileo's assertion that the 'book' of the 'universe' 'is written in the language of mathematics'.[27]

In Descartes' view, the physical universe is entirely distinct from consciousness:

I knew I was a substance whose whole essence or nature is simply to think, and which does not require any place, or depend on any material thing, in order to exist. Accordingly this "I" – that is, the soul by which I am what I am – is entirely distinct from the body[28]

Hence the dualistic mind/body distinction found in Descartes' writings between the mind, or *res cogitans* ('thinking thing', which has no physical extension) and the body, or *res extensa* ('extended thing', which has no consciousness).[29] In the ensuing centuries, the body (or matter) emerged as the dominant partner, so that it started to seem plausible that the mind would prove to be no more than a side-effect of physical processes.

Epiphenomenalism

In 1978 the biologist Edward O. Wilson expressed his belief that, in the future, 'The mind will be more precisely explained as an epiphenomenon of the neuronal machinery of the brain'.[30] This is an example of the epiphenomenalist position, which was defined in four propositions by C. D. Broad (1887–1971):

(1) Certain bodily events cause certain mental events. (2) No mental event plays any part in the causation of any bodily event. (3) No mental event plays any part in the causation of any other mental event. Consequently (4) all mental events are caused by bodily events and by them only.[31]

There are a variety of closely overlapping epiphenomenalist views including 'illusionism' which is advocated, for instance, by Daniel Dennett and Keith Frankish.[32] In introducing this approach, Frankish drew a parallel with the choice between a blue or a red pill in the film *The Matrix*: 'I am going to offer you a different pill which – if it works – will convince you that your own consciousness is a sort of illusion, a fiction created by your brain to help you keep track of its activities'.[33]

Galen Strawson has referred to such a denial of consciousness's existence as 'the silliest claim that has ever been made' and 'the Great Silliness'.[34] The rush to eschew the animistic beliefs that often underpin 'wretched subjects' stems, I suggest, from an assurance of epistemological absolutism that was articulated by Descartes: 'the very fact that God is not a deceiver, and the consequent impossibility of there being any falsity in my opinions which cannot be corrected by some other faculty supplied by God, offers me a sure hope that I can attain the truth even in these matters.'[35] Under this view, our birthright as human beings is certainty in all things, from which it follows that whatever cannot be proved to exist, must not exist – even if ultimately, as is the case with epiphenomenalism, what does not exist is ourselves.

There is perhaps a parallel here with the conclusion reached by Geoffrey Dean and his colleagues in regard to astrology: 'to adequately test astrology the participation of the astrologer must be eliminated', so any complications that preclude certainty would be discarded.[36] In the testing of astrology, as with the formulation of epiphenomenalism, consciousness is seen as a fly in the ointment of certainty. Another factor to be dismissed in the quest for certainty, the relevance of which will emerge towards the end of this paper, is emotion. As the neuroscientist Antonio Damasio put it: 'Throughout most of the twentieth century, emotion was not trusted in the laboratory... not only was emotion not rational, even studying it was probably not rational'.[37] He pinned much of the blame for this on Descartes.[38]

Science has moved on from the Cartesian apartheid between mind and matter. Hence, for example, Werner Heisenberg (1901–1976) wrote:

> When we speak of the picture of nature in the exact science of our age, we do not mean a picture of nature so much as a *picture of our relationships with nature*. The old division of the world into objective processes in space and time and the mind in which these processes are mirrored – in other words, the Cartesian difference between *res cogitans* and *res extensa* – is no longer a suitable starting point for our understanding of modern science... Science no longer confronts nature as an objective observer, but sees itself as an actor in this interplay between man and nature.[39]

The science whose trajectory was shaped by Descartes and Galileo, amongst others, and which eroded belief in the reality of consciousness, has now reinstated consciousness. Hence, as Mary Midgley put it, 'In many areas, the advantages of ignoring ourselves have run out'.[40] This rehabilitation of consciousness surely makes panpsychism more plausible in principle. Even were it to be proven, however, it is by no means certain what consequences this would have for astrology.

The Celestial Body Problem

A problem for astrology in a panpsychic universe would be that it could be rendered superfluous by *Psi*. (I use the term in the same broad sense as was advocated by its originators, Robert H. Thouless (1894–1984) and Bertold

Paul Wiesner (1901–1972), comprising related terms such as 'extra-sensory perception' and 'psychokinesis'.[41]) The issue can be seen in the judgement of the psychologist and statistician Suitbert Ertel (1932–2017), at the conclusion of a discussion of tests of astrologers:

> Confirmations of classical astrological predictions... do not verify astrological beliefs. Correct astrological diagnoses, if they occur, might be due, e.g., to paranormal intuitions of psi-gifted astrologers. Parapsychological phenomena are likely to eventually become reconcilable with the growing body of scientific knowledge; astrology is far from having the same chance.[42]

This issue was also raised by the professor of philosophy Stephen E. Braude. Discussing his wife Gina's astrological work he observed that her 'accuracy in astrological forecasting seems conspicuously tied to quite specific features of the chart wheels she calculates'; at the same time, however, he felt 'there has to be more to the story – in particular a psychic element, whether it's Gina's extrasensory and wide-ranging scanning for relevant information, her psychokinetic nudging of events, or her telepathic influence'.[43]

Panpsychism may make Psi phenomena somewhat plausible, but this creates a problem for astrology regarding the status of the celestial bodies. The issue may be framed by a comparison with systems of divination such as the *I Ching* or tarot. One will sometimes encounter the idea that in casting divinatory tokens (such as yarrow stalks, or coins, or cards) a meaningful arrangement can be created by a form of Psi; for instance, perhaps the unconscious mind uses psychokinesis to influence the fall of the tokens, thereby conveying its greater insights.[44] The locations of the planets at any time is however – unlike the fall of yarrow stalks – known in advance. Hence it can be argued that panpsychism undermines astrology in two ways. First, the 'tokens' of astrology – celestial bodies – seem precisely the type of object that would not co-operate with Psi, on account both of their mass, their distance from the Earth, and their inexorable movement. Second, it seems that panpsychism would in any case remove the need for tokens of any kind. This last point requires elaboration.

I take it that in discussing astrology one discusses a craft in which the astronomical positions of the celestial bodies play a key role. This is in line with Curry's definition, cited earlier. It is necessary to reiterate this because, as has just been discussed, seemingly astrological phenomena might be explicable through the exercise of Psi – thereby bypassing the celestial bodies and ensuring that whatever took place, it would not strictly be astrology. Indeed some commentators – the psychologists Rollo May (1909–1994) and Thomas Moore are examples – see a useful role for 'astrology', but only for so long as it is a purely subjective tool, a 'myth' or 'mythology of the soul' with no necessary connection to the physical world and its celestial bodies.[45]

The issue of whether astrology does, or does not, have a necessary connection to astronomical bodies can be illustrated through the idea that astrology is a language. This was advocated in modern times by, amongst others, Dane Rudhyar (1895–1985). Rudhyar compared astrology to a language (sometimes to algebra), and on one occasion said that the natal horoscope is 'the message of the universe to you – a message in the celestial language of symbols'.[46] The bare statement that astrology is a language is compatible with the idea of it being a purely subjective mythological system. When, however, Rudhyar's additional clause is added – that astrology is a language *which the universe uses to convey messages to us* – then what is being claimed is not entirely in the realm of the subjective. There would need to be some correlation between the positions of the planets and whatever message the universe wants to convey, just as there would be a correlation between words used and a speaker's intended message.

The existence of a problem, verging on paradox, in astrological thought on this issue was identified by Nicholas Campion. After establishing that the description of astrology as 'a symbolic language' is popular amongst astrologers, he remarked that the interpretation of astrology's symbolism was often attributed mainly to the astrologer's intuition, yet with the positions of the celestial bodies still (somehow) crucial. Hence the problem 'that astrology can simultaneously lack any content or connection with astronomical order, yet make definite statements which are justified by that order'.[47] This is the same problem that Stephen Braude raised.[48] In order to pursue the question of if, and how, panpsychism might apply here, I will consider an article by the astrologer David Hamblin in which he argued a case for panpsychism as an explanatory system for astrology.[49]

David Hamblin's Panpsychic Model

Under Hamblin's account, there is a cosmic hierarchy wherein 'At each level, the organisms are in service to the organisms at the next level up in the hierarchy, even though they may not be aware of this'.[50] The particular relevance of this is that the Earth – which Hamblin identifies as 'Gaia' – 'is at a higher level of consciousness than ourselves… [and] contains within herself the sum total of all the "consciousnesses" of all the creatures on her surface'.[51] This includes astrological knowledge:

when Venus moves into Gemini, she starts to behave in a Geminian way because Gaia is telling her that these are the qualities of this particular area of the sky. Venus, like the other planets, is Gaia's pupil and is reflecting back to Gaia the information that Gaia has given to her.[52]

This is the *type* of explanation that would be needed to integrate astrology into a panpsychic cosmos, in that it provides a necessary role for the celestial bodies. Further, it attempts to address the 'celestial body problem' by having Venus et al. reflect astrologers' interpretations back into reality. I believe, however, that there are two problems in the detail of Hamblin's explanatory model, to which I now turn.

The Combination Problem

In Hamblin's account, Gaia possesses a digest of all the astrological thought of the creatures on her surface. It is not clear how this concept could navigate past the 'combination problem', a well-established challenge for panpsychism.[53] The gist of the problem was formulated by William James:

> Take a sentence of a dozen words, and take twelve men and tell to each one word. Then stand the men in a row or jam them in a bunch, and let each think of his word as intently as he will; nowhere will there be a consciousness of the whole sentence... The private minds do not agglomerate into a higher compound mind.[54]

There are missing steps between thoughts existing in the minds of individuals, and Gaia's arrival at a comprehensive overview. The issue here would be particularly acute in the case of astrology, because of the lack of agreement between astrologers over technical matters. Thus to take Hamblin's example, when a western astrologer would say 'Venus has entered Gemini', a practitioner of *jyotish* – the horoscopic tradition which is practised mainly on the Indian subcontinent – would consider Venus to be a few degrees into the sign of Taurus. So that even if Gaia *were* somehow able to extract and subsume all the astrological thought arising in humanity, the agglomeration of astrological perspectives could not be distilled into the coherent, unitary account that would be necessary for Hamblin's theory to work.

Given this problem, it seems that in order for something like Hamblin's model to function, it would be necessary for a level of responsiveness to exist from the celestial bodies to astrologers *on an individual basis*, in which the idiosyncrasies of each astrologer's approach would be acknowledged and incorporated. The approach would then be similar to the view of 'astrology as divination' which has been advocated by Geoffrey Cornelius and Maggie Hyde.[55] This is to say that astrology would be a dialogical process, taking place within a responsive cosmos – to use terms advocated by Lindsay Radermacher and James Brockbank, respectively, in discussions of the philosophy and cosmology that could inform astrology as divination.[56]

Relationship of Mind and Cosmos

The second problem I see in Hamblin's account is that consciousness is largely treated as if it were a physical force. For instance, the account of the celestial bodies storing and replaying astrological data from human consciousnesses, routed through Gaia, resembles a computer backup system, with planets functioning like hard drives. The question can be asked whether this exhausts the possible manifestations of consciousness.

There is precedent for this question in the history of philosophy. Whitehead accused Descartes of failing to explore the nature of consciousness after arriving at his *cogito*: 'like Columbus who never visited America, Descartes missed the full sweep of his own discovery, and... continued to construe the functionings of the subjective enjoyment of experience according to the substance-quality categories.'[57] Whitehead's position was distilled by Pierfrancesco Basile: 'The paradox of Descartes' philosophy is that he divorced the subject from the material world, but at the same time continued to interpret it in terms of ontological categories derived from that world, as if the self were a "thing"'.[58] In order to draw out an alternative to self-as-thing, with particular relevance to this discussion, I will draw on William James's discussion of *intimacy*.

In defining intimacy, James took aim at any system which 'leaves the human subject outside the deepest reality in the universe', characterising and advocating an approach opposed to such alienation:[59]

> From a pragmatic point of view the difference between living against a background of foreignness and one of intimacy means the difference between a general habit of wariness and one of trust. One might call it a social difference, for after all, the common *socius* of us all is the great universe whose children we are.[60]

In James's late philosophy, intimacy emerged as, in David C. Lamberth's words, 'James's most general criterion for distinguishing good philosophy'.[61] The breadth of the term's reach is matched by the complexity of its significance –

Lamberth characterised it as 'a phenomenological affect, a variable, concrete and independent feature of real metaphysical relations, and ultimately... an ideal for human action'.[62]

I should register two caveats at this point. First, in introducing the term 'intimacy' in its Jamesian sense I do not wish to smuggle into the discussion the lofty valuation James assigned to it; in this paper I use the term solely to help articulate two different ways of viewing the world. Second, a somewhat related point, James spoke more of pantheism – the denial that God and the world are ontologically distinct – than of panpsychism and so in quoting him it may seem that I am conflating the two terms.[63] James however used the term 'panpsychism' in contexts where, at the least, its meaning overlapped substantially with the meaning of pantheism.[64] As Lamberth remarked, '[a] number of James's comments about pantheism could be read panpsychically... Where one would close the floodgate on this effort, however, is unclear'.[65] Certainly, pantheism and panpsychism were closely related terms for James, and he is not alone in this; for instance, Macquarrie observed that 'pantheism often combines with a doctrine of panpsychism'.[66] In what follows I take it that James's panpsychism is, for the purpose of this discussion at least, practically indistinguishable from his pantheism.

James applied the criterion of intimacy to pantheism and found it necessary to distinguish 'two subspecies [of pantheism], of which the one is more monistic, the other more pluralistic in form'.[67] This yielded a distinction between *monistic pantheism*[68] and *pluralistic pantheism*.[69] He characterised monistic pantheism by citing Spinoza's contention that 'all things are in God, and so depend on him, that without him they could neither exist nor be conceived...'.[70] Spinoza's monistic pantheism was not satisfactory, in James's view, because of 'the impossibility of being intimate with *his* God'.[71] James's objection was that a monistic account of 'Absolute Mind' 'does not account for our finite consciousness'.[72] The point here is that under a thorough-going monist account, 'nothing exists but as the Absolute Mind knows it'.[73] This would deny all reality to human experiences of 'change... history... novelties, struggles, losses, gains', with the 'Absolute Mind' disengaged from the vicissitudes of individual human lives.[74]

If monistic pantheism were invoked as an explanatory system for astrology, similar problems would arise, for horoscopes are read in order to gain insight into human issues – career and relationships for instance – to which monistic pantheism would deny reality and significance. There is therefore nothing in monistic pantheism that could explain why astrology would function. To my mind, Hamblin's account has much in common with monistic pantheism. Although he portrays the celestial bodies as reflecting back humanity's astrological concepts, there is no indication of why they might see this as something worthwhile, nor of how those concepts would be connected to the issues (such as 'should I accept this job offer') that might be of interest to individual human beings. In fact, under Hamblin's account the consciousnesses of the beings who inhabit the Earth would be reduced to little more than epiphenomena whose purpose is to serve the consciousness of Gaia.

I would like to suggest that a significant problem in Hamblin's account arises from the absence, in it, of the possibility of intimacy between individual beings and the cosmos in which they live. Such an absence typifies much contemporary scientific discourse. Thus Mary Midgley remarked that 'hostile imagery about nature' of the kind seen in the writings of Francis Bacon (1561–1626) has become the norm in science, whilst 'affectionate and respectful imagery such as [Marsilio] Ficino used' is not allowed.[75] Hence, she argued, no modern scientist 'could ever dare to use terms such as *love* for forces of attraction, though today equally anthropomorphic – but hostile – words such as *spite*, *cheat*, *selfish* and *grudging* are the accepted coin of sociobiological discourse'.[76] If Hamblin allowed that love between parts of the cosmos could play a decisive role then his model would not be far away from the Neoplatonic one advanced by Ficino when he suggested that 'the parts of this great animal, that is all the bodies of the world... borrow and lend natures to and from each other. From this common relationship is born a common love; from love, a common attraction. And this is the true magic'.[77]

Although, as Midgley remarked, 'love' is not part of contemporary scientific argot, explorations in neuroscience suggest that the exclusion of emotion may restrict our vision. The research of Antonio Damasio, referred to earlier, is relevant. Surveying the neurological research he had amassed, he concluded,

> Well-targeted and well-deployed emotion seems to be a support system without which the edifice of reason cannot operate properly. These results and their interpretation called into question the idea of dismissing emotion as a luxury or a nuisance or a mere evolutionary vestige.[78]

If consciousness pervades the cosmos, as panpsychism suggests, and if a quality approximated by the word 'emotion' is an integral feature of that consciousness, then a universe of the kind advocated by Ficino begins to seem possible once more.[79] Since Patrizi held Ficino in high esteem, such a perspective would (incidentally) be consonant with the intentions of the man who coined the term 'panpsychism'.

At this point, however, the 'celestial body problem' rears its head once more. A strength of Hamblin's account is that it integrates the physical planets into the functioning of astrology. An explanation based in Ficinian love seems as though it might bypass the celestial bodies altogether, just as (in Ertel's account, cited earlier) Psi might do. Astrology continues to seem a problematic hybrid, needing celestial bodies to function both as material entities and as signifiers of meaning and agents of dialogue for human beings. If these dual roles are to be reconciled, it seems to me that the celestial bodies need to be seen as constituent parts of a language – as already discussed – taking place within what might be dubbed anthropic panpsychism. This will require some explanation, and I will try to open the theme up by considering mathematics.

Mathematics and the Anthropic Principle

Descartes was pleased to take the advances occasioned by mathematics and its extrapolation into the physical sciences as evidence for God's bestowal of the means whereby humanity could arrive at certainty. The *provenance* of mathematics however is a question with the potential to erode that certainty. This can be summarised by observing that, according to Darwin's theory of natural selection, the human organism has evolved to relate to the world in a way that allows us to survive. As Steven Pinker put it, 'Our minds evolved by natural selection to solve problems that were life-and-death matters to our ancestors, not to commune with correctness'.[80] Until very recently in human history there would have been no benefit in formulating calculus, therefore no reason for such a faculty to develop.

Albert Einstein referred to this problem as 'an enigma... which in all ages has agitated inquiring minds. How can it be that mathematics, being after all a product of human thought which is independent of experience, is so admirably appropriate to the objects of reality?'[81] Einstein's distinction between 'human thought' and 'objects of reality' here is revealing: given this kind of dualistic separation, it is difficult indeed to see how mind could penetrate the mysteries of the physical universe. So the existence of mathematics, and particularly its successful application through the physical sciences, can be taken to argue for a rapprochement between mind and matter of the kind embodied in panpsychism.

An argument with possible relevance can be found in the work of Carl Jung. In describing one of his astrological experiments, Jung wrote that 'a secret, mutual connivance existed between the material and the psychic state of the astrologer'.[82] This has emerged as a key phrase in discussions of synchronicity, and divination, in relation to astrology.[83] In order to address the question of how the human mind could conceive a mathematical language so efficacious that it seems to map and to open out unimaginable dimensions of physical reality, it might be conjectured that there is a secret – and systemic – mutual connivance between the human mind and the cosmos in which we live, which finds expression in the laws of mathematics.

With this postulation of connivance between the cosmos and the beings which inhabit it, one enters the outskirts of the *anthropic principle*. Brandon Carter coined this term in 1974.[84] He characterised it as a measured adjustment against 'exaggerated subservience to the "Copernican principle"', arguing: 'Copernicus taught us... that we must not assume gratuitously that we occupy a privileged *central* position in the Universe. Unfortunately there has been a strong... tendency to extend this to a most questionable dogma to the effect that our situation cannot be privileged in any sense'.[85] Writing twenty-nine years after Carter's original formulation, Bostrom estimated that more than thirty variants of the anthropic principle (on a spectrum from 'weak' to 'strong') had been proposed.[86] The particular form that would be most relevant here would come from the 'strong' end of the spectrum: 'The strong anthropic principle suggests that the fact that we exist imposes constraints not just on our *environment* but on the possible *form and content of the laws of nature themselves*'.[87]

Pursuing such a possibility, the physicist and science writer Paul Davies raised the question, '*Why* is nature shadowed by a mathematical reality?'[88] He concluded:

> I am convinced that human understanding of nature through science, rational reasoning and mathematics points to a much deeper connection between life, mind and cosmos... life, mind and physical law are part of a common scheme, mutually supporting. Somehow, the universe has engineered its own self awareness.[89]

The question arises as to whether the calculation of quantities and forces through applied mathematics exhausts what the universe's self-awareness is capable of, or whether it has another dimension – a more qualitative, relational side – and, if so, whether that other dimension can find expression through astrology. Rudhyar remarked that 'astrology and mathematics... invest with coherence, pattern, logic and order whatever substantial reality is associated with them'.[90] His equation of the two disciplines has always struck me as one of his more exuberant claims, and yet the anthropic principle seems as if it could, in principle at least, support such a possibility. Although the two disciplines – mathematics and astrology – function differently in many ways, it is possible that each is a language through which the cosmos (so to speak) reaches out to meet the individual, providing enough structure and orientation for meaningful interaction and discovery in specific enquiries.

The classical scholar Crystal Addey wrote that, in Neoplatonic theurgy, 'theurgic symbols were considered to have an ontological link with the deity from which they were derived'.[91] In this setting, a symbol 'could be a physical object such as a plant, gemstone, herb or type of incense'.[92] It has emerged in this paper that panpsychism can be interpreted (with a little work) as incorporating an ontological link between individual human beings, celestial bodies, and the more-than-human (however one might conceive thereof). Under this account, not only would rocks be conscious; some of them might, as it were, talk to us.

I am aware that this possibility will stretch the belief of many. That may however be the point. The Roman astrologer Marcus Manilius (fl. first century CE) wrote that astrology had been given to humankind 'that awe might be roused not only by the appearance but by the power of things, and that mankind might learn wherein lay God's greatest power'.[93] An astrology which functioned as a reliable information system, operating through easily-discerned principles, would not fulfil this function.[94] On this basis, and with apologies to Niels Bohr, I acknowledge that this theory of astrology as a manifestation of anthropic panpsychism may be crazy, yet wonder, is it crazy enough?[95]

Conclusions

In the wake of the scientific revolution the view burgeoned that it would be possible to explain the entirety of the world as we experience it, *including the fact of this experiencing*, exclusively in terms of material science. The existence of consciousness itself has however remained inexplicable within this frame of reference. Lacking a viable account of how or why an entirely material cosmos would generate consciousness (or even the appearance thereof), it behoves us at least to consider the possibility that consciousness subsists in all materiality. This principle is embodied in panpsychism, a position which negates Cartesian dualism as an ontological absolute.

If mind is inseparable from matter, many consequences follow for the relationship of humanity to the cosmos. Some of these have been examined in this paper, taking astrology both as a subject of interest in its own right and as an illustrative example of some of the issues that must arise whenever the possibility of meaningful interaction between human beings and their cosmic environs is discussed. Given a panpsychic universe, some long-standing criticisms of astrology lose purchase. The basis of those criticisms can broadly be grouped into two types. The first is the lack of a causal physical mechanism by which astrology could work. The second is a paucity of simple correspondence between astrological factors and facts in the world, of the kind whereby (say) Mars in one part of the sky at birth would map onto one type of event in the world, such as a particular choice of career.[96] Both criticisms presuppose a need for evidence that would be, or would follow, a mechanical process. Both therefore rest upon the assumption that a true astrology would function as if the cosmos were a great machine. If the cosmos has non-machine-like characteristics – if it is in some way conscious, animate – and if astrological work depends upon this quality, then it would follow that much evaluation of astrology has been misguided. This should be a challenge to any critic of astrology who aspires to scientific and philosophical coherence. By the same token there is a challenge to those astrologers, and clients of astrologers, who believe that astrology can and should deliver information on demand, as if one were eliciting information from a cosmic predecessor of Google. In this paper I have touched on the account of astrology *as divination*; this casts the work of the astrologer as dialogical and hence more enigmatic, nuanced and context-dependent than would be the case if astrology functioned as a simple information system.

There can be no absolute and definitive conclusion here, only conditional statements. One option is as follows. *If* panpsychism is a valid account, *then* consequences follow for our relationship to the cosmos which *might* extend so far as to support an account of astrology as divination. I have argued that in order for astrology, as generally understood and defined, to be encompassed it would be necessary to factor in meaningful reciprocity between the cosmos and individual human beings which would encompass matter (celestial bodies) and mind (the conceptual apparatus and judgements of an astrologer). I discussed this potential manifestation of panpsychism by reference to the anthropic principle, and also – referring back to the origins of the term 'panpsychism' – to concepts of an ordered, loving, cosmos as found, for instance, in the works of Marsilio Ficino. Given this historical context, panpsychism and astrology can be seen as ideas which were shouldered to one side by the scientific revolution, but which might repay fresh evaluation.

There is an alternative possibility. If the 'hard problem of consciousness' were to be explained on an entirely material basis, that would fill the ontological vacuum which panpsychism might otherwise occupy. This would banish the prospect of meaningful interaction between the consciousness of the individual and the larger universe. It would do so since – given the reach of epiphenomenalism – it would banish the very idea of a conscious individual. It should be challenging, therefore, for a materialist critic of panpsychism to find a way to challenge the idea of consciousness's ubiquity that would not simultaneously undermine any basis upon which there would really be a conscious individual such as themselves to be aware of such an issue – let alone to weigh it and arrive at a rationally-based conclusion. Crazy as panpsychism may appear, therefore, it may not be as crazy as an alternative position which, as it is being made, disproves the existence of the one making it and any basis in reality their argument could have.

Notes

1.   Thus, for instance, Gallup polls in America, Canada and the UK, conducted in 2005, suggested that 25% of people in each country believe in 'Astrology, or that the stars and planets can affect people's lives'. Nicholas Campion has suggested that this figure may be an underestimate, arguing that polls showing 70% of people believe in astrology may be nearer the mark. Alec Gallup and Frank Newport, eds, *The Gallup Poll: Public Opinion 2005* (Lanham, MD: Rowman & Littlefield, 2007), p. 221. Repeated at http://www.gallup.com/poll/19558/paranormal-beliefs-come-supernaturally-some.aspx (accessed 2 April 2021). Nicholas Campion, *Astrology and Popular Religion* (Farnham: Ashgate, 2012), p. 1, p. 157 – full analysis of sources is in the note to table 11.5 at p. 157.

2.   For 'absurd', see John Searle, 'Consciousness & the Philosophers', *New York Review of Books* 44, no. 4 (6 March 1997): p. 45; for 'crazy', see Philip Goff, 'Panpsychism is crazy, but it's also most probably true', at https://aeon.co/ideas/panpsychism-is-crazy-but-its-also-most-probably-true (accessed 23 January 2021).

3.   A succinct example that encompasses both types of objection is Richard Dawkins' complaint that 'astrology has nothing going for it at all, neither evidence nor any inkling of a rationale which might prompt us to look for evidence', Richard Dawkins, 'The Real Romance in the Stars', *Independent on Sunday*, 31 December 1995, p. 18.

4.   Illustrative quotations: 'The changing nature of Qi between a material substance and an ethereal, subtle force is central to the Chinese medicine view of body and mind as an integrated unit', Giovanni Maciocia, *The Foundations of Chinese Medicine – A Comprehensive Text for Acupuncturists and Herbalists* (New York: Churchill Livingstone, 1989), p. 2; 'Simplistically speaking, the universe is the macrocosm and the human body is a microcosm within it', Zhanwen Liu, Liang Liu et al., eds, *Essentials of Chinese Medicine*, Volume 1 (Dordrecht: Springer, 2009), p. 37.

5.   David J. Chalmers, 'Facing up to the Problem of Consciousness', *Journal of Consciousness Studies* 2, no. 3 (1995): pp. 200–01.

6.   Gottfried Leibniz, *The Monadology and Other Philosophical Writings*, trans. Robert Latta (1714; London: Oxford University Press, 1898), pp. 227–28, *Monadology* section 17; Thomas H. Huxley, *The Elements of Physiology and Hygiene; a Text-Book for Educational Institutions* (New York: Appleton, 1868), p. 178, Chap. IX, para 238; William James, 'Human Immortality: Two Supposed Objections to the Doctrine', in William James and Gerald E. Myers, eds, *William James: Writings 1878 – 1899* (1898; New York: The Library of America, 1992), p. 1113.

7.   Thomas Nagel, *Mortal Questions* (Cambridge: Cambridge University Press, 1979), p. 187.

8.   Patrick Curry, 'Astrology', in Kelly Boyd, ed., *Encyclopaedia of Historians and Historical Writing (Vol.1)* (London: Fitzroy Dearborn, 1999), p. 55.

9.   In what follows, references to 'celestial bodies' should be understood also to imply other horoscopic factors – it would be tedious to repeat this each time.

10. Alfred North Whitehead, *Adventures of Ideas* (Cambridge: Cambridge University Press, 1933), pp. 244–45; A. S. Eddington, *Space Time and Gravitation* (London: Cambridge University Press, 1920), p. 200.

11. David Skrbina, *Panpsychism in the West* (Cambridge, MA: Massachusetts Institute of Technology, 2005), p. 16. There is also a revised edition published 2017.

12. Discussed at Skrbina, *Panpsychism in the West*, pp. 15–19, and chapters 2–9, respectively.

13. Francesco Patrizi, *Nova de Universis Philosophia [New Philosophy of the Universe]*, 2nd edn (Ferrara, 1591; Venice: Robertus Meiettus, 1593). 'Pampsychia' is the title of the third section, pp. 47–60. Cited as the first use of the term by, e.g., Skrbina, *Panpsychism in the West*, p. 70. The term actually used was 'pampsychia', an archaic form – Skrbina remarks that at it is not clear why Patrizi used this, since 'panpsychia' would have been more consistent usage (Skrbina, *Panpsychism in the West*, p. 275 n.3).

14. Paul Oskar Kristeller, *Eight Philosophers of the Italian Renaissance* (Stanford, CA: Stanford University Press, 1964), p. 122.

15. Patrizi, *Nova de Universis Philosophie*, p. 115.

16. 'Patritius ille, cum ratione insanire', Johannes Kepler, *Astronomia Nova* (Prague, 1609) p. 2.

17. Skrbina, *Panpsychism in the West*, p. 19.

18. Edward B. Tylor, *Primitive Culture* Vol. 1, 4th edn (1871; London: John Murray, 1903), p. 129.

19. Franz Cumont, *Astrology and Religion Among the Greeks and Romans* (New York: G. P. Putnam's Sons, 1912), p. 10.

20. Marc Edmund Jones, *Astrology, How and Why it Works* (1945; London: Routledge & Kegan Paul, 1977), p. 15; Dane Rudhyar, *The Astrology of Personality*, 3rd edn (1936; New York: Doubleday 1970), pp. 7–8.

21. Graham Harvey, *Animism: Respecting the World*, 2nd edn (2005; London: C. Hurst & Co, 2017), p. xxvi.

22. Harvey, *Animism*, p. 3, p. xvii.

23. Skrbina, *Panpsychism in the West*, p. 17.

24. I acknowledge that the term 'rock' would be at best a loose characterisation of the four gas giants Jupiter, Saturn, Uranus and Neptune, and the Sun (a star constituted from hot plasma).

25. René Descartes, *Principles of Philosophy*, in *The Philosophical Writings of Descartes, Volume 1*, trans. John Cottingham, Robert Stoothoff, and Dugald Murdoch (1644; Cambridge University Press, 1985), p. 279 (Part Four, section 187 [314]).

26. Descartes, *Principles of Philosophy*, p. 247 (Part Two, section 64 [78]).

27. Galileo Galilei, *The Assayer [Il Saggiatore]*, in Stillman Drake, trans. and ed., *Discoveries and Opinions of Galileo* (1623; Garden City, NY: Doubleday Anchor, 1957), pp. 237–38.

28. René Descartes, *Discourse on Method (Part Four)*, in *The Philosophical Writings of Descartes, Volume I*, trans. John Cottingham, Robert Stoothoff and Dugald Murdoch (1644; Cambridge: Cambridge University Press, 1985), p. 127 [32].

29. René Descartes, *Meditations on First Philosophy (Meditation 6)*, in *The Philosophical Writings of Descartes, Volume I*, trans. John Cottingham, Robert Stoothoff and Dugald Murdoch (1644; Cambridge: Cambridge University Press, 1985), p. 54, section 78.

30. Edward O. Wilson, *On Human Nature* (Cambridge, MA: Harvard University Press, 1978), p. 195.

31. C. D. Broad, *The Mind and its Place in Nature* (New York: Harcourt, Brace & Company, 1925), p. 118.

32. Daniel C. Dennett, 'Illusionism as the Obvious Default Theory of Consciousness', *Journal of Consciousness Studies* 23, no. 11-12 (2016): pp. 65–72; Keith Frankish, 'Illusionism as a Theory of Consciousness', *Journal of Consciousness Studies* 23, no. 11-12 (2016): pp. 11–39.

33. Keith Frankish, 'The Consciousness Illusion', *Aeon* website 26 September 2019, at https://aeon.co/essays/what-if-your-consciousness-is-an-illusion-created-by-your-brain (accessed 28 March 2021).

34. Galen Strawson, 'The Silliest Claim', in *Things that Bother Me: Death, Freedom, the Self, Etc.* (New York: New York Review Books, 2018), p. 130.

35. The term 'wretched subjects' is an allusion to Otto Neugebauer, 'The Study of Wretched Subjects', *Isis* 42, no. 2 (June 1951): pp. 111, in which the author briefly explains 'why a serious scholar might spend years on the study of wretched subjects like ancient astrology'. Rene Descartes, *Meditations on First Philosophy* (Sixth Meditation [80]), trans. John Cottingham, in Rene Descartes, *The Philosophical Writings of Descartes*, Vol. II, trans. John Cottingham, Robert Stoothoff and Dugald Murdoch (Cambrdige: Cambridge University Press, 1984), pp. 55–56.

36. Geoffrey Dean, assisted by Arthur Mather and 52 collaborators, *Recent Advances in Natal Astrology: A Critical Review, 1900 – 1976* (Subiaco, Western Australia: Analogic, 1977), p. 554.

37. Antonio Damasio, *The Feeling of What Happens* (London: Vintage/Random, 2000), p. 39; Antonio Damasio, *Descartes' Error: Emotion, Reason, and the Human Brain*, revised edn (1994; London: Vintage/Random, 2006).

38. Damasio, *Descartes' Error*.

39. Werner Heisenberg, *Das Naturbild der Heutigen Physik (The Physicist's Conception of Nature)*, trans. Arnold J. Pomerans (Hamburg: Rohwolt, 1955; London: Hutchinson Scientific and Technical, 1958), pp. 28–29.

40. Mary Midgley, *Science and Poetry* (London: Routledge, 2001), p. 84.

41. Robert H. Thouless, 'The Present Position of Experimental Research into Telepathy and Related Phenomena', *Proceedings of the Society for Psychical Research* 47, Part 166 (1942): pp. 1–19. In this first published reference to Psi phenomena, Thouless described it as 'a term proposed by Dr Wiesner' (p. 5). Psychokinesis was added to ESP as a component of Psi in R. H. Thouless and B. P. Wiesner, 'The PSI Processes in Normal and "Paranormal" Psychology', *Proceedings of the Society for Psychical Research* 48 (Part 174) (1947): p. 179.

42. Suitbert Ertel, 'Appraisal of Shawn Carlson's Renowned Astrology Tests', *Journal of Scientific Exploration* 23, no. 2 (2009): p. 134.

43. Stephen E. Braude, *The Gold Leaf Lady and Other Parapsychological Investigations* (Chicago, IL: University of Chicago Press, 2007), p. 173.

44. See for example, Lance Storm, 'A Parapsychological Investigation of the I Ching: Seeking Psi in an Ancient Chinese System of Divination', *Australian Journal of Parapsychology* 2, no. 1 (2002): pp. 44–62.

45. Rollo May, *The Cry for Myth* (New York: Delta, 1991), p.22 n.1; Thomas Moore, *The Re-Enchantment of Everyday Life* (New York: Harper Collins, 1996), p. 317.

46. Dane Rudhyar, 'The Birth Chart as a Celestial Message from the Universal Whole to an Individual Part' (talk given to the 1976 Convention of the American Federation of Astrologers), at http://www.khaldea.com/rudhyar/astroarticles/celestialmessage.shtml (accessed 6 June 2021). Earlier examples of the language analogy in Rudhyar's work occur at *Astrology of Personality*, p. 48; *From Humanistic to Transpersonal Astrology* (Palo Alto, CA: The Seed Center, 1975 [1972 as *My Stand on Astrology*, expanded for 1975 republication]), p. 26.

47. Nicholas Campion, 'Is Astrology a Symbolic Language?', in Nicholas Campion

and Liz Greene, eds, *Sky and Symbol: The Proceedings of the Ninth Annual Conference of the Sophia Centre for the Study of Cosmology in Culture, University of Wales, Trinity Saint David, 4-5 June 2011* (Ceredigion: Sophia Centre Press, 2013), p. 45. Campion associated this problem particularly with the thought of the astrologer Dane Rudhyar.

48. Braude, *The Gold Leaf Lady*, p. 173.

49. David Hamblin, 'A Theory of How Astrology Works: The Planets as Conscious Beings', *The Astrological Journal* 62, no. 5 (September/October 2020): pp. 37–41.

50. Hamblin, 'A Theory of How Astrology Works', p. 39.

51. Hamblin, 'A Theory of How Astrology Works', p. 39.

52. Hamblin, 'A Theory of How Astrology Works', p. 39.

53. See, e.g., Philip Goff, *Galileo's Error: Foundations for a New Science of Consciousness* (London: Rider, 2019), pp. 161–69.

54. William James, *The Principles of Psychology* Vol. 1 (New York: Henry Holt and Company, 1890), p. 160.

55. Geoffrey Cornelius, *The Moment of Astrology*, 2nd edn (Bournemouth: Wessex Astrologer, 2003); Maggie Hyde, *Jung and Astrology* (London: Aquarian/Harper Collins, 1992).

56. Lindsay Radermacher, 'The Role of Dialogue in Astrological Divination' (MPhil dissertation, University of Kent, 2011), at http://www.cosmocritic.com/pdfs/Radermacher_Lindsay_Dialogue_in_Astrological_Divination.pdf [accessed 2 April 2021]); James Brockbank, 'The Responsive Cosmos: An Enquiry into the Theoretical Foundation of Astrology' (unpublished doctoral thesis, University of Kent, 2011). At http://www.cosmocritic.com/pdfs/Brockbank_James_Responsive_Cosmos.pdf (accessed 2 April 2021).

57. Alfred North Whitehead, *Process and Reality: an Essay in Cosmology (Corrected Edition* with corrections by David Ray Griffin and Donald W. Sherburne, eds) (1929: New York: The Free Press/MacMillan, 1978), p. 159.

58. Pierfrancesco Basile, *Whitehead's Metaphysics of Power: Reconstructing Modern Philosophy* (Edinburgh: Edinburgh University Press, 2017), p. 40.

59. William James, 'A Pluralistic Universe', in William James, *William James: Writings 1902 – 1910*, ed. Bruce Kuklick (1909; New York: The Library of America, 1987), p. 641.

60. James, 'A Pluralistic Universe', p. 644.

61. David C. Lamberth, *William James and the Metaphysics of Experience* (Cambridge: Cambridge University Press, 1999), p.156. Cf Levinson's suggestion that 'Intimacy was the principle of order in James's hierarchy of universes from 1904 on', Henry Paul Levinson, *The Religious Investigations of William James* (Chapel Hill, NC: University of North Carolina Press, 1981), p. 192.

62. David C. Lamberth, 'Interpreting the universe after a social analogy: Intimacy, panpsychism, and a finite god in a pluralistic universe', in Ruth Anna Putnam, ed., *The Cambridge Companion to William James* (Cambridge: Cambridge University Press, 1997), p. 245.

63. 'Although pantheists differ among themselves at many points, they all agree in denying the basic theistic claim that God and the world are ontologically distinct'. H.P. Owen, *Concepts of Deity* (London: MacMillan, 1971), p. 65.

64. For a discussion of James's panpsychism, see David Skrbina, *Panpsychism in the West* (Cambridge, MA: MIT Press, 2005), pp. 145-49 and Lamberth, *William James and the Metaphysics of Experience*, pp. 185–96.

65. Lamberth, *William James and the Metaphysics of Experience*, p. 189 n.138.

66. John Macquarrie, *In Search of Deity* (London: SCM, 1984), pp. 52–53.

67. James, 'A Pluralistic Universe', p. 644.

68. James, 'A Pluralistic Universe', p. 645.

69. James, 'A Pluralistic Universe', p. 645.

70. Benedict De Spinoza, *The Ethics*, in: *The Chief Works of Benedict De Spinoza*, trans. R. H. M. Elwes (1677; New York: Dover, 1955), p. 74. James quoted this passage in 'Some Problems of Philosophy: A Beginning of an Introduction to Philosophy', in William James, *William James: Writings 1902 – 1910*, ed. Bruce Kuklick (New York, NY: The Library of America, 1987 [1911]) p. 1043 n.2.

71. James, 'Pluralistic Universe', p. 650. Original emphasis.

72. James, 'Some Problems', p. 1052. The numbering of the four points here follows James's text.

73. James, 'Some Problems', p. 1052.

74. James, 'Some Problems', pp. 1052–53.

75. Midgley, *Science and Poetry*, p. 45.

76. Midgley, *Science and Poetry*, p. 45. Original emphases.

77. Marsilio Ficino in Marsilio Ficino, *Commentary on Plato's Symposium on Love*, trans. Sears Jayne (Speech VI) (Woodstock CT: Spring, 1985), p. 127.

78. Damasio, *The Feeling of What Happens*, p. 42.

79. I should acknowledge that I am taking Ficino as a convenient figurehead for elements of Neoplatonic thought; a full comparative analysis from that perspective would have *greatly* increased the size of this paper.

80. Steven Pinker, *How the Mind Works* (London: Penguin, 1998), p. 561.

81. Albert Einstein; G. B. Jeffery and W. Perrett, trans., *Sidelights on Relativity* (London: Methuen, 1922), p. 28.

82. C. G. Jung, 'Synchronicity: An Acausal Connecting Principle' [1952], in C. G. Jung, *The Structure and Dynamics of the Psyche: Collected Works* Vol. 8, 2nd edn, trans. R. F. C. Hull (1960; London: Routledge, 1969), p. 478 [905].

83. It provides the title for chapter 10 of Hyde, *Jung and Astrology*, pp. 172–91, and appears repeatedly in Cornelius, *The Moment of Astrology*, p. 77, p. 222, p. 227, p. 299.

84. Brandon Carter, 'Large number coincidences and the anthropic principle in cosmology', in M. S. Longair, ed., *Confrontation of Cosmological Theories with Observational Data* (Dordrecht: Reidel, 1974), pp. 291–98.

85. Carter, 'Large number coincidences', p. 291.

86. Nick Bostrom, *Anthropic Bias – Observation Selection Effects in Science and Philosophy* (New York: Routledge, 2002), p. 6.

87. Stephen W. Hawking and Leonard Mlodinow, *The Grand Design* (London: Transworld/Bantam, 2010), p. 197. Original emphases.

88. Paul Davies, *The Goldilocks Enigma* (London: Penguin, 2006), p. 10.

89. Paul Davies, *The Goldilocks Enigma*, p. 262.

90. Rudhyar, *The Astrology of Personality*, p. 49.

91. Crystal Addey, 'The Connected Cosmos: Harmony, Cosmology and Theurgy in Neoplatonism', in Nicholas Campion, ed., *The Harmony Debates: Exploring a Practical Philosophy for a Sustainable Future* (Ceredigion, Wales: Sophia Centre Press, 2020) p. 144.

92. Addey, 'The Connected Cosmos', p. 144.

93. Marcus Manilius, *Astronomica*, ed. and trans. G. P. Goold (1977: Cambridge, MA.: Harvard University Press, 1997). p. 7 (Book 1, 34-7).

94. I discuss the idea of astrology as an agent of cosmic awe in more detail in chapters 6 & 7 of my doctoral thesis, 'Astrology and Truth: A Context in Contemporary Epistemology' (unpublished doctoral thesis, University of Wales Trinity St. David, 2020), at www.cosmocritic.com/pdfs/Phillipson_Garry_Astrology_and_Truth.pdf {accessed 2 July 2021).

95. I allude here to the remark made by Niels Bohr to Wolfgang Pauli: 'We are all

agreed that your theory is crazy. The question which divides us is whether it is crazy enough to have a chance of being correct'. Reported by Freeman J. Dyson, 'Innovation in Physics', *Scientific American* 199, no. 3 (September 1958): p. 80.

96. This is an allusion to the work of Michel and Francoise Gauquelin which suggested several such correlations including, most famously, that between the placement of Mars and a medical career. A summary can be found in Michel Gauquelin, *Neo Astrology: A Copernican Revolution*, trans. Stela Tomašević (London: Arkana, 1991).

THE SOPHIA CENTRE
UNIVERSITY OF WALES TRINITY SAINT DAVID

http://www.uwtsd.ac.uk/sophia/

The Sophia Centre for the Study of Cosmology in Culture is a teaching and research centre within the Institute of Education and Humanities at the University of Wales Trinity Saint David. The Centre works from a humanities and social-science perspective and follows research methodologies from anthropology, history, philosophy, archaeology, sociology and the study of religions. The Centre's two academic goals are:

1. to undertake the academic and critical examination of astrology and its practice;

2. to pursue research, scholarship and teaching in the relationship between astrological, astronomical and cosmological beliefs and theories, and society, politics, religion and the arts, past and present.

The Centre's creation of the MA in Cultural Astronomy and Astrology in 2002 marked the first formal use of the terms cultural astronomy and astrology at a university in the UK. Cultural astronomy is defined as the study of the application of beliefs about the stars and sky to all aspects of human culture, from religion and science to the arts and literature. It also includes skyscape archaeology (which incorporates archaeoastronomy) the study of astronomical alignments, orientation and symbolism in architecture, ancient and modern, within wider cultural contexts, along with ethnoastronomy, that branch of ethnography which is concerned with societal relationships with, and attitudes to, the sky. Astrology itself is the practice of relating the heavenly bodies to lives and events on earth, and the tradition that has thus been generated. Cultural astrology is, in parallel with cultural astronomy, the application of this tradition to religion, science, the arts and all facets of culture.

The Centre's wider goal is stated in its title – to 'study cosmology in culture'. From an anthropological perspective, a cosmology is a view of what the cosmos is, how it works and how human beings engage with it. How do we live in, relate to, participate with, describe and portray the sky, stars and cosmos? As Gavin Pretor-Pinney said 'We don't live beneath the sky. We live within it.'.* This enables us to tackle a wide range of topics, from Egyptian sky religion and Babylonian astrology, to astronomy in surrealist painting, astrology in contemporary culture, the nature of sacred space, and the politics and ethics of the space race. The centre promotes research in the subject area, holds seminars and conferences, is associated with the Sophia Centre Press and the publication *Culture and Cosmos*, supervises PhD students, and supports the *Journal of Skyscape Archaeology*.

* Gavin Pretor-Pinney, 'Cloudy with a Chance of Joy', TED talk, June 2013,

ABOUT THE CONTRIBUTORS

AKINDYNOS KANIAMOS graduated with a MA in Cultural Astronomy and Astrology in 2017. He is currently a PhD student at the École Pratique des Hautes Études (EPHE) in Paris, completing his thesis entitled 'Astral Divinisation in Neoplatonism. Theory and Ritual Practices of Celestial Soteriology in Late Antiquity' ('La divinisation astrale dans le néoplatonisme. Théories et pratiques rituelles de sotériologie céleste dans l'Antiquité tardive').

ALINA PELTEACU holds a MA in Cultural Astronomy and Astrology from the University of Wales Trinity Saint David (2018). Her research interests include the sky and psyche, which formed the basis of her dissertation. She currently manages the publishing house Pro Cultura, in Bucharest. Her publishing projects include Romanian translation of *Astrology and Cosmology in the World Religions* by Nicholas Campion (2019).

CHRIS MITCHELL graduated from Bath Spa University College in 2008 with an MA in Cultural Astronomy and Astrology examining the development of the zodiac from its Babylonian origins. He gained his PhD from the University of Leicester in 2020 where he investigated a twelfth-century astrological manuscript and is the author of *England's First Astrology Book: Roger of Hereford's Judicial Astrology*, based on his PhD. Chris is a tutor on the Cultural Astronomy and Astrology MA at the University of Wales Trinity Saint David.

CRYSTAL EVES completed her MA in Cultural Astronomy and Astrology in 2021 with a thesis exploring spatio-temporal representation and the language of astrology. Crystal has a voracious interest in the subjects of time, human rhythms, psychology, and personal knowledge management. As such, she is a member of the Canadian Chronobiological Society and the Canadian Positive Psychology Association and has foundational training in psychoanalysis through the Toronto Institute for Contemporary Psychoanalysis.

FRANCES CLYNES is a tutor at the University of Wales Trinity Saint David, teaching on the MA in Cultural Astronomy and Astrology. She was awarded her PhD in 2016 for 'An Examination of the Impact of the Internet on Modern Western Astrology'. Her publications include 'Cyberspace and the Sacred Sky', *Cosmologies: Proceedings of the Seventh Annual Sophia Centre Conference 2009*, ed. Nicholas Campion, (Lampeter: Sophia Centre Press, 2010), pp. 137-151; 'Sacred Sky and Cyberspace', *The Inspiration of Astronomical Phenomena VI, Astronomical Society of the Pacific Conference Series, Vol. 441*, ed. Enrico Maria Corsini, (Astronomical Society of the Pacific: San Francisco 2011), pp. 343-349; 'The Enchanting Heavens', *Astronomy and Civilization in the New Enlightenment: Passion of the Skies*, eds. Anna-Teresa Tymieniecka and Attila Grandpierre (Heidelberg: Springer, 2011), pp. 61-67; and 'The Role of Solar Deities in Irish Megalithic Monuments', *Culture and Cosmos*, Vol 24 nos 1 and 2, Spring Summer and Autumn Winter 2020. She was on the organising committee of the 2016 conference of the European Society for Astronomy in Culture and five Sophia Centre conference.

JAYNE LOGAN graduated with aMA in Cultural Astronomy and Astrology in 2020 Jayne's life-long engagement with personal development has gradually morphed from mainstream to esoteric pursuits. Her dissertation, 'The Nature of the Soul in Contemporary Western Astrology', prompted her to segue into the practice of evolutionary astrology after experiencing the transformative potential of this approach. She is currently engaged in research focused on developing the potential of astro-genealogy while also working with clients seeking to understand their own evolution within the context of family and ancestral dynamics.

JENN ZAHRT, PhD is an author, translator, publisher, and teacher of cultural astronomy and astrology, and is an Honorary Research Fellow at the University of Wales Trinity Saint David. She is a company director of the Sophia Centre Press and deputy editor of the peer-reviewed journal *Culture and Cosmos*. In 2021 she became the Director of the Celestial Arts Education Library Institute in Olympia, Washington.

GARRY PHILLIPSON is a part-time tutor for the Sophia Centre, University of Wales Trinity Saint. David. His doctoral thesis, completed in 2020, *Astrology and Truth: A Context in Contemporary Epistemology,* explored issues previously raised in his book *Astrology in the Year Zero* (2000). Garry has also discussed related questions in journals including *Organization* (with Prof. Peter Case), *Correlation*, and the *Journal for the Study of Religion, Nature and Culture*.

KARINE DILANIAN graduated from the MA in Cultural Astronomy and Astrology in 2014 with her dissertation on 'An examination of theories of light in relation to the practice of astrology'. Her publications include *The Kepler Project. Kepler's Astrology: Phase 2. Astrological Manuscripts of Johannes Kepler* (2017). Karine has organised international astrological conferences in Moscow since 1993. From 2012, these became International Academic Conferences on the Study of Astronomy and Astrology in Culture; among them is the 2019 Saint Petersburg conference dedicated to the 400th anniversary of Johannes Kepler's *Harmony of the World*.

KIM FARNELL completed her MA in Cultural Astronomy and Astrology in 2005, focusing on the history of Sun sign astrology. Currently, she is pursuing a PhD examining the relationship between the horoscope column and women's magazines. She is the author of several books, including *Modern Astrologers* (2018) a biography of the astrologers Alan and Bessie Leo, *Cheiro the Wonderful* (2022), a biography of the palmist Cheiro, and *The True History of Sun Sign Astrology* (2022).

LAURA ANDRIKOPOULOS graduated with her MA in Cultural Astronomy and Astrology in 2011, having written her dissertation on the relationship between the beliefs of astrologers and the theory of secularisation. She is currently completing her PhD with the Sophia Centre on the subject of the psychologisation of astrology in the twentieth century and was a tutor on the ‹Sky and Psyche› module between 2013 and 2020. She has published papers in *Culture and Cosmos* on the themes of the use of the term 'inscapes' in cultural astronomy and on psychological astrology and disenchantment.

M. A. RASHED earned her MA in Cultural Astronomy from the University of Wales Trinity Saint David in 2017. Her master's dissertation, entitled 'Cosmic Chaos in Islamic Apocalyptic Eschatology,' was short-listed for the 2018 Master's in Cultural Astronomy and Astrology Alumni Association Dissertation Prize. Rashed is the author of 'Harmony in Islamic Cosmology: Subjugation, Sujūd and Oneness in Islamic Philosophical Thought,' *The Harmony Debates* (ed. Nicholas Campion, Lampeter: Sophia Centre Press, 2019). In 2020 she won first place in the American Association of Teachers of Arabic Translation

Contest, non-literary category, for her translation of a medieval Islamic work on Sufism. She presented her paper titled, on 'Astrology, Magic, and Free Will in the Discourse of Abū Ya'qūb al-Kindī' 2021 Annual Meeting of the American Academy of Religion. Rashed is currently in her third year of her doctoral studies in the Department of Religion, University of Rice, where investigating the transmission of ideas between the Islamic Orient and Latin West from the cosmological perspective of cultural astronomy.

INDEX

Please note, for Arabic names, those prefixed by *al* are alphabetised according to the letter following the particle; those beginning with *Ibn/Abd/Abu* are alphabetised according to those elements.